Discover
Rome

Experience the best
of Rome

This edition written and researched by

Abigail Blasi
Duncan Garwood

Discover Rome

Ancient Rome (p47)

No other city has such an evocative ancient heart.

Don't Miss: Colosseum, Palatino, Roman Forum

Centro Storico (p69)

The city's tangled historic centre is packed with incredible sights.

Don't Miss: Pantheon

Tridente, Trevi & the Quirinale (p99)

Glamorous, debonair and touristy – this is Rome's designer-clad soul.

Monti, Esquilino & San Lorenzo (p121)

Busy areas, speckled by glittering churches and some cool restaurants.

San Giovanni to Testaccio (p141)

Monumental basilicas, towering ruins, traditional trattorias and thumping nightlife.

Don't Miss: Basilica di San Giovanni in Laterano

Southern Rome (p155)

Encompassing the beautiful, historic Appian Way and ancient catacombs.

Villa Borghese & Northern Rome (p203)

Vatican City, Borgo & Prati (p183)

Tridente, Trevi & the Quirinale (p99)

Centro Storico (p69)

Monti, Esquilino & San Lorenzo (p121)

Ancient Rome (p47)

Trastevere & Gianicolo (p167)

San Giovanni to Testaccio (p141)

Southern Rome (p155)

Trastevere & Gianicolo (p167)

Enchantingly pretty, with tangled lanes, ochre palazzi and a boho vibe.

Vatican City, Borgo & Prati (p183)

Home to a stunning wealth of artistic treasures.

Don't Miss: Vatican Museums, St Peter's Basilica

Villa Borghese & Northern Rome (p203)

Encompasses the glorious park of Villa Borghese and the city's cultural hub.

Contents

Plan Your Trip   Discover Rome

Welcome to Rome

Rome is a seductive, thrilling city, created through the alchemy of history, genius and the hot Mediterranean sun.

With an artistic heritage dating back to Etruscan times, the city is packed with masterpieces, particularly from the ancient, Renaissance and baroque eras. Throughout history, Rome has played a starring role in the major upheavals of Western art and the results are there for all to see – amazing classical carvings, stunning Renaissance frescoes and breathtaking baroque statuary. Walk around the centre and, even without trying, you'll come across works by the greats of the artistic pantheon – sculptures by Michelangelo, paintings by Caravaggio, frescoes by Raphael and fountains by Bernini. In Rome, art is not locked away from view, it's all around you.

Once *caput mundi* (capital of the world), the glittering hub of the vast Roman Empire, Rome was the seat of papal power for centuries. The legacies of its past are embodied in awe-inspiring buildings such as the Roman Forum, the Pantheon and the Vatican, which contemporary Romans navigate with an uncanny air of nonchalant cool. Rome was a city that counted, and this is writ large on its historic streets – the Colosseum evokes glorious imperial days, the Circo Massimo conjures up images of wild chariot races, Castel Sant'Angelo testifies to violent dramas and St Peter's Basilica stands as a monument to artistic genius and papal ambition.

But Rome is as much about lapping up the lifestyle as it is about gorging on art and historic sights. And there's no better way of getting into the spirit of things than by eating and drinking well. Food and wine are as important to Roman social life as those other pillars: family and football, and the hundreds of pizzerias, trattorias, restaurants and gelaterie in the city buzz and bubble over with life. Whether it gets to you through its art, its architecture, its pasta or its vibrant sense of life, Rome is a city that encourages devotion.

> **Rome is a city that encourages devotion**

Fontana dei Quattro Fiumi and Chiesa di Sant'Agnese in Agone, Piazza Navona (p79)

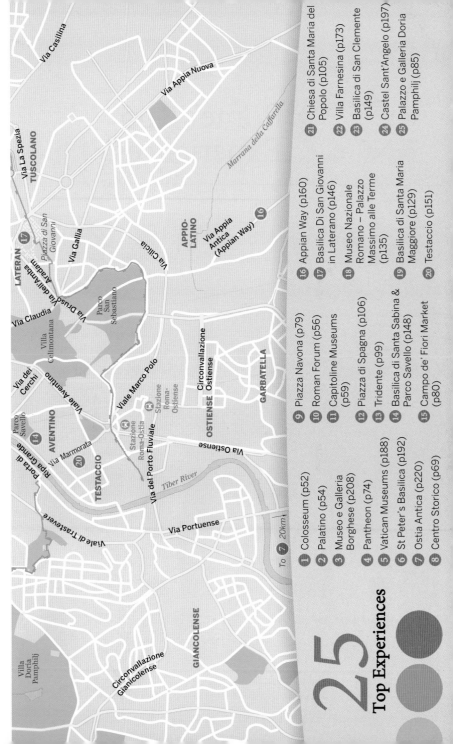

25 Top Experiences

25 Rome's Top Experiences

Colosseum (p52)

Rome's most iconic monument, the Colosseum is a compelling sight. You'll know what it looks like but no photograph can prepare you for the thrill of seeing it for the first time. For 2000 years, this muscular arena has stood as the symbol of Roman power, as the striking embodiment of the terrible awe that Rome once inspired. As you climb its steeply stacked stands, try to imagine them full of frenzied spectators screaming for blood – a chilling thought.

GEOFF STRINGER/LONELY PLANET IMAGES ©

②

Palatino (p54)

Rome's seven hills offer some superb vantage points. One of the best is the Palatino (Palatine hill), a gorgeous green expanse of evocative ruins, towering pine trees and sweeping views that rises above the Roman Forum. This is where it all began, where Romulus supposedly killed Remus and founded the city in 753 BC, and where the ancient Roman emperors lived in unimaginable luxury.

Museo e Galleria Borghese (p208)

Everybody's heard of Michelangelo and the Sistine Chapel, but Rome is as much about baroque art as it is the Renaissance, and the lovely Museo e Galleria Borghese is the place to see it. You'll need to book ahead but it's a small price to pay to see Bernini's amazing baroque sculptures, as well as works by Canova, Caravaggio, Raphael and Titian. And when you've finished, the surrounding Villa Borghese park is the perfect place to digest what you've just seen. Statue of Apollo and Daphne by Gian Lorenzo Bernini

ARALDO DE LUCA/CORBIS ©

The Best...
Free Sights

PANTHEON
An architectural wonder, ancient Rome's most complete building. (p74)

ST PETER'S BASILICA
Glittering with imposing splendour, full of artistic riches, topped by Michelangelo's dome. (p192)

PIAZZA NAVONA
Huge lozenge-shaped piazza, ripe for people-watching and filled with baroque fountains. (p79)

VILLA BORGHESE
Bucolic landscape of tree-shaded gardens, dotted by lakes and statuary. (p211)

BASILICA DI SANTA MARIA MAGGIORE
Glorious patriarchal basilica featuring exquisite mosaics. (p129)

BASILICA DI SAN GIOVANNI IN LATERANO
Rome's cathedral, with a façade surmounted by 7m-high figures and a Borromini-designed interior. (p146)

The Best...
Ancient Rome

COLOSSEUM
This mammoth stadium hosted fights between gladiators and wild beasts. (p52)

PANTHEON
An architectural masterpiece, over 2000 years old. (p74)

PALATINO
A garden-cloaked hill, dotted by ruined imperial palaces. (p54)

ROMAN FORUM
Once the beating heart of Imperial Rome, the Forum still has an extraordinary resonance. (p56)

BASILICA DI SAN CLEMENTE
Descend beneath this church to discover an ancient pagan temple. (p149)

OSTIA ANTICA
Conjures up ancient life better than any inner city sight. (p220)

Pantheon (p74)

The best preserved of Rome's ancient monuments, the Pantheon is an astounding building. Its huge columned portico and thick-set walls impress, but it's only when you get inside that you get the full measure of the place. It's vast, and you'll feel very small as you look up at the record-breaking dome soaring above your head. Adding to the effect are the shafts of light that stream in through the central oculus (the circular opening at the dome's apex), illuminating the royal tombs set into the circular marble-clad walls.

DAVID TOMLINSON/LONELY PLANET IMAGES ©

Vatican Museums (p188)

Rome boasts many artistic highlights, but few are as overpowering as Michelangelo's frescoes in the Sistine Chapel. A kaleidoscopic barrage of colours and images, they are the grand finale to the Vatican Museums. Inside the vast complex, kilometres of corridors are lined with classical sculptures, paintings and tapestries, leading inexorably towards the Raphael Rooms and, beyond that, the Sistine Chapel. Interior staircase

HANAN ISACHAR/LONELY PLANET IMAGES ©

St Peter's Basilica (p192)

You don't have to be a believer to be bowled over by St Peter's. Everything about the place is astonishing, from the sweeping piazza that announces it to the grandiose facade and unbelievably opulent interior. Topping everything is Michelangelo's extraordinary dome, a mould-breaking masterpiece of Renaissance architecture and one of Rome's landmark sights.

RICHARD I'ANSON/LONELY PLANET IMAGES ©

MARTIN MOOS/LONELY PLANET IMAGES ©

Ostia Antica (p220)

Ostia Antica is an ancient Roman port that fell into disuse, and remains in parts as well preserved as Pompeii. Make the journey out here and you'll find that the complex, combining housing, baths, theatre, temples and latrines, is easily on a par with the more famous sites in the city centre. Walk along the central strip, the Decumanus Maximus, or potter around the Thermopolium, an ancient cafe, and you'll get a much better idea of what a working Roman town looked like than you ever will by exploring the Roman Forum.

Dining al Fresco in the Centro Storico (p86)

Eating out is one of the great pleasures of Rome, especially in summer when it's warm enough to dine al fresco. There's nothing like sitting out on a beautiful cobbled lane to dine on fine Italian food and lusty local wine, while all around you the city plays out its daily show. And with everything from refined romantic restaurants to brash, noisy pizzerias and sumptuous gelaterie you'll be sure to find somewhere to suit your style. Piazza della Rotonda

8

RUSSELL MOUNTFORD/LONELY PLANET IMAGES ©

The Best...
Churches

ST PETER'S BASILICA
Christendom's mightiest church, St Peter's is awe-inspiring. (p192)

BASILICA DI SANTA SABINA
One of Rome's earliest churches, this 4th-century masterpiece has a colonnaded interior and glorious simplicity. (p148)

BASILICA DI SANTA MARIA MAGGIORE
Adorned by glimmering 5th-century mosaics, this great patriarchal basilica is an ecclesiastical extravaganza. (p129)

BASILICA DI SAN CLEMENTE
This is a marvel of Rome – descend three levels to discover layers of history. (p149)

BASILICA DI SANTA MARIA IN TRASTEVERE
The glittering façade and interior mosaics of this beautiful church are mesmerisingly pretty. (p175)

Piazza Navona (p79)

Hanging out on Rome's showcase piazzas is part and parcel of Roman life. For millennia, the city's public spaces have been at the heart of city living, hosting markets, ceremonies, games and even executions, and still today they attract cheerful, milling crowds of locals, tourists, hipsters, diners and touts. Piazza Navona is arguably the most spectacular, a huge space that was built over a 1st-century stadium, and which hosted the city market for centuries. It's an ever-changing tableau, with its frenzied baroque fountains, street artists and pavement cafes. Fontana del Nettuno

⑨

The Best...
Underground

BASILICA DI SAN CLEMENTE
Descend into the bowels of this multi-layered basilica to discover a pagan temple and a 1st-century house. (p149)

VATICAN GROTTOES
Extending beneath St Peter's Basilica, these underground chambers contain the tombs of several popes. (p195)

CATACOMBS
Via Appia Antica is riddled with underground tunnels (the catacombs) where the early Christians buried their dead. (p160)

COLOSSEUM
Recently opened to guided tours, the hypogeum is the complex of corridors and lifts that lay beneath the arena. (p53)

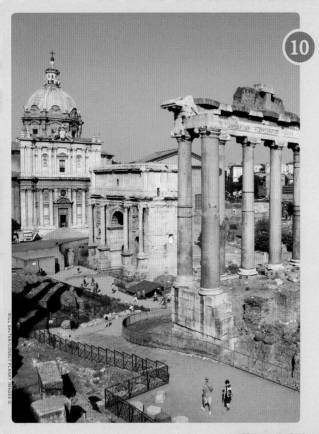

Roman Forum (p56)

To walk through the tumbledown ruins of the Roman Forum is to retrace the footsteps of the great figures of Roman history, people like Julius Caesar and Pompey, who both led triumphal marches up Via Sacra, the Forum's central axis. The Forum is today one of Rome's most visited sights but crowds are nothing new here. In ancient times this was the city's busy, chaotic centre, humming with activity as everyone from senators to slaves went about their daily business.

Capitoline Museums (p59)

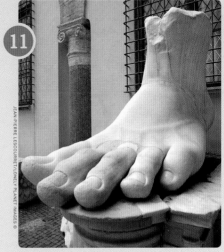

In ancient times, the Campidoglio (Capitoline hill) was home to Rome's two most important temples. Nowadays, the main reason to make the short, steep climb to the top is to admire the views and visit the Capitoline Museums on Piazza del Campidoglio. The world's oldest public museums, these harbour some fantastic classical statuary, including the celebrated *Lupa Capitolina* (Capitoline Wolf), an icon of early Etruscan art, and some really wonderful paintings. And be sure to bring your camera for the masonry littered around the entrance courtyard. Foot from the statue of the Emperor Constantine

JEAN-PIERRE LESCOURRET/LONELY PLANET IMAGES ©

12

People-Watching on Piazza di Spagna (p106)

Rising from Piazza di Spagna, the Spanish Steps have long been a prime people-watching spot. Visitors have been hanging out here since the 18th century. In the 19th century Dickens described seeing artists' models here, touting for work in the morning. Today the Steps are still continually thronged. There are local Lotharios flirting with the foreigners, red-faced tourists catching their breath, and hawkers selling their plastic tat. Below the Steps, you can window-shop or flex your credit card at the area's flagship designer stores.

WILL SALTER/LONELY PLANET IMAGES ©

13

Window-Shopping in Tridente (p116)

Below the Spanish Steps lies Rome's most exclusive shopping district – a glittering grid of streets lined by small boutiques with work-of-art window displays. All of fashion's big guns are here: Dolce & Gabbana, Gucci, Bulgari, Valentino, Prada, Fendi and more. Even though it caters to high-rolling shoppers, the district has an individual, neighbourhood-type feel, and there are also a few small artisan workshops (often hidden away on the first floor) where you can buy a bespoke bag, belt or marble carving.

Basilica di Santa Sabina & Parco Savello (p148)

The Basilica di Santa Sabina is a beautiful and tranquil edifice, dating from the 4th century, with an atmosphere quite unlike any other church in Rome. It has its original wood-carved doors, which bear one of the earliest renditions of the crucifixion, and is lined by 24 huge Corinthian columns that were constructed especially for the basilica. Alongside the church lies the lovely little Parco Savello, an orange garden with splendidly romantic views over the city. View of Basilica di Santa Sabino from Parco Savello

14

The Best...
Wine Bars

PALATIUM
Showcasing the best of Lazio's produce and wine, this is a contemporary take on the wine bar. (p113)

CASA BLEVE
In a column-lined atrium topped by stained glass, this is an elegant gourmet delight. (p89)

VINERIA ROSCIOLI SALUMERIA
This brick-arched place harbours mouth-watering foodstuffs and serves sophisticated Italian food – the wine list runs to 1100 labels. (p90)

CAVOUR 313
Close to the Forum, this offers pub-like, wood-panelled cosiness and 1200-plus labels of wine. (p67)

The Best...
Ice Cream Shops

ALBERTO PICA
Old-school gelateria, particularly famous for its rice varieties. (p91)

FIOR DI LUNA
Tiny Trastevere gelateria specialising in seasonal flavours, using the finest ingredients. (p178)

PALAZZO DEL FREDDO DI GIOVANNI FASSI
Great back-in-time barn of a place, offering fantastic classic flavours. (p134)

SAN CRISPINO
Sells what is believed by many to be Rome's best ice cream, with fresh, seasonal flavours served in tubs only. (p87)

Browsing the Campo de' Fiori Market (p80)

Rome's most central food and flower market – selling plump olives, many varieties of cheese, bread, fish, seasonal fruit and veg, and flowers – fills the charismatic Campo de' Fiori ('field of flowers') every day until around 2pm. It might be the most touristy of all Rome's markets, and a little pricier than others, but the produce is still fresh and alluring, and it's a lovely place to browse. The square itself feels particularly vibrant, and is as much a magnet for locals as it is for tourists – not only for its market, but also for drinks in the evening, when it draws a young and lively crowd.

TOP: WAYNE FOODEN/PHOTOLIBRARY © LEFT: WILL SALTER/LONELY PLANET IMAGES ©

Walking or Cycling the Appian Way (p160)

The Appian Way once formed the route to Brindisi in the south of Italy. It's an extraordinary experience to walk along the ancient 'Queen of Roads', which extends 560km in total, its huge cobbles worn smooth by millennia of feet. The road is lined by the ruins of Roman country villas and grandiose funerary monuments, which indicate the considerable status of the deceased even in death. You can also hire bicycles to explore.

16

© LOUIS MAZZATENTA/GETTY IMAGES ©

RUSSELL MOUNTFORD/LONELY PLANET IMAGES ©

Basilica di San Giovanni in Laterano (p146)

17

You'll feel very small as you explore the echoing baroque interior of Rome's oldest Christian basilica. The monumental Basilica di San Giovanni in Laterano, Rome's cathedral, is an exercise in sumptuous, overpowering splendour: from its façade topped by towering, 7m-high figures of Christ with St John the Baptist, John the Evangelist and the 12 apostles, to the swirling Cosmati flooring and 17th-century Borromini architecture of the interior,

Museo Nazionale Romano – Palazzo Massimo alle Terme (p135)

One of Rome's finest, this light-filled museum is packed with spectacular classical art, yet it remains off the beaten track in its location close to Termini station. Sculptural highlights include the mesmerising *Boxer* and the 2nd-century-BC *Sleeping Hermaphrodite*. The museum's sensational frescoes on the third floor, however, blow everything else away – in particular an entire room in which is depicted a paradisiacal garden from Villa Livia, one of the homes of Emperor Augustus' wife Livia. Boxer

18

The Best...
Shops

CONFETTERIA MORIONDO & GARIGLIO
A magical-seeming, stuck-in-time chocolate shop. (p97)

LUCIA ODESCALCHI
Exotic, thoroughly modern jewellery; works of art housed in a palace. (p119)

ARMANDO RIODA
Artisans in an upstairs workroom create luscious handbags at non-designer prices. (p116)

VERTECCHI
Has great notebooks with Rome covers, plus beautiful paper. (p116)

BOTTEGA DI MARMORARO
Have the motto of your choice carved into a marble slab at this delightful oddity. (p117)

Basilica di Santa Maria Maggiore (p129)

19

Featuring a lavish interior, the Basilica di Santa Maria Maggiore is one of the capital's great churches, dating from the 5th century. Perched atop Esquilino hill, it was built following a 'miracle', when snow fell in April. One of Rome's four patriarchal basilicas, its treasures include beautiful 14th-century mosaics on the facade, a 14th-century Romanesque bell tower (the highest in Rome), 5th-century mosaics lining the apse, an exquisite Cosmatesque floor and a gilded coffered ceiling dating from the 15th century.

RUSSELL MOUNTFORD/LONELY PLANET IMAGES ©

The Best...
Pizzerie

PIZZERIA IVO
Trastevere staple serves up delicious, fresh, sizzling, thin-base pizzas with a wealth of toppings. (p179)

PANATTONI
Streetside seating and fine, traditional Roman pizzas close to the river in Trastevere. (p178)

PIZZERIA DA BAFFETTO
Wham-bam service and paper-thin pizzas sizzling with toppings at this Rome institution. (p87)

PIZZARIUM
The Michelangelo of *pizza al taglio* (by the slice), Gabriele Bonci, creates masterpieces at this place in the Vatican neighbourhood. (p201)

FORNO DI CAMPO DE' FIORI
If angels made *pizza al taglio*, this is how it would taste, particularly the pizza *bianca* (white) and *rossa* (red). (p90)

OWEN FRANKEN/CORBIS ©

20 Roman Cuisine in Testaccio (p152)

Centred on Rome's former slaughterhouse, Testaccio is the spiritual home of 'blood-and-guts' Roman cooking – from the days when every bit of the animal counted. The area's popular trattorias and restaurants are the place to try it. They specialise in offal, with dishes such as *rigatoni con la pajata* (pasta cooked with the intestines of a milk-fed calf) and *coda alla vaccinara* (tail cooked butcher's style), though the restaurants also serve up less challenging Roman favourites such as *bucatini all'amatriciana* (pasta with pancetta and tomato sauce).

Chiesa di Santa Maria del Popolo (p105)

One of Rome's earliest and richest Renaissance churches, the Chiesa di Santa Maria del Popolo was worked on by artists such as Pinturicchio, in the 15th century, and Bramante and Bernini, who added later architectural elements. Today the church is an incredible repository of art: noble families commissioned the lavish chapels, which were decorated by Caravaggio, Bernini, Raphael and others.

Villa Farnesina (p173)

Villa Farnesina was built in the early 16th century for Agostino Chigi, the immensely wealthy papal banker. The building has a classic Renaissance design – a symmetrical construction with two wings – but it's the interior that's particularly breathtaking. It features some awe-inspiring frescoes by Sebastiano del Piombo and the villa's original architect, Baldassare Peruzzi, who had formerly worked as Bramante's assistant. Most masterful of all, however, are the decorations by Raphael, whose most famous work here is the *Triumph of Galatea*.

Basilica di San Clemente (p149)

Descend through Rome's multilayered past. The 12th-century basilica, with its beautiful apse mosaics, is built above a 4th-century church lined with faded frescoes, which, in turn, stands over a 2nd-century Mithraic temple, complete with altar and a 1st-century Roman house. Beneath everything are foundations dating to the Roman Republic. You can also peer through a hole at an underground channel, whose waters run beneath the Colosseum. Mosaics in the 12th-century basilica

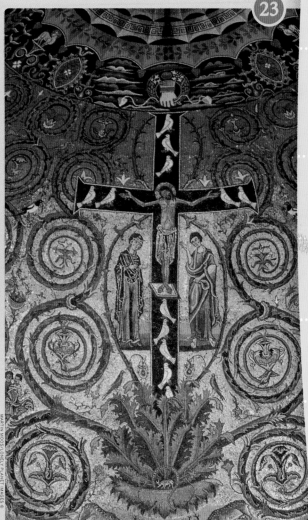

The Best... Kids' Stuff

EXPLORA
Small interactive and fun museum, where under-12s can play at being grownups in the model supermarket, bank and post office. (p214)

COLOSSEUM
Fire up the imagination with tales of gladiators and wild beasts at Rome's ancient stadium. (p52)

PALATINO
Rambling ruins and an enchanted atmosphere make this a great place to explore and have a picnic. (p54)

VILLA BORGHESE
Central Rome's largest park is perfect for boating, picnicking and cycling. (p211)

OSTIA ANTICA
A whole ruined city to run around, with plenty of entertaining nooks and crannies. (p220)

MARTIN MOOS/LONELY PLANET IMAGES ©

Castel Sant'Angelo (p197)

This great drum of a castle was originally a mausoleum for the emperor Hadrian, but was converted into a papal fortress in the 6th century. The castle has a secret 13th-century passageway to the Vatican palaces, and has served as sanctuary to many popes in times of danger. With lavish Renaissance interiors on the upper floors, it also has stupendous views from the terrace, immortalised by Puccini in his opera *Tosca*.

View from Castel Sant'Angelo

The Best...
Restaurants

L'ASINO D'ORO
Fantastic food, stunning value and Umbrian flavours in the charming Monti district. (p133)

LA ROSETTA
Sublime, classy fish restaurant in view of the Pantheon. (p86)

GLASS HOSTARIA
Italian cuisine as creative art in Trastevere. (p178)

OPEN COLONNA
Cooking with verve, wit and flair under a glass roof, plus cheap lunch menus. (p135)

TRATTORIA MONTI
Family-run, elegant treasure offers up delicious dishes from the Marche region. (p134)

AGATA E ROMEO
Grande dame of creative cooking in Rome, with innovative takes on Roman favourites and a splendid wine list. (p134)

ALINARI ARCHIVES/CORBIS ©

25

Palazzo e Galleria Doria Pamphilj (p85)

This central palazzo looks unprepossessing from without, but step inside and you'll find a lavish 18th-century interior resembling a mini Versailles, lined with glittering gilt-framed mirrors and deep-red silk. Its purpose-built galleries house one of Rome's richest private art collections – that of the Doria Pamphilj family – with painting-crammed walls covered in works by Raphael, Tintoretto, Brueghel, Titian, Caravaggio, Velázquez and Bernini. Exhibition Hall

Top Days in
Rome

Ancient Rome

The Colosseum is an appropriate high on which to start your odyssey in Rome. Next, head to the nearby crumbling scenic ruins of the Palatino, followed by the Roman Forum. After lunch climb to Piazza del Campidoglio, the Capitoline Museums and the 360-degree views from Il Vittoriano.

① Colosseum (p52)

Rome's great gladiatorial arena is a fitting start to your first day. Visit its broken interior and imagine the roar of the crowd.

COLOSSEUM ◐ PALATINO

Walk south down the Via di San Gregorio to the Palatino.

② Palatino (p54)

Included on the Colosseum ticket, the gardens and ruins of the Palatino are an atmospheric place to wander, with great views across Circo Massimo and the Roman Forum.

PALATINO ◐ ROMAN FORUM

Return on foot along the Via di San Gregorio towards the Colosseum, where you'll turn left onto the Via Sacra to approach the entrance to the Forum.

③ Roman Forum (p56)

You've seen where its citizens relaxed and played, now visit ancient Rome's administrative and political heart.

ROMAN FORUM ◐ HOSTARIA DA NERONE

Exit the Forum onto Largo Romolo e Remo, walk back past the Colosseum and turn left into Via N Salvi to find Hostaria da Nerone.

④ Lunch at Hostaria da Nerone (p66)

This tucked-away restaurant near the Forum and the Colosseum is an excellent, unfussy choice.

HOSTARIA DA NERONE ◐ CAMPIDOGLIO & CAPITOLINE MUSEUMS

Return to Largo C Ricci, walk along Via dei Fori Imperiali, then turn left onto Via di Tuliano; walk up the hill to reach the Campidoglio and its museums.

⑤ Campidoglio (p59) & Capitoline Museums (p59)

With wonderful views over the Forum, the piazza atop the Capitoline Hill (Campidoglio) was designed by Michelangelo and is flanked by the world's oldest national museums.

CAMPIDOGLIO & CAPITOLINE MUSEUMS ◐ IL VITTORIANO

Descend from the Campidoglio via the sweeping staircase, La Cordonata, and you'll arrive in front of Il Vittoriano.

⑥ Il Vittoriano (p63)

Il Vittoriano is an ostentatious, overpowering mountain of white marble. Love it or hate it, take the glass lift to the top and you'll be rewarded by 360-degree views.

Colosseum.
RICHARD I'ANSON/LONELY PLANET IMAGES ©

Vatican City & Centro Storico

On day two, hit the Vatican. Blow your mind on the Sistine Chapel and Vatican Museums, then complete your tour at St Peter's Basilica. Dedicate the afternoon to sniffing around the historic centre, including Piazza Navona and the Pantheon.

1 Vatican Museums (p188)

With over 7km of exhibits, it'd be hard to see it all in a morning, but make a beeline for the Pinacoteca, the Museo Pio-Clementino, Galleria delle Carte Geografiche, Stanze di Raffaello (Raphael Rooms) and the Sistine Chapel.

VATICAN MUSEUMS ➲ DINO & TONY

From the Vatican Museums entrance, turn right and then take a left up Via Leone IV, walking around 300m to reach small neighbourhood osteria, Dino & Tony.

2 Lunch at Dino & Tony (p200)

Head to this local osteria for excellent and bountiful antipasti and *rigatoni alla' ama-triciana* (pasta with pancetta and tomato), the signature dish, which will set you up for the afternoon.

DINO & TONY ➲ ST PETER'S BASILICA

From the restaurant, walk back down Via Leone IV, then follow the Vatican wall to reach St Peter's Basilica.

3 St Peter's Basilica (p192)

Approaching St Peter's Piazza from the side, you'll see it as Bernini intended: a surprise. Visit this beautiful public square and the church itself, home to Michelange-lo's Pietá and a breathtaking dome – it's worth climbing the latter for astounding views.

ST PETER'S BASILICA ➲ CASTEL SANT'ANGELO

From St Peter's Piazza, walk along the Borgo Sant'Angelo, following the fortified wall of the elevated walkway, to reach Castel Sant'Angelo.

4 Castel Sant'Angelo (p197)

If you're not feeling overwhelmed by sight-seeing, visit the interior of this ancient Roman tomb that became a fortress.

CASTEL SANT'ANGELO ➲ PIAZZA NAVONA

Cross the river via the pedestrianised Ponte Sant'Angelo, then follow the river eastwards for around 300m before turning right inland at the next bridge, following Via G Zanardelli to reach Piazza Navona.

5 Piazza Navona (p79)

This vast baroque square is a showpiece of the Centro Storico, and full of vibrant life. The lozenge-shaped space is an echo of its ancient origins as the site of a stadium.

PIAZZA NAVONA ➲ PANTHEON

It's a short walk eastwards from Piazza Navona to Piazza della Rotonda, where you'll find the Pantheon.

6 Pantheon (p74)

This 2000-year-old temple, now a church, is an extraordinary building, whose innova-tive design has served to inspire genera-tions of architects and engineers.

PANTHEON ➲ LA ROSETTA

There are plenty of excellent restaurants around the Pantheon, and La Rosetta, within sight of the temple, is one of Rome's best fish restaurants.

7 Dinner at La Rosetta (p86)

Splash out and dine at La Rosetta. Alterna-tively, try traditional favourite Armando al Pantheon (p87), or hob nob with journal-ists and politicians at Osteria Sostegno (p87).

Piazza Navona
GEOFF STRINGER/LONELY PLANET IMAGES ©

Villa Borghese, Tridente & Trevi

Start your day at the brilliant Museo e Galleria Borghese, before rambling around the shady avenues of the surrounding park of Villa Borghese. Next explore Tridente, including the Spanish Steps and Via Condotti, before heading to the Trevi Fountain.

DAY
3

1 Galleria e Museo Borghese (p208)

Book ahead and start your day with the marvellous collection of the Galleria e Museo Borghese, housed in the lavish and *bijou* Casino Borghese.

GALLERIA E MUSEO BORGHESE ❂ PINCIO

🟢 Take a stroll through Villa Borghese towards the Pincio.

2 Pincio (p104)

Meander through the lovely, rambling park of Villa Borghese (p211), formerly the playground of the mighty Borghese family. You'll pass the Piazza di Sienna, a historic racecourse, and walk along tree-shaded lanes to reach the Pincio, which offers great views across Rome.

PINCIO ❂ SPANISH STEPS

🟢 From the Pincio you can exit along Viale G D'Annunzio to reach the top of the Spanish Steps.

3 Spanish Steps (p106)

The Spanish Steps (Scalineta della Trinitá dei Monti) is a glorious flight of ornamental rococo steps, with views over the glittering, designer-store-packed streets of Tridente district and the Piazza di Spagna.

SPANISH STEPS ❂ VIA CONDOTTI

🟢 Walk down the Spanish Steps to Via Condotti.

4 Via Condotti (p116)

Via Condotti is Rome's most exclusive shopping street, lined by big-name designers and jewellers such as Prada, Bulgari, Fendi and Salvatore Ferragamo. Even if you haven't got cash to splash, it's well worth a wander to window shop and check out some of the outfits on the informal catwalk of the street.

VIA CONDOTTI ❂ PALATIUM

🟢 From Via Condotti turn south along Via Belsiana to reach the wine bar Palatium.

5 Lunch at Palatium (p113)

Specialising in produce from Lazio, this sleek wine bar is a great place to try local wines and delicacies, such as Frascati white wine and porchetta (pork roasted with herbs).

PALATIUM ❂ PIAZZA DEL POPOLO

🟢 Returning along Via Belsiana, turn right at Via Vittoria, then left at Via del Babuino, to reach Piazza del Popolo.

6 Piazza del Popolo (p104)

The huge, oval Piazza del Popolo dates from the 16th century and is overlooked by Chiesa di Santa Maria del Popolo (p105), which contains a remarkable array of masterpieces.

PIAZZA DEL POPOLO ❂ TREVI FOUNTAIN

🟢 From Piazza del Popolo, walk back along Via del Corso (or hop on minibus 119), then turn left up Via Sabini to reach the Trevi Fountain.

7 Trevi Fountain (p109)

End your day at this foaming, fantastical baroque fountain, designed by Nicola Salvi, where you can toss in a coin to ensure a return visit to Rome.

Trevi Fountain
TONYBURNS/LONELY PLANET IMAGES ©

DAY 4

Southern Rome, Monti & Trastevere

On your fourth day, venture out to Via Appia Antica and the catacombs. Start the afternoon by visiting the Museo Nazionale Romano – Palazzo Massimo alle Terme, then drop by the Basilica di Santa Maria Maggiore. Finish with an evening in Trastevere.

① Catacombe di San Sebastiano (p160)

Start your day underground, by taking a tour of one of the three networks of catacombs that are open to the public. It's a fascinating and chilling experience to see the tunnels where early Christians buried their dead.

CATACOMBE DI SAN SEBASTIANO ⊙ VILLA DI MASSENZIO

⊕ Walk around 100m south along the Via Appia and you will see the Villa di Massenzio on your left.

② Villa di Massenzio (p161)

The best preserved part of Maxentius' 4th-century ruined palace is the Circo di Massenzio, which was once a racetrack with capacity for 10,000 people.

VILLA DI MASSENZIO ⊙ MAUSOLEO DI CECILIA METELLA

⊕ Walk on 50m or so onwards along the Via Appia and you'll see the Tomb of Cecilia Metella.

③ Mausoleo di Cecilia Metella (p161)

With travertine walls and an interior decorated with a sculpted frieze bearing Gaelic shields, ox skulls and festoons, this great, rotund tomb is an imposing sight.

MAUSOLEO DI CECILIA METELLA ⊙ RISTORANTE CECILIA METELLA

⊕ From the tomb, walk around 200m back up the road to the Ristorante Cecilia Metella.

④ Lunch at Ristorante Cecilia Metella (p165)

Have lunch at this long-standing, family-run restaurant, which proffers Roman favourites served by smartly dressed waiters, and surrounded by kempt gardens.

Catacombe di San Sebastiano
RAIMUND KUTTER/IMAGEBROKER ©

RISTORANTE CECILIA METELLA ⊙ PALAZZO MASSIMO ALLE TERME

🚌 After lunch, hop on a bus or the Archaobus back to Termini station, to visit the Palazzo Massimo alle Terme.

⑤ Palazzo Massimo alle Terme (p135)

This light-filled museum holds part of the Museo Nazionale Romano collection, with a splendid array of classical carving and an unparalleled selection of ancient Roman frescoes.

PALAZZO MASSIMO ALLE TERME ⊙ BASILICA DI SANTA MARIA MAGGIORE

⊕ From the museum walk about 200m southwest along Via Massimo d'Azeglio to reach Santa Maria Maggiore.

⑥ Basilica di Santa Maria Maggiore (p129)

One of Rome's four patriarchal basilicas, this monumental church stands on the summit of the Esquilino hill, on the spot where snow is said to have miraculously fallen in the summer of AD 358.

BASILICA DI SANTA MARIA MAGGIORE ⊙ TRASTEVERE

🚌 From Termini station, which is a short walk from the basilica, you can take a tram or bus to Trastevere.

⑦ Trastevere (p167)

Spend the evening wandering the charismatic streets of Trastevere. This district is as popular with locals as it is with tourists, and is a beguiling place for an evening stroll before settling on a place for dinner.

Month by Month

January

🔒 Winter Sales

Running from early January to mid-February, the winter sales offer savings of between 20% and 50%. Action is particularly frenzied around Piazza di Spagna and on Via del Corso.

February

✳️ Carnevale

The week before Lent is a technicolour spectacle as children take to the streets in fancy dress and throw *coriandoli* (coloured confetti) over each other. Costumed processions add to the fun – see www .carnevale.roma.it for details.

March

🏃 Maratona di Roma

Sight-seeing becomes sport at Rome's annual marathon. The 42km route starts and finishes near the Colosseum, taking in many of the city's big sights. Details online at www .maratonadiroma.it.

April

✳️ Easter

In the capital of the Catholic world, Easter is big business. On Good Friday the pope leads a candlelit procession around the Colosseum. At noon on Easter Sunday he blesses the crowds in Piazza San Pietro.

◎ Settimana della Cultura

During Culture Week admission is free to many state-run monuments, museums, galleries and otherwise closed sites. Dates change annually so check www.beniculturali.it (in Italian).

✳️ Natale Di Roma

Rome celebrates its birthday on 21 April with music, historical recreations, fireworks and free entry to many museums. Events are staged throughout the city but the focus is Campidoglio and Circo Massimo.

◎ Mostra Delle Azalee

From mid-April to early May, the Spanish Steps are decorated with 600 vases of blooming, brightly coloured azaleas – a perfect photo opportunity.

May

☆ Primo Maggio

Hundreds of thousands of fans troop to Piazza di San Giovanni in Laterano for Rome's annual May Day rock concert. It's a mostly Italian affair with big-name local performers but you might catch the occasional foreign guest star.

Performance at the Roman Forum during the Estate Romana

FRANCO ORIGLIA/GETTY IMAGES ©

 June

 Estate Romana

Between June and October, Rome's big summer festival involves everything from concerts to book fairs, puppet shows and late-night museum openings. Check the website – www.estateromana.comune.roma.it.

Roma Incontro Il Mondo

Villa Ada is transformed into a colourful multi-ethnic village for this popular annual event. There's a laid-back party vibe and an excellent programme of concerts. Check www.villaada.org.

Festa dei Santi Pietro e Paolo

On 29 June, Romans celebrate their two patron saints, Peter and Paul, with a mass at St Peter's Basilica and a street fair on Via Ostiense near the Basilica di San Paolo Fuori le Mura.

 July

Villa Celimontana Jazz

Rome's best jazz festival is held in the ravishing Villa Celimontana park on Celio hill. Concerts are held every night in July, attracting quality performers and passionate audiences. Get programme details at www.villacelimontanajazz.com.

Festa di Noantri

Trastevere celebrates its roots with a raucous street party in the last two weeks of July. Centred on Piazza Santa Maria in Trastevere, events kick off with a religious procession and continue with much eating, drinking, dancing and praying.

 August

 Festa della Madonna della Neve

On 5 August, rose petals are showered on celebrants in the Basilica di Santa Maria Maggiore to commemorate a miraculous 4th-century snowfall. This impressive miracle is celebrated at the Basilica di Santa Maria Maggiore on 5 August.

 October

Romaeuropa

Established international performers join emerging stars at Rome's premier dance and drama festival. Events, staged throughout October and November, range from avant-garde dance performances to installations, multimedia shows, recitals and readings. Get details at http://romaeuropa.net/.

Festival Internazionale del Film di Roma

Held at the Auditorium Parco della Musica, Rome's film festival rolls out the red carpet for Hollywood hotshots and bigwigs from Italian cinema. Consult the programme at www.romacinemafest.org.

 November

Roma Jazz Festival

Jazz masters descend on the Auditorium Parco della Musica for the three-week Roma Jazz Festival (www.romajazzfestival.it).

Festival Internazionale di Musica e Arte Sacra

Over four days in mid-November, the Vienna Philharmonic Orchestra and other top ensembles perform a series of classical concerts in Rome's four papal basilicas. Check the programme on www.festivalmusicaeartesacra.net.

 December

Piazza Navona Christmas Fair

Rome's most beautiful baroque square becomes a big, brash marketplace as brightly lit market stalls set up shop, selling everything from nativity scenes to teeth-cracking *torrone* (nougat), until Epiphany on 6 January.

What's New

For this new edition of Discover Rome, our authors have hunted down the fresh, the transformed, the hot and the happening. These are some of our favourites. For up-to-the-minute recommendations, see lonelyplanet.com/Rome.

1 MAXXI
A stunning work of modern architecture, the Museo Nazionale delle Arti del XXI Secolo (MAXXI) has finally opened its doors to the public more than 10 years after it was commissioned. (p213)

2 MUSEO NAZIONALE ROMANO – PALAZZO MASSIMO ALLE TERME
The superb Roman frescoes on the 3rd floor are looking better than ever thanks to a new layout that better reflects they way they would have originally been placed. (p135)

3 BEER
Rome's beer drinkers have never had it so good as a trend for artisanal brews sweeps the city. Have a taste at Open Baladin (p94) or Ma Che Siete Venuti a Fà. (p179)

4 SALOTTO LOCARNO
This debonair art deco bar in the gorgeous Locarno Hotel is the perfect place to dress up and drink elegant cocktails. (p115)

5 VILLA SPALLETTI TRIVELLI
Live like a local aristocrat at this refined city-centre country house, a fabulous addition to Rome's luxury accommodation scene. (p263)

6 L'ASINO D'ORO
This minimalist trattoria brings the earthy tastes of the Umbrian countryside to the bohemian lanes of the Monti district. (p133)

7 BABUINO 181
Beautifully renovated old palazzo between Piazza del Popolo and Piazza di Spagna, offering discreet luxury. (p263)

8 PASTIFICIO SAN LORENZO
One of Rome's hot dining venues is this chic restaurant in the industrial-arthouse setting of San Lorenzo's Pastificio Cerere. (p137)

9 SWEETY ROME
Sumptuous iced cupcakes, brunch and pancakes are on offer at this little cafe just off Via Nazionale. (p134)

10 LUCIA ODESCALCHI
Jewellery designer Luca Odescalchi has open a new showroom and shop in the beautiful surrounds of her family palace, in the former archive room. (p119)

Get Inspired

Books

o **I, Claudius** (Robert Graves) Understand the intrigue and entanglements of imperial Rome with this rollicking read.

o **Imperium** (Robert Harris) Fictional and well-researched biography of Cicero brings the ancient Roman emperor to life.

o **Michelangelo & the Pope's Ceiling** (Ross King) Fascinating account of the painting of the Sistine Chapel.

o **Roman Tales** (Alberto Moravia) Short stories set in Rome's poorest neighbourhoods.

Films

o **The Talented Mr Ripley** Murderous intrigue on Piazza di Spagna and in other Italian locations.

o **Roma Città Aperta** (Rome Open City) A neorealist study of desperation in Nazi-occupied Rome.

o **Il Divo** (The Deity) Impressionistic, compelling story of Italian politician Giulio Andreotti.

o **La Dolce Vita** Federico Fellini film that epitomised an era and gave us the term 'paparazzi'.

♫ Music

o **Three Coins in the Fountain** (Frank Sinatra) Classic, velvet-voiced theme for a somewhat cheesy 1954 film.

o **Fellini Jazz** (Enrico Pieranunzi) Sizzling jazz by one of Rome's most renowned musicians.

o **Concert at the Vatican** (Sistine Chapel Choir) Choral classics to get you in the mood for the heart of Christendom.

o **Rome** (Danger Mouse & Daniele Luppi) Music inspired by the Roman spaghetti westerns, featuring vocals by Jack White and Norah Jones.

Websites

o **Lonely Planet** (www.lonelyplanet.com /rome) Destination lowdown, hotels and traveller forum.

o **060608** (www.060608 .it) Rome's official tourist website.

o **Revealed Rome** (www .revealedrome.com) Insider tips on things to see and do.

o **Pierreci** (www.pierreci .it) Information and ticket booking for Rome's monuments.

Short on time?

This list will give you an instant insight into the city.

Read *Rome* (Robert Hughes) is a sweeping, entertaining analysis covering the city's art, architecture and history.

See Gregory Peck and Audrey Hepburn fall in love and whizz around on a Vespa in the enchanting romance, *Roman Holiday*.

Hear Puccini's *Tosca* is the ultimate Rome opera: at its climax Tosca throws herself off the terrace of Castel Sant'Angelo.

Log on In Rome Now (www .inromenow.com) is an up-to-date English-language site, with the low-down on cultural happenings in the Eternal City.

Statue in the Trevi Fountain (p109)

Need to Know

Currency
Euro (€)

Language
Italian

Visas
Not required by EU citizens. Not required by nationals of Australia, Canada, New Zealand and the USA for stays of up to 90 days.

Money
ATMs are widespread. Credit cards are accepted in larger hotels and restaurants.

Mobile Phones
Local SIM cards can be used in European, Australian and unlocked US phones. Other phones must be set to roaming.

Time
Western European Time (GMT/UTC plus one hour).

Wi-Fi
In some cafes, hotels and various public spaces in the city. Sometimes free.

Tipping
Bars: small change (eg €0.20–0.50); hotel porters: €3–5; restaurants: €1 per person (with service charge) or 10% (without).

For more information, see Survival Guide (p271).

When to Go

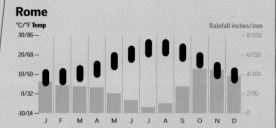

Rome

In spring (April to June) and early autumn (September and October) there's good weather and many festivals and outdoor events. It's also busy and peak rates apply.

Advance Planning

Two months Book high season accommodation.

Three to four weeks Check for concerts at www.auditorium.it, www.operaroma.it and www.circoloartisti.it.

One to two weeks Reserve tables at A-list restaurants. Sort out tickets to the Pope's weekly audience at St Peter's.

Few days Check www.estateromana.comune.roma.it for free summer events. Phone for tickets for the Museo e Galleria Borghese (compulsory) and book for the Vatican Museums (advisable to avoid queues).

Your Daily Budget

Budget less than €70
- Dorm beds €15–35
- Pizza meal plus beer €15
- Save by drinking coffee standing at the bar
- Have an *aperitivo* (aperative) and eat for the price of a drink

Midrange €70–200
- Double room €120–250
- Three-course restaurant meal €30–50
- OK to mix and match courses when eating out
- B&Bs are often better value than hotels in the same category

Top End over €200
- Double room €250 plus
- City taxi ride €5–15
- Auditorium concert tickets €25–90

Arriving in Rome

Leonardo da Vinci (Fiumicino) Airport Direct trains to Stazione Termini 6.38am–11.38pm, €14; slower trains to Trastevere, Ostiense and Tiburtina stations, 5.43am–11.38pm, €8; buses to Stazione Termini 8.30am–12.30am and at 1.15am, 2.15am, 3.30am and 5am, €4.50–8; private transfers €25–37 per person; taxis €40.

Ciampino Airport Buses to Stazione Termini 7.45am–12.15am, €4–6; private transfers €25–37 per person; taxis €30.

Getting Around

Rome's public transport system includes buses, trams, metro and a suburban train network. The main hub is Stazione Termini, the only point at which the city's two metro lines cross. The metro is quicker than surface transport but the network is limited and the bus is often a better bet. Children under 10 travel free.

○ **Metro** Two lines A (orange) and B (blue). Runs 5.30am to 11.30pm (to 1.30am on Friday and Saturday).

○ **Buses** Most routes pass through Stazione Termini. Buses run 5.30am until midnight, with limited services throughout the night.

Sleeping

Rome is expensive and with the city busy year-round, you'll want to book as far ahead as you can to secure the best deal and the place you want.

Accommodation options range from palatial five-star hotels to hostels, B&Bs, convents and *pensioni*. Hostels are the cheapest, offering dorm beds and private rooms. Bed and breakfasts range from simple home-style set-ups to chic boutique outfits with prices to match, while religious institutions provide basic, value-for-money accommodation but may insist on a curfew. Hotels are plentiful and there are many budget, family-run *pensioni* in the Termini area.

Useful Websites

○ **060608** (www.060608.it) Lists all official accommodation options (with prices).

○ **Santa Susanna** (www.santasusanna.org /comingToRome/convents.html) Has information on religious accommodation.

○ **Bed & Breakfast Italia** (www.bbitalia.com) Rome's longest-established B&B network.

What to Bring

○ **Sun hat** If you're travelling from May to September.

○ **Comfortable shoes** So you can wander and sightsee to your heart's and feet's content.

○ **Smart clothes** At least one smart outfit, to fit in with the Italian *bella figura*.

○ **Regular medications** Those available over the counter – such as antihistamine or paracetamol – tend to be fairly expensive in Italy.

Be Forewarned

○ **Petty crime** Pickpocketing can be an annoyance in Rome. Keep your valuables out of reach, particularly on public transport.

○ **Safety** Rome is a fairly safe city, but use your common sense and don't wander dark, deserted areas late at night.

○ **Closures** Many restaurants and businesses in Rome close during the month of August – this is the holiday month for most Italians, and the summer is at its hottest.

Organised Tours

Taking a tour is a good way of seeing a lot in a short time or investigating a sight in depth. There are several outfits running hop-on hop-off bus tours, typically costing about €20 per person. Both the Colosseum and Vatican Museums offer official guided tours, but for a more personalised service you'll be better off with a private guide. For more details see p269.

Ancient Rome

Just south of the city centre, this area contains the great ruins of the ancient city, all concentrated within strolling distance. There are two focal points: the Colosseum to the east and the Campidoglio (Capitoline hill) to the west. In between lie the forums: the more famous Roman Forum on the left of Via dei Fori Imperiali, as you walk up from the Colosseum, and the Imperial Forums on the right. Rising above the Roman Forum is the Palatino, the imperial city's most exclusive neighbourhood, dotted by ruined palaces, and behind that is the Circo Massimo, ancient Rome's racecourse. Continuing northwest from the Circo Massimo brings you to the Forum Boarium, a former cattle market and river port, where you'll find the Bocca della Verità, Rome's mythical lie detector.

To explore the area, the obvious starting point is the Colosseum, which is easily accessible by metro.

Palatino ruins (p58)
SFAGNAN/DREAMSTIME.COM ©

Ancient Rome Highlights

Colosseum (p52)

Built in the 1st century, on a site formerly occupied by Nero's ornamental lake in the grounds of his palace Domus Aurea, Rome's towering gladiatorial amphitheatre is both an architectural masterpiece – the blueprint for much modern stadium design – and a stark, spine-tingling reminder of the brutality of ancient times. Here, crowds of up to 50,000 used to roar for blood as gladiators and unfortunates fought wild beasts for entertainment.

WIBOWO RUSLI/LONELY PLANET IMAGES ©

Palatino (p54)

Explore the vestiges of lost empires by wandering around the haunting and evocative ruins of the Palatino. Ancient Rome's most exclusive neighbourhood sprawls across a richly verdant hill and overlooks the huge oval of Circo Massimo, the ancient racecourse, which had capacity for a quarter of the city's population. It's easy to imagine the emperors cheering on the chariot races from the peak of the hill.

RICHARD I'ANSO/LONELY PLANET IMAGES ©

Capitoline Museums (p59)

Come face to face with centuries of awe-inspiring art at the world's oldest national museums, housed in twin *palazzi* that face each other across Michelangelo's perfect piazza. The collection ranges from ancient sculpture, such as the emotive *Dying Gaul*, to Bernini's frenetic *Medusa*, and upstairs is the masterpiece-filled Pinacoteca, with works by Caravaggio, Titian, Tintoretto, Reni, van Dyck and Rubens. Statue of Romulus and Remus being fed by the Capitoline Wolf

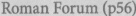

Roman Forum (p56)

The Roman Forum, the sometime political heart of the Empire, might be a shadow of its former glory, but there's something undeniably amazing about walking down the Via Sacra, its once-grand thoroughfare. It only takes a little bit of imagination to transform the slightly shambolic collection of stones into the grandiose ensemble of marble-clad temples, proud basilicas and vibrant public spaces it once was.

Il Vittoriano (p63)

Il Vittoriano, the vast marble monument built in 1885 to commemorate Italian unification and honour Vittorio Emanuele II, Italy's first king, might be an undeniable white monstrosity, but it offers some of the finest 360-degree views in Rome. Take the glass lift up and survey the grandeur of the city spread out all around you.

Ancient Rome Walk

Follow in the footsteps of an ancient Roman on this meander around the imperial city's heartland, with its many magnificent ruins.

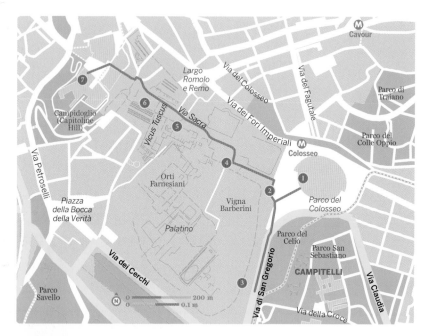

WALK FACTS
- **Start** Colosseum
- **Finish** Piazza del Campidoglio
- **Distance** 1.2km
- **Duration** Three hours

❶ Colosseum

However many times you set eyes on this vast, millennia-old stadium (p52), it never ceases to amaze. It's particularly awe-inspiring from the exterior, which is remarkably complete, having survived raids for its marble, sacking and earthquakes. This is the perfect place to start your walk around the heart of Ancient Rome.

❷ Arco di Costantino

Just beside the Colosseum is this beautifully carved triumphal arch (p58), built in 312 to commemorate Constantine's victory over Maxentius at the Battle of Ponte Milvio. However, as the empire was becoming increasingly strapped for cash, the arch was constructed from other, earlier monuments, some of them dating as far back as AD 82.

❸ Palatino

From the Arco di Costantino, it's about 400m south along Via di San Gregorio to the **Palatino** (p54). This was Ancient Rome's most sought-after neighbourhood, where the emperor lived alongside the cream of imperial society. The ruins are not always easy to make sense of, but their scale gives some sense of the luxury in which the ancient VIPs liked to live. You can still make out parts of the **Domus Augustana**, the emperor's private residence, and the **Domus Flavia**, where he would hold official audiences.

Arco di Tito

Head north, descending the Palatine hill, and enter the Roman Forum near the **Arco di Tito**, another great triumphal arch. This one commemorates the Sack of Jerusalem in AD 79. The reliefs beneath the arch show scenes from Titus's triumphal parade along the Via Sacra, the main road running through the Forum.

Casa delle Vestali

Bear right and head along the Via Sacra. Follow the path down and, after a few hundred metres, you'll come to the **Casa delle Vestali** (p57), where the legendary Vestal Virgins lived, tending to their duties and guarding their virtue.

Basilica Giulia & the Curia

Beyond the three columns of the Tempio di Castore e Polluce, you'll see a flattened area littered with column bases and brick stumps. This is the **Basilica Giulia**, where lawyers and magistrates worked to dispense justice in the crowded law courts. Meanwhile, senators debated matters of state at the **Curia**, over on the other side of the Forum.

Campidoglio & the Capitoline

From near the Curia, exit the Forum and climb up the **Campidoglio** (Capitoline hill; p59) to the magnificent **Capitoline Museums** (p59). If you're after a long, leisurely lunch, descend the flight of steps leading to Via d'Aracoeli, and head for a restaurant in the Ghetto, Rome's historic Jewish quarter (p91). If all you want is a snack, try the lovely **Caffè Capitolino** (p67) behind the museums.

★★★ The Best...

PLACES TO EAT

Hostaria da Nerone Old-school trattoria where hearty pasta dishes will set you up for sightseeing. (p66)

San Teodoro Smart seafood restaurant with a chic interior and attractive outdoor terrace. (p67)

Ara Coeli Artisanal ice-creamery, handily placed a few steps down from the Campidoglio. (p67)

PLACES TO DRINK

Caffè Capitolino Cafe at the Capitoline Museums, with stupendous views over Rome's rooftops. (p67)

Cavour 313 Wood-panelled wine bar with the cosiness of a pub, a fantastic wine list, and moreish snacks. (p67)

LOOKOUTS

Il Vittoriano You can almost forgive the monument's monstrosity when you see the 360-degree views from the top. (p63)

Orti Farnesiani The Farnese 16th-century botanical gardens on the Palatino have views over to the Colosseum. (p55)

Tabularium, Capitoline Museums The former hall of records, perched on Capitoline hill, provides a balcony over the Roman Forum. (p59)

Statue in Piazza del Campidoglio
WITOLD SKRYPCZAK/LONELY PLANET IMAGES ©

Don't Miss
Colosseum

A monument to raw, merciless power, the Colosseum (Colosseo) is the most thrilling of Rome's ancient sights. It's not just the amazing completeness of the place, or its size, but the sense of violent history that resonates: it was here that gladiators met in mortal combat and condemned prisoners fought off wild beasts in front of baying, bloodthirsty crowds.

Map p60

📞 06 399 67 700

www.pierreci.it

Piazza del Colosseo

Adult/reduced incl Roman Forum & Palatino €12/7.50, audioguides €5.50

🕗 8.30am-1hr before sunset

Ⓜ Colosseo

History

Built by Vespasian (r AD 69–79) in the grounds of Nero's vast Domus Aurea complex, the Colosseum was inaugurated in AD 80. The 50,000-seat arena was originally known as the Flavian Amphitheatre, and although it was Rome's most fearful arena, it wasn't the biggest – the Circo Massimo could hold up to 250,000 people.

The name Colosseum, when introduced in medieval times, was not a reference to its size but to the *Colosso di Nerone,* a giant statue of Nero that stood nearby.

With the fall of the Roman empire in the 6th century, the Colosseum was abandoned and gradually became overgrown. In the Middle Ages it became a fortress, occupied by two of the city's warrior families, the Frangipani and the Annibaldi.

Exterior

The outer walls have three levels of arches, articulated by Ionic, Doric and Corinthian columns. They were originally covered in travertine, and marble statues once filled the niches on the 2nd and 3rd storeys. The upper level had supports for 240 masts that held up a canvas awning over the arena. The entrance arches, known as *vomitoria,* allowed the spectators to enter and be seated in a matter of minutes.

Interior

The interior was divided into the arena, *cavea* and podium. The arena had a wooden floor covered in sand to prevent the combatants from slipping and to soak up the blood. It could also be flooded for mock sea battles. Trapdoors led down to the hypogeum, an underground complex of corridors, cages and lifts beneath the arena floor.

Hypogeum

The hypogeum, along with the top tier, have recently been opened to the public. Visits, which cost €8 on top of the normal Colosseum ticket and are by guided tour only, require advance booking.

Don't Miss List

BY VINCENZO MACCARRONE,
COLOSSEUM
STAFF MEMBER

1 ARENA
The arena had a wooden floor covered in sand to prevent combatants from slipping and to soak up blood. Gladiators arrived directly from their training ground via underground passageways, and were hoisted onto the arena by a complicated system of pulleys.

2 CAVEA AND PODIUM
The cavea, for spectator seating, was divided into three tiers: knights in the lowest, wealthy citizens in the middle and plebs at the top. The podium – close to the action but protected by nets made of hemp – was reserved for emperors, senators and VIPs.

3 FACADE
The exterior mimics the Teatro di Marcello (p81); the walls were once clad in travertine, with statues in the niches on the 2nd and 3rd storeys. On the top level are holes that held wooden masts supporting the Velarium (a canvas awning over the arena).

4 TEMPORARY EXHIBITIONS
The 2nd floor hosts some fantastic exhibitions, either about the Colosseum or on the wider history of Rome. Walk past the bookshop to the end of the corridor and look out towards the eastern side of the Roman Forum – there's a wonderful view from here of the Tempio di Venere e Roma (Temple of Venus and Rome), hard to see from the ground.

5 THE PERFECT PHOTO
Towards closing time, the Colosseum is bathed in a beautiful light. For great views of the building, head up Colle Oppio (Oppio Hill) right above the Colosseo metro station, or up Colle Celio (Celio Hill) opposite the Palatino and Colosseum exit.

Don't Miss
Palatino

Sandwiched between the Roman Forum and the Circo Massimo, the Palatino (Palatine hill) is an atmospheric area of towering pine trees, majestic ruins and memorable views. According to legend, this is where Romulus and Remus were saved by a wolf and where Romulus founded Rome in 753 BC. Archaeological evidence cannot prove the legend but it has dated human habitation to the 8th century BC. As the most central of Rome's seven hills, and because it was close to the Roman Forum, the Palatino was ancient Rome's poshest neighbourhood.

Map p60

☎ 06 399 67 700

www.pierreci.it

Via di San Gregorio 30

Adult/reduced incl Colosseum & Roman Forum €12/7.50, audioguides €5;

⏰ 8.30am-1hr before sunset

Ⓜ Colosseo

Stadio & Domus Augustana

On entering the Palatino from Via di San Gregorio, head uphill until you come to the first recognisable construction, the **stadio**. This sunken area, part of the main imperial palace, was used by the emperor for private games. Next to the stadio are the ruins of the **Domus Augustana**, the emperor's private residence. Over two levels, rooms lead off a *peristilio* (garden courtyard) on each floor. You can't get to the lower level, but from above you can see the basin of a fountain and, beyond it, rooms that were paved with coloured marble.

Museo Palatino & Domus Flavia

The **Museo Palatino** (admission incl in Palatino ticket; ⊙8am-4pm) houses a small collection of finds from the Palatino. On the other side of the Museo Palatino is the **Domus Flavia**, the public part of Domitian's palace complex.

Casa di Livia & Casa di Augusto

Among the best-preserved buildings on the Palatino is the **Casa di Livia,** northwest of the Domus Flavia. Home to Augustus' wife Livia, it was built around an atrium leading onto what were once frescoed reception rooms. In front is the **Casa di Augusto** (⊙11am-4.30pm Mon, Wed, Sat & Sun), Augustus' separate residence, which contains superb frescoes in vivid colours.

Orti Farnesiani & Criptoportico

In the northwest corner of the Palatino, **Orti Farnesiani** is one of Europe's earliest botanical gardens. Named after Cardinal Alessandro Farnese, who had them laid out in the mid-16th century, they boast lovely perfumed hedges and shady pines.

Near the Orti Farnesiani, the **criptoportico** is a 128m tunnel where Caligula is said to have been murdered and which Nero used to connect his Domus Aurea with the Palatino. Lit by a series of windows, it is now used to stage temporary exhibitions.

1 **HUT VILLAGE**
This is the sacred place of the origin of Rome. Here Romulus decided to locate his primitive city, formed of mud and straw huts. The holes for the planks in the tufa rock are still visible today, and recent studies have identified Romulus' hut.

2 **AUGUSTUS COMPLEX: HOUSE OF AUGUSTUS AND HOUSE OF LIVIA**
Ottaviani Augustus, the first emperor, chose to live close to the hut of Romulus during his long reign. This was a complex of buildings rather than a single palace, and contains perhaps the most important and refined series of frescoes of the Roman tradition.

3 **CRIPTOPORTICO OF NERO**
This is a long enclosed corridor, which was used to link the various nuclei of the imperial palace in the Julius–Claudium period. It was also used after the building of the Domus Flavia. According to literary sources, it's thought that it might have been the corridor where Caligula was killed.

4 **DOMUS FLAVIA AND THE STADIUM**
The Flavian emperors, together with the architect Rabirio, built the residential palace par excellence. Rabirio's articulated architecture is enriched by fountains and gardens. Particularly interesting is the stadium, which was used by the imperial family as an area for walks, exercise and leisure time (*otium*).

5 **FARNESI GARDENS, WITH VIEWS OVER THE ROMAN FORUM AND THE CITY**
By the mid-15th century, what remained of the Tiberian palace was covered by the vegetable patches of Farnesi, created by Cardinal Alessandro Farnese (nephew of Pope Paul III). The magnificent gardens have undergone several changes over the centuries. Currently, major excavations are taking place to bring the ancient Tiberian palace to life.

Don't Miss
Roman Forum

Once the gleaming heart of the ancient world, a grandiose ensemble of marble-clad temples, proud basilicas and vibrant public spaces, the Roman Forum (Foro Romano) is now a collection of impressive but badly labelled ruins that can leave you drained and confused. But if you can set your imagination going, there's something undeniably compelling about walking in the footsteps of Julius Caesar and the great emperors of Roman history. For more detail, see p64.

Map p60

☎ 06 399 67 700

www.pierreci.it

Largo della Salara Vecchia

Adult/reduced incl Colosseum & Palatino €12/7.50, audioguides €5;

🕑 8.30am-1hr before sunset

Ⓜ Colosseo

Via Sacra Towards Campidoglio

Entering the Forum from Largo della Salara Vecchia – you can also enter directly from the Palatino – you'll see the **Tempio di Antonino e Faustina** ahead to your left. Erected in AD 141, this was later transformed into a church, so the soaring columns now frame the **Chiesa di San Lorenzo in Miranda**. To your right the **Basilica Fulvia Aemilia**, built in 179 BC, was a 100m-long public hall, with a two-storey porticoed facade.

At the end of the short path, you come to **Via Sacra,** the Forum's main throughfare. Opposite the basilica stands the **Tempio di Giulio Cesare** (Temple of Julius Caesar) built by Augustus in 29 BC. Head right up Via Sacra and you reach the **Curia,** the meeting place of the Roman Senate. This was rebuilt on various occasions and what you see today is a 1937 reconstruction of Diocletian's Curia.

In front of the Curia, and hidden by scaffolding, is the **Lapis Niger**, a large piece of black marble that covered a sacred area said to be the tomb of Romulus.

At the end of Via Sacra stands the 23m-high **Arco di Settimio Severo** (Arch of Septimius Severus), dedicated to the eponymous emperor and his two sons, Caracalla and Geta. Nearby, at the foot of the Tempio di Saturno, is the Millarium Aureum, from where distances to the ancient city were measured.

On your left are the remains of the **Rostrum**, an elaborate podium where Shakespeare had Mark Antony make his famous 'Friends, Romans, countrymen...' speech. In front of this, the **Colonna di Foca** (Column of Phocus) marks the centre of the Piazza del Foro, the forum's main square.

The eight granite columns that rise up behind the Colonna are all that remain of the **Tempio di Saturno** (Temple of Saturn), an important temple that doubled as the state treasury. Behind it are (from north to south): the ruins of the **Tempio della Concordia** (Temple of Concord), the **Tempio di Vespasiano** (Temple of Vespasian and Titus) and the **Portico degli Dei Consenti**.

Tempio di Castore e Polluce & Casa delle Vestali

Passing over to the path that runs parallel to Via Sacra, you'll see the stubby ruins of the **Basilica Giulia**, which was begun by Julius Caesar and finished by Augustus. At the end of the basilica, the three columns you see belong to the 5th-century BC **Tempio di Castore e Polluce** (Temple of Castor and Pollux). Near the temple, the **Chiesa di Santa Maria Antiqua** is the oldest Christian church in the Forum, and the **Casa delle Vestali** (House of the Vestal Virgins) was home to the virgins who tended the flame in the adjoining **Tempio di Vesta**.

Via Sacra Towards the Colosseum

Heading up Via Sacra past the **Tempio di Romolo** (Temple of Romulus), you come to the **Basilica di Massenzio**, the largest building on the forum. Started by the Emperor Maxentius and finished by Constantine (it's also known as the Basilica di Costantino), it covered an area of approximately 100m by 65m.

Continuing, you come to the **Arco di Tito** (Arch of Titus), built in AD 81 to celebrate Vespasian and Titus' victories against Jerusalem.

Vestal Virgins

Every year, six physically perfect patrician girls between the ages of six and 10 were chosen by lottery to serve Vesta, goddess of hearth and household. Once selected, they faced a 30-year period of chaste servitude at the Tempio di Vesta. During this time their main duty was to ensure that the temple's sacred fire never went out. If a priestess were to lose her virginity she risked being buried alive and the offending man being flogged to death.

Discover Ancient Rome

 Getting There & Away

○ **Bus** Frequent buses head to Piazza Venezia, including numbers 40, 64, 87, 170, 492, 916 and H.

○ **Metro** Metro line B has stops at the Colosseum (Colosseo) and Circo Massimo. At Termini follow signs for metro Line B direzione Laurentina.

 Sights

Colosseum & Palatino

Colosseum Monument
See p52.

Arco di Costantino Monument
Map p60 (Via di San Gregorio; Ⓜ Colosseo) The Arco di Costantino (Arch of Constantine) was built in 312 to commemorate Constantine's victory over his rival Maxentius at the Battle of Ponte Milvio. One of the last great Roman monuments, it incorporates stonework dating to Domitian's reign (AD 81–96) and eight large medallions produced in Hadrian's time (117–138).

Palatino Ancient Ruins
See p54.

Circo Massimo Historical Site
Map p60 (Via del Circo Massimo; Ⓜ Circo Massimo) Now just a basin of grass, gravel and dust, the Circo Massimo (Circus Maximus) was 1st-century Rome's biggest stadium with a capacity of 250,000. The 600m racetrack circled a wooden dividing island with ornate lap indicators and Egyptian obelisks.

Forums & Around

Before venturing into the forums, take a minute to prepare yourself at the **Centro Espositivo Informativo** (Map p60; ☏ 06 679 77 02; Via dei Fori Imperiali; ☺ 9.30am-6.30pm; Ⓜ Colosseo), an information centre dedicated to the area.

Roman Forum Ancient Ruins
See p56 and p64.

Arco di Costantino
JAN BUTCHOFSKY/CORBIS ©

Basilica di SS Cosma e Damiano
Church

Map p60 (Via dei Fori Imperiali; ⏲9am-1pm & 3-7pm; MColosseo) Backing onto the Roman Forum, this 6th-century basilica incorporates parts of the **Foro di Vespasiano** and **Tempio di Romolo**, visible through the glass wall at the end of the nave. The real reason to visit, though, are the vibrant 6th-century apse mosaics, depicting Christ's Second Coming.

Imperial Forums
Ruins

Map p60 (MColosseo) The ruins over the road from the Roman Forum are known collectively as the Imperial Forums (Fori Imperiali). Constructed between 42 BC and AD 112, they were largely buried in 1933 when Mussolini built Via dei Fori Imperiali. Excavations have since unearthed much of them but visits are limited to the Mercati di Traiano (Trajan's Markets), accessible through the Museo dei Fori Imperiali.

Little recognisable remains of the Foro di Traiano (Trajan's Forum), except for some pillars from the **Basilica Ulpia** and the **Colonna di Traiano** (Trajan's Column), whose minutely detailed reliefs celebrate Trajan's military victories over the Dacians (from modern-day Romania).

To the southeast, three temple columns rise from Foro di Augusto (Augustus' Forum), now mostly under Via dei Fori Imperiali. The 30m-high wall behind the forum was built to protect it from the frequent fires in the area.

The Foro di Nerva (Nerva's Forum) was also buried by Mussolini's road-building, although part of a temple dedicated to Minerva still stands. Over the road, three columns are the most visible remains of the Foro di Cesare (Caesar's Forum).

Mercati di Traiano Museo dei Fori Imperiali
Museum

Map p60 (☎06 06 08; www.mercatiditraiano .it; Via IV Novembre 94; adult/reduced €11/9; ⏲9am-7pm Tue-Sun, last entry 6pm) Housed in Trajan's 2nd-century market complex, this striking museum provides a fascinating introduction to the Imperial Forums with detailed explanatory panels and a smattering of archaeological artefacts.

Carcere Mamertino
Historical Site

Map p60; Clivo Argentario 1; €10; ⏲9.30am-7pm summer, 9.30am-5pm winter, last admission 40min before closing time; 🚌Piazza Venezia) At the foot of the Campidoglio, the Mamertine Prison was ancient Rome's maximum-security prison. St Peter did time here and while imprisoned supposedly created a miraculous stream of water to baptise his jailers.

Campidoglio

Rising above the Roman Forum, the Campidoglio (Capitoline hill) was one of the seven hills on which Rome was founded. At its summit were Rome's two most important temples: one dedicated to Jupiter Capitolinus (a descendant of Jupiter, the Roman equivalent of Zeus) and the other (which housed Rome's mint) to the goddess Juno Moneta.

Capitoline Museums
Museums

Map p60 (☎06 06 08; www.museicapitolini.org; Piazza del Campidoglio 1; adult/reduced €12/10, audioguides €5; ⏲9am-8pm Tue-Sun, last admission 7pm; 🚌Piazza Venezia) The world's oldest national museums are housed in two stately *palazzi* on the Michelangelo-designed Piazza del Campidoglio. Their origins date to 1471, when Pope Sixtus IV donated a number of bronze statues to the city, forming the nucleus of what is now one of Italy's finest collections of classical art.

Start at the Palazzo dei Conservatori. Before you head upstairs, take a moment to admire the ancient masonry around the ground-floor courtyard, most notably a mammoth head, hand and foot. These all came from a 12m-high statue of Constantine that originally stood in the Basilica di Massenzio in the Roman Forum.

Of the sculpture on the 1st floor, the Etruscan *Lupa Capitolina* (Capitoline Wolf) is the most famous. Located in the Sala Della Lupa, this 5th-century-BC bronze wolf stands over her suckling wards Romulus and Remus, who were added to the composition in 1471.

The 2nd floor is given over to the Pinacoteca, the museum's picture gallery, with paintings by such heavyweights as

Ancient Rome

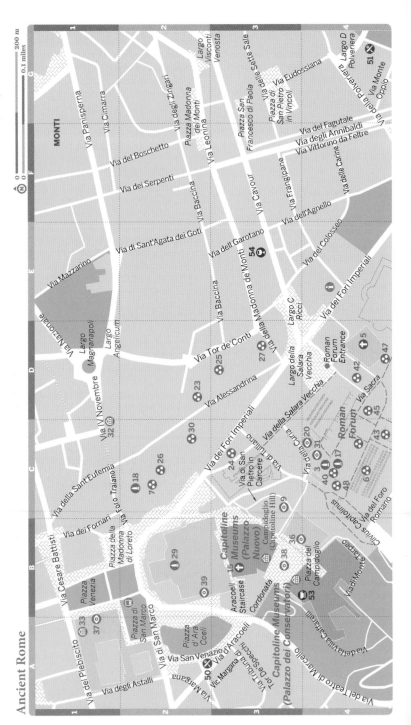

200 m
0.1 miles

MONTI

Via Panisperna
Via Cimarra
Via degli Zingari
Largo Visconti Venosta
Via Madonna dei Monti
Piazza Madonna dei Monti
Piazza San Francesco di Paola
Via delle Sette Sale
Via Eudossiana
Piazza di San Pietro in Vincoli
Largo D Polveriera
Via del Boschetto
Via Leonina
Via del Fagutale
Via degli Annibaldi
Via Vittorino da Feltre
51

Via dei Serpenti
Via del Monte Oppio

Via di Sant'Agata dei Goti
Via Baccina
Via Cavour
Via Frangipane
Via delle Carine Ant

Via Mazzarino
Via dell'Agnello

Via del Garotano
54
Via del Colosseo

Largo Magnanapoli
Largo Angelicum
Via Baccina

Via Nazionale

Via Tor de'Conti
Largo C. Ricci
Via dei Fori Imperiali
27
Largo della Salara Vecchia
25
23

Via IV Novembre
32
Via Alessandrina
Roman Forum Entrance
5
42
47
30
Via della Madonna dei Monti
Via della Salara Vecchia

Via dei Fori Imperiali
24
Via di San Pietro in Carcere
Via di Tulliano
20
Via Sacra
45

Via della Sant'Eufemia
18
7
26
31
17
43

Via della Foro Traiano
Roman Forum
48
6

Via dei Fornari
3
40

Piazza della Madonna di Loreto
9
Clivus Capitolinus
Via del Foro Romano

Via Cesare Battisti
29
Campidoglio (Capitoline Hill)
38
36
Clivus Capitolinus

Piazza Venezia
Capitoline Museums (Palazzo Nuovo)
15
Piazza del Campidoglio

Via del Plebiscito
33
37
Aracoeli Staircase
Cordonata
53
Via di Monte

Piazza di San Marco
39

Via di San Marco
Piazza d'Ara Coeli
Capitoline Museums (Palazzo dei Conservatori)
Via del Teatro di Marcello

Via San Venazio
50
Via d'Aracoeli
Vic Margana
Tor De'specchi
Via 17 Tribuna d'Aracoeli

Via Marsana
Via della Villa Caffarelli

Via degli Astalli

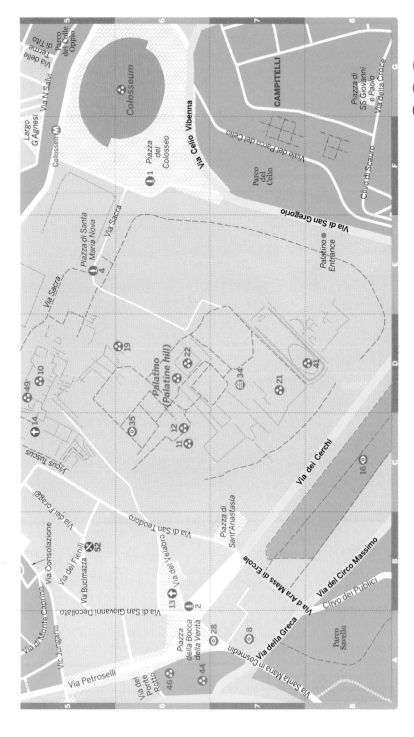

61

Ancient Rome

Titian, Tintoretto, Reni, van Dyck and Rubens. Sala di Santa Petronilla has a number of important canvases, including two by Caravaggio: *La Buona Ventura* (The Fortune Teller; 1595), which shows a gypsy pretending to read a young man's hand but actually stealing his ring, and *San Giovanni Battista* (John the Baptist; 1602), a sensual and unusual depiction of the saint.

A tunnel links Palazzo dei Conservatori to Palazzo Nuovo on the other side of the square via the Tabularium, ancient Rome's central archive, beneath Palazzo Senatorio.

Palazzo Nuovo contains some real show-stoppers. Chief among them is the *Galata Morente* (Dying Gaul) in the Sala del Gladiatore. Also in this room, the *Satiro in Riposo* (Resting Satyr) is said to have inspired Nathaniel Hawthorne to write his novel *The Marble Faun*.

Piazza del Campidoglio   Piazza

Map p60 (🚇 Piazza Venezia) Designed by Michelangelo in 1538, this elegant piazza is one of Rome's most beautiful squares. You can reach it from the Roman Forum but the most dramatic approach is via the

Cordonata, the graceful staircase that leads up from Piazza d'Ara Coeli. At the top of the stairs, the piazza is bordered by three *palazzi*: **Palazzo Nuovo** to the left, **Palazzo Senatorio** straight ahead and **Palazzo dei Conservatori** on the right. Together, Palazzo Nuovo and Palazzo dei Conservatori house the **Capitoline Museums**, while Palazzo Senatorio is home to Rome's city council.

In the centre, the bronze equestrian **statue of Marcus Aurelius** is a copy. The original, which dates from the 2nd century AD, is in the Capitoline Museums.

Chiesa di Santa Maria in Aracoeli   Church

Map p60 (Piazza Santa Maria in Aracoeli; ⏱9am-12.30pm & 3-6.30pm; 🚇Piazza Venezia) Marking the highest point of the Campidoglio, this 6th-century church sits on the site of the Roman temple to Juno Moneta. Features to note include the Cosmatesque floor and an important 15th-century fresco by Pinturicchio.

Piazza Venezia
Il Vittoriano   Monument

Map p60 (Piazza Venezia; admission free; ⏱9.30am-5.30pm summer, 9.30am-4.30pm winter; 🚇Piazza Venezia) Love it or loathe it, as most locals do, you can't ignore Il Vittoriano, the massive mountain of white marble that towers over Piazza Venezia. Known also as the Altare della Patria (Altar of the Fatherland), it was begun in 1885 to commemorate Italian unification and honour Vittorio Emanuele II, Italy's first king and the subject of its gargantuan equestrian statue. It also hosts the Tomb of the Unknown Soldier.

Whatever you might think of this monument, there's no denying that the 360-degree views from the top are quite stunning. To get to the top, take the glass lift, **Roma dal Cielo** (adult/reduced €7/3.50; ⏱9.30am-6.30pm Mon-Thu, to 7.30pm Fri-Sun), from the side of the building.

Palazzo Venezia   Museum

Map p60 (🚇Piazza Venezia) On the western side of Piazza Venezia, this was the first of Rome's great Renaissance palaces, built between 1455 and 1464. For centuries it served as the embassy of the Venetian Republic, although its best known resident was Mussolini, who famously made speeches from its balcony.

Palazzo Nuovo

Roman Forum

In ancient times, a forum was a market place, civic centre and religious complex all rolled into one, and the greatest of all was the Roman Forum (Foro Romano). Situated between the Palatino (Palatine Hill), ancient Rome's most exclusive neighbourhood, and the Campidoglio (Capitoline Hill), it was the city's busy, bustling centre. On any given day it teemed with activity. Senators debated affairs of state in the **Curia** ❶, shoppers thronged the squares and traffic-free streets, crowds gathered under the **Colonna di Foca** ❷ to listen to politicians holding forth from the **Rostrum** ❷. Elsewhere, lawyers worked the courts in basilicas including the **Basilica di Massenzio** ❸, while the Vestal Virgins quietly went about their business in the **Casa delle Vestali** ❹.

Special occasions were also celebrated in the Forum: religious holidays were marked with ceremonies at temples such as the **Tempio di Saturno** ❺ and the **Tempio di Castore e Polluce** ❻, and military victories were honoured with dramatic processions up Via Sacra and the building of monumental arches like the **Arco di Settimio Severo** ❼ and the **Arco di Tito** ❽.

The ruins you see today are impressive but they can be confusing without a clear picture of what the Forum once looked like. This spread shows the Forum in its heyday, complete with temples, civic buildings and towering monuments to heroes of the Roman Empire.

TOP TIPS

Get grandstand views of the Forum from the Palatino and Campidoglio.

Visit first thing in the morning or late afternoon; crowds are worst between 11am and 2pm.

In summer it gets hot in the Forum and there's little shade, so take a hat and plenty of water.

Colonna di Foca & Rostrum

The free-standing, 13.5m-high Column of Phocus is the Forum's youngest monument, dating to AD 608. Behind it, the Rostrum provided a suitably grandiose platform for pontificating public speakers.

Campidoglio (Capitoline Hill)

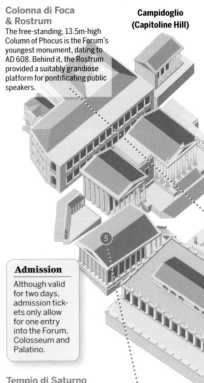

Admission

Although valid for two days, admission tickets only allow for one entry into the Forum, Colosseum and Palatino.

Tempio di Saturno

Ancient Rome's Fort Knox, the Temple of Saturn was the city treasury. In Caesar's day it housed 13 tonnes of gold, 114 tonnes of silver and 30 million *sestertii* worth of silver coins.

JONATHAN SMITH / LONELY PLANET IMAGES ©

GEOFF STRINGER / LONELY PLANET IMAGES ©

Tempio di Castore e Polluce

Only three columns of the Temple of Castor and Pollux remain. The temple was dedicated to the Heavenly Twins after they supposedly led the Romans to victory over the Etruscans.

Arco di Settimio Severo

One of the Forum's signature monuments, this imposing triumphal arch commemorates the military victories of Septimius Severus. Relief panels depict his campaigns against the Parthians.

Curia

This big barnlike building was the official seat of the Roman Senate. Most of what you see is a reconstruction, but the interior marble floor dates to the 3rd-century reign of Diocletian.

Basilica di Massenzio

Marvel at the scale of this vast 4th-century basilica. In its original form the central hall was divided into enormous naves; now only part of the northern nave survives.

Julius Caesar RIP

Julius Caesar was cremated on the site where the Tempio di Giulio Cesare now stands.

Via Sacra

Tempio di Giulio Cesare

Casa delle Vestali

White statues line the grassy atrium of what was once the luxurious 50-room home of the Vestal Virgins. The virgins played an important role in Roman religion, serving the goddess Vesta.

Arco di Tito

Said to be the inspiration for the Arc de Triomphe in Paris, the well-preserved Arch of Titus was built by the emperor Domitian to honour his elder brother Titus.

Nowadays, the *palazzo* houses the **Museo Nazionale del Palazzo Venezia** (Map p60; 06 678 01 31; Via del Plebiscito 118; adult/reduced €4/2; ⊙8.30am-7.30pm Tue-Sun) with its collection of superb Byzantine and early Renaissance paintings, jewellery, ceramics, arms and armour.

Forum Boarium & Around

Bocca della Verità   Monument

Map p60 (Piazza della Bocca della Verità 18; donation €0.50; ⊙9.30am-4.50pm; ▣Via dei Cerchi) A round piece of marble that was once part of an ancient fountain, or possibly an ancient manhole cover, the *Bocca della Verità* (Mouth of Truth) is one of Rome's most photographed curiosities. According to legend, if you put your hand in the carved mouth and tell a lie, it will bite your hand off.

The mouth lives in the portico of the **Chiesa di Santa Maria in Cosmedin,** one of Rome's most beautiful medieval churches. Originally built in the 8th century, the church was given a major revamp in the 12th century, when the bell tower and portico were added and the floor was decorated with Cosmati inlaid marble.

Forum Boarium   Historical Site

Map p60 (Piazza della Bocca della Verità; ▣Via dei Cerchi) Car-choked Piazza della Bocca della Verità stands on what was once ancient Rome's cattle market (Forum Boarium). Opposite Chiesa Santa Maria in Cosmedin are two tiny Roman temples dating to the 2nd century BC: the round **Tempio di Ercole Vincitore** and the **Tempio di Portunus,** dedicated to the god of rivers and ports, Portunus. Just off the piazza, the **Arco di Giano** (Arch of Janus) is a four-sided Roman arch that once covered a crossroads. Beyond it is the medieval **Chiesa di San Giorgio in Velabro** (Map p60; Via del Velabro 19; ⊙10am-12.30pm & 4-6.30pm Tue, Fri & Sat), a beautiful church whose original 7th-century portico was destroyed by a Mafia bomb attack in 1993.

⊗ Eating

Hostaria da Nerone   Trattoria €€

Map p60 (06 481 79 52; Via delle Terme di Tito; meals €35; ⊙Mon-Sat lunch & dinner; Ⓜ Colosseo) This old-school, family-run trattoria is not the place for a romantic dinner or a special-occasion splurge

Forum Boarium

but if you're after a good earthy meal after a day's sightseeing, it does the job admirably. Tourists tuck into classic Roman pastas and salads outside while in the yellowing, woody interior visiting businessmen cut deals over saltimbocca and tiramisu.

San Teodoro
Modern Italian €€€

Map p60 (📞 06 678 09 33; www.st-teodoro. it; Via dei Fienili 49-50; meals €80; 🕐 Mon-Sat lunch & dinner; 🚌 Via del Teatro di Marcello) Hidden away on a picturesque corner behind the Palatino, San Teodoro is a refined seafood restaurant. Sit in the cool, minimalist interior or outside on the covered terrace and enjoy sophisticated creations like lasagne with zucchini flowers, scampi and pecorino cheese.

Ara Coeli
Gelateria €

Map p60 (Piazza d'Ara Coeli 9; 🕐 11am-11pm; 🚌 Piazza Venezia) Close to the base of the Campidoglio, Ara Coeli has more than 40 flavours of excellent organic ice cream, semicold varieties, Sicilian *granita* (flavoured shaved ice) and yoghurt.

 Drinking & Nightlife

Caffè Capitolino
Cafe

Map p60 (Capitoline Museums, Piazzale Caffarelli 4; 🕐 Tue-Sun; 🚌 Piazza Venezia) Hidden behind the Capitoline Museums, this stylish rooftop cafe commands memorable views. It's a good place to take a museum timeout and relax with a drink or snack (*panini,* salads and pizza), although you don't need a ticket to drink here – it's accessible via an independent entrance on Piazzale Caffarelli.

Cavour 313
Wine Bar

Map p60 (📞 06 678 54 96; www.cavour313 .it; Via Cavour 313; 🕐 10am-3.30pm & 7pm-midnight; Ⓜ Cavour) Close to the Forum, wood-panelled, intimate wine bar Cavour 313 attracts everyone from actors to politicians to tourists. Sink into its pub-like cosiness and while away hours over sensational wine (over 1200 labels) accompanied by cold cuts and cheese or a light meal.

Centro Storico

Rome's historic centre has astounding masterpieces around every corner, making sightseeing as effortless as taking a stroll. The Pantheon, a jaw-dropping piece of architectural genius, is a short walk from stadium-sized Piazza Navona. Art is thick on the ground in these parts, and many of the centre's churches harbour extraordinary frescoes and sculptures. The area is also full of life: it's a magnet for tourists and hip Romans heading for its bohemian boutiques, cool bars and popular pizzerias.

Over on the other side of Corso Vittorio Emanuele II, the main road that bisects the area, all streets lead to Campo de' Fiori, home to a colourful daily market and hectic late-night drinking scene, linked by a lane to the breathtaking, graceful Piazza Farnese. From here you can shop your way down to the medieval Jewish Ghetto, an atmospheric district of romantic corners and authentic eateries.

Piazza della Rotonda (p73)
GEOFF STRINGER/LONELY PLANET IMAGES ©

Centro Storico Highlights

Pantheon (p74)

As you step into this ancient temple, now a church, you'll feel the same sense of awe that the ancients must have felt 2000 years ago. Above you soars the world's largest unreinforced concrete dome, made all the more extraordinary by its central oculus – an opening to the sky that ensures your eyes are drawn to the heavens.

PHILIP & KAREN SMITH/LONELY PLANET IMAGES ©

Piazza Navona (p79)

This vast piazza was built over the remains of 1st-century-AD Stadio di Domiziano. It's exuberant and vibrant, full of locals as well as tourists. The piazza hosted Rome's main market for almost 300 years, and today, ringed by pavement cafes and centred on baroque fountains, it ebbs and flows with technicolour crowds. Fontana del Moro

DIANA MAYFIELD/LONELY PLANET IMAGES ©

Palazzo e Galleria Doria Pamphilj (p85)

3

Despite the opulence of the Galleria Doria Pamphilj collection, there's something very accessible about this fabulous group of artworks. The wealth of masterpieces is housed in a gilded series of rooms, on an intimate scale that makes them feel like private apartments. The audioguide, narrated by Jonathan Pamphilj, gives it an additional personal touch.

4

Chiesa di San Luigi dei Francesi (p81)

A few paces from Piazza Navona, the Chiesa di San Luigi dei Francesi is the church of Rome's French community, and contains Caravaggio's Matthew cycle, which is among his earliest religious works. The paintings are startling in their lack of glorification of the sacred, with an earthy realism that renders the subjects tangibly human and makes them all the more moving.

5

Jewish Ghetto (p80)

There's a atmosphere unique to the Jewish Ghetto, with its narrow lanes, famous yet unsigned bakeries, and small piazzas. Although the area is very central – a few streets away from Piazza Venezia – it's much more peaceful and calm than the surrounding streets, and is a splendid place to dine on Roman-Jewish cuisine.

Centro Storico Walk

Rome's Centro Storico is punctuated by beautiful piazzas – from the theatrical splendour of Piazza Navona to the technicolour market of Campo de' Fiori. This walk will take you around the historic centre's most beautiful public spaces, with opportunities to visit its major sights on the way.

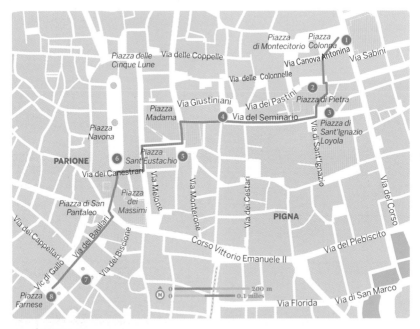

WALK FACTS
- **Start** Piazza Colonna
- **Finish** Piazza Farnese
- **Distance** 1.5km
- **Duration** Two hours

① Piazza Colonna

Start in this grand square (p85), at Rome's political heart. It's dominated by the 30m-high **Colonna di Marco Aurelio** and flanked by **Palazzo Chigi**, the official residence of the Italian prime minister. Next door is the equally impressive seat of the Chamber of Deputies, **Palazzo di Montecitorio**, which faces its own, eponymous piazza.

② Piazza di Pietra

From Piazza Colonna follow Via dei Bergamaschi down to **Piazza di Pietra** (p85), an elegant, oblong space overlooked by the 11 weather-worn columns of the 2nd-century **Tempio di Adriano**. The building that integrates them was once the Roman stock exchange. There are several elegant little bars and a stylish restaurant on the square.

③ Piazza di Sant'Ignazio Loyola

Continue past the columns down Via de' Burro to **Piazza di Sant'Ignazio Loyola** (p86), a small theatrical piazza. It's overlooked by the church of the same name, which contains a remarkable trompe d'oeil: the ceiling was painted by artist

Andrea Pozzo to look like the receding interior of a dome.

 Piazza della Rotonda

From here, it's a short walk along Via del Seminario to busy Piazza della Rotonda, dominated by the **Pantheon** (p74), which is also known as Santa Maria Rotonda, hence the piazza's name. Enter the breathtakingly complete, sometime Roman temple to gaze upwards at its audacious oculus: the building is open to the heavens.

 Piazza Sant'Eustachio

Leaving the Pantheon, head up Salita dei Crescenzi and then go left along Via Sant'Eustachio to **Piazza Sant'Eustachio**. On this small, workaday square you'll find the **Caffè Sant'Eustachio** (p93), a busy and unremarkable-looking cafe that serves the best espresso in town.

 Piazza Navona

Follow Via degli Staderari to Corso del Rinascimento, drop a quick left followed by a short right and you're into Rome's showpiece square, **Piazza Navona** (p79). Here, among the street artists, tourists and pigeons, you can compare the two giants of Roman baroque – Gian Lorenzo Bernini, creator of the **Fontana dei Quattro Fiumi**, and Francesco Borromini, author of the **Chiesa di Sant'Agnese in Agone**.

 Campo de' Fiori

Exit the piazza southwards, cross Corso Vittorio Emanuele II, the busy road that bisects the historic centre, and follow Via dei Baullari to the noisy market square, **Campo de' Fiori** (p80). The 'field of flowers' is filled with a daily flower-and-food market, which finishes at around 2pm.

 Piazza Farnese

Just beyond the Campo, **Piazza Farnese** presents an altogether more sober spectacle, overshadowed by the Renaissance **Palazzo Farnese** (p80) and decorated by two imposing fountains constructed out of recycled Roman bathtubs.

 The Best...

PLACES TO EAT

Casa Coppelle An intimate restaurant, serving sophisticated Italian cooking. (p86)

Giggetto al Portico d'Ottavia Classic Roman–Jewish restaurant. (p91)

Pizzeria da Baffetto Frenetic, atmospheric pizzeria. (p87)

La Rosetta A classic fish restaurant that exudes class. (p86)

PLACES TO DRINK

Caffè Sant'Eustachio A contender for the title of Rome's best coffee. (p93)

Open Baladin Artisanal beers are the capital's latest craze; try them out at this dedicated bar. (p94)

Salotto 42 A chic living-room-style place, with views of Tempio Adriana. (p94)

Etablì A rambling, laid-back yet upmarket bar, with a French-rustic decor. (p93)

ART CHURCHES

Chiesa di San Luigi dei Francesi Has glorious Caravaggio paintings. (p81)

Chiesa del Gesú A golden ensemble of Counter-Reformation pomp. (p77)

Chiesa di Sant'Ignazio di Loyola Houses a remarkable trompe d'oeil ceiling. (p86)

Chiesa di Santa Maria Sopra Minerva Rome's only Gothic church. (p76)

Restaurant in Piazza della Rotonda

Don't Miss
Pantheon

Along with the Colosseum, the Pantheon is one of Rome's iconic sights. A striking 2000-year-old temple, now a church, it is the city's best preserved ancient monument and one of the most influential buildings in the Western world. Over the centuries its innovative design and revolutionary structure have inspired generations of architects and engineers.

Map p82

Piazza della Rotonda

Admission free

Audioguide €5

⊙8.30am-7.30pm Mon-Sat, 9am-6pm Sun

🚊🚌Largo di Torre Argentina

History

In its current form the Pantheon dates to around AD 120, when the emperor Hadrian built over an earlier temple.

Hadrian's temple was dedicated to the classical gods – hence the name Pantheon, a derivation of the Greek words *pan* (all) and *theos* (god) – but in AD 608 it was consecrated as a Christian church in honour of the Madonna and all martyrs after the Byzantine emperor Phocus donated it to Pope Boniface IV. Thanks to this consecration the Pantheon was spared the worst of the medieval plundering that reduced many of Rome's ancient buildings to their bare bones. However, it wasn't totally safe from plundering hands. The gilded-bronze roof tiles were removed and, in the 17th century, the Barberini Pope Urban VIII had the portico's bronze ceiling melted down to make 80 canons for Castel Sant'Angelo and the baldachino over the main altar of St Peter's Basilica.

Exterior

Most impressively, the monumental entrance portico is made up of 16 Corinthian columns, each 13m high and made of Egyptian granite, supporting a triangular pediment. Little remains of the ancient decor, although rivets and holes in the brickwork indicate where the marble-veneer panels were once placed, and the towering 20-tonne bronze doors are 16th-century restorations of the originals.

Interior

Although impressive from outside, it's only when you get inside the Pantheon that you can really appreciate its full size. With light streaming in through the oculus (the 8.7m-diameter hole in the centre of the dome), the marble-clad interior seems absolutely vast, an effect that was deliberately designed to cut worshippers down to size in the face of the gods.

Opposite the entrance is the church's main altar, over which hangs a 7th-century icon of the Madonna and Child. To the left (as you look in from the entrance) is the tomb of Raphael, marked by Lorenzetto's 1520 sculpture of the *Madonna del Sasso* (Madonna of the Rock), and next door, the tombs of King Umberto I and Margherita of Savoy. Over on the opposite side of the rotunda is the tomb of King Vittorio Emanuele II.

Dome

The Pantheon's dome, considered the Romans' most important architectural achievement, was the largest in the world until the 15th century and is still today the largest unreinforced concrete dome ever built. Its harmonious appearance is due to a precisely calibrated symmetry – the diameter is equal to the building's interior height of 43.3m. Light enters through the central oculus, which served as a symbolic connection between the temple and the gods as well as an important structural role – it absorbs and redistributes the huge tensile forces.

Inscription

For centuries the Latin inscription over the Pantheon's entrance led historians to believe that the current temple was Marcus Agrippa's original. However, excavations in the 19th century revealed traces of an earlier temple, and scholars realised that Hadrian had simply reinstated Agrippa's original inscription over his new temple.

Pantheon in the Rain

According to the attendants who work at the Pantheon, the question tourists most often ask is: what happens when it rains? The answer is that the rainwater drains away through 22 almost-invisible holes in the sloping marble floor.

Discover
Centro Storico

🔄 Getting There & Away

o **Bus** The best way to access the *centro storico*. A whole fleet serve the area from Termini, including Nos 40 and 64, which both stop at Largo di Torre Argentina and continue down Corso Vittorio Emanuele II. From Barberini metro station, bus 116 stops at Corso Rinascimento (for Piazza Navona), Piazza Farnese and Via Giulia.

o **Metro** There are no metro stations in the neighbourhood but it's within walking distance of Barberini, Spagna and Flaminio stations, all on line A.

o **Tram** No 8 connects Largo di Torre Argentina with Trastevere.

👁 Sights

Bound by the River Tiber and Via del Corso, the *centro storico* (historic centre) is made for aimless wandering. You'll come across some of Rome's great sights: the Pantheon, Piazza Navona and Campo de' Fiori, as well as a host of monuments, museums and churches. To the south, the Jewish Ghetto is an atmospheric area studded with artisans' studios, vintage clothes shops and kosher bakeries; it has been home to Rome's Jewish community since the 2nd century BC.

Pantheon & Around

Pantheon   Church
See p74.

Elefantino   Monument
Map p82 (Piazza della Minerva; 🚏Largo di Torre Argentina) A short skip south of the Pantheon stands the Elefantino, a curious and much-loved sculpture of a puzzled elephant carrying a 6th-century-BC Egyptian obelisk. Unveiled in 1667 and designed to glorify Pope Alexander VII, the elephant, symbolising strength and wisdom, was sculpted by Ercole Ferrata to a design by Bernini.

Chiesa di Santa Maria Sopra Minerva   Church
Map p82 (Piazza della Minerva; 🕗8am-7pm Mon-Fri, 8am-1pm & 3.30-7pm Sat & Sun; 🚏🚏Largo di Torre Argentina) Built on the site of an ancient temple to Minerva, the Dominican Chiesa di Santa Maria Sopra Minerva is Rome's only Gothic church, although little remains of the original 13th-century design.

Pantheon
JEAN-PIERRE LESCOURRET/LONELY PLANET IMAGES ©

Inside, in the Cappella Carafa (also called the Cappella della Annunciazione), you'll find two superb 15th-century frescoes by Filippino Lippi and the majestic tomb of Pope Paul IV. Left of the high altar is one of Michelangelo's lesser-known sculptures, *Cristo Risorto* (Christ Bearing the Cross; 1520). An altarpiece of the Madonna and Child in the second chapel in the northern transept is attributed to Fra Angelico, the Dominican friar and painter, who is also buried in the church. The body of St Catherine of Siena, minus her head (which is in Siena), lies under the high altar, and the tombs of two Medici popes, Leo X and Clement VII, are in the apse.

Largo di Torre Argentina   Ancient Ruins

Map p82 (Largo di Torre Argentina) A busy transport hub, Largo di Torre Argentina is set around the sunken **Area Sacra** and the remains of four Republican-era temples, all built between the 2nd and 4th centuries BC. These ruins are off-limits to humans but home to a thriving population of 250 stray cats and a **cat sanctuary** (www.romancats.com; ◷noon-6pm).

Chiesa del Gesù   Church

Map p82 (www.chiesadelgesu.org; Piazza del Gesù; ◷7am-noon & 4-7.45pm; Largo di Torre Argentina) An imposing example of late 16th-century Counter-Reformation architecture, this is Rome's most important Jesuit church. The facade by Giacomo della Porta is impressive, but it's the awesome gold and marble interior that is the real attraction. Of the art on display, the most astounding work is the *Trionfo del Nome di Gesù* (Triumph of the Name of Jesus), the swirling, hypnotic vault fresco by Giovanni Battista Gaulli (aka Il Baciccia), who also painted the cupola frescoes and designed the stucco decoration.

Baroque master Andrea Pozzo designed the **Cappella di Sant'Ignazio** in the northern transept. Here you'll find the tomb of Ignatius Loyola, the Spanish soldier and saint who founded the Jesuits in 1540.

The Spanish saint lived in the church from 1544 until his death in 1556. His private **rooms** (◷4-6pm Mon-Sat, 10am-noon Sun), with a masterful trompe l'oeil by Andrea del Pozzo, are right of the main church.

Piazza Navona & Around

Chiesa di Santa Maria della Pace & Chiostro del Bramante
Church

Map p82 (📞06 686 09 035; www.chiostrodelbramante.it; Vicolo dell'Arco della Pace 5; exhibitions adult/reduced €10/8; ⏱church 9am-noon Mon, Wed & Sat, cloisters 10am-11pm daily, exhibitions 10am-8pm Tue- Sun; 🚌Corso Vittorio Emanuele II) Tucked away in the backstreets near Piazza Navona, this small 15th- century church boasts an elaborate porticoed exterior and a minor Raphael fresco, *Sibille* (Sibyls). Next door, the Chiostro del Bramante (Bramante Cloisters) is a masterpiece of Renaissance styling, its classic lines providing a marked counterpoint to the church's undulating facade.

Pasquino
Monument

Map p82 (Piazza Pasquino; 🚌Corso Vittorio Emanuele II) Recently scrubbed back to a virginal white, this unassuming sculpture is Rome's most famous 'talking statue'. During the 16th century, when there were no safe outlets for dissent, a Vatican tailor named Pasquino began sticking notes to the statue with satirical verses lampooning the church and aristocracy.

Chiesa di Sant'Ivo alla Sapienza
Church

Map p82 (Corso del Rinascimento 40; ⏱9am-noon Sun; 🚌Corso del Rinascimento) Hidden in the porticoed courtyard of **Palazzo della Sapienza**, this tiny church is a masterpiece of baroque architecture. Built by Francesco Borromini between 1642 and 1660, and based on an incredibly complex geometric plan, it combines alternating convex and concave walls with a circular interior topped by a twisted spire.

Chiesa di Sant'Agostino
Church

Map p82 (Piazza di Sant'Agostino; ⏱7.45am-noon & 4-7.30pm; 🚌Corso del Rinascimento) This early Renaissance church is a favourite of soon-to-be mums, who pop in to pay their respects to Jacopo Sansovino's sculpture of the Virgin Mary, the *Madonna del Parto* (1521). The Madonna also features in Caravaggio's *Madonna dei Pellegrini* (Madonna of the Pilgrims), which caused uproar when it was unveiled in 1604, due to its depiction of Mary as barefoot and her two devoted pilgrims as filthy beggars. Painting almost a century before, Raphael provoked no such scandal with his fresco of *Isaiah,* visible on the third pilaster on the left in the nave.

Chiesa di Sant'Agostino

PAOLO CORDELLI/LONELY PLANET IMAGES ©

GEOFF STRINGER/LONELY PLANET IMAGES ©

Don't Miss
Piazza Navona

With its ornate fountains, exuberant baroque palazzi and pavement cafes, Piazza Navona is central Rome's showcase square.

Like many of the city's great landmarks, it sits on the site of an ancient monument, in this case the 1st-century-AD **Stadio di Domiziano** (📞06 0608; Piazza Tor Sanguigna 13; ⏰closed for restoration).

Of the piazza's three fountains, it's Gian Lorenzo Bernini's high-camp **Fontana dei Quattro Fiumi** (Fountain of the Four Rivers) that dominates. Commissioned by Pope Innocent X and completed in 1651, it depicts the Nile, Ganges, Danube and Plate, representing the then-known four continents of the world, and is festooned with a palm tree, lion and horse, and topped by an obelisk.

The **Fontana del Moro** at the southern end of the square was designed by Giacomo della Porta in 1576. Bernini added the Moor holding a dolphin in the mid-17th century, but the surrounding Tritons are 19th-century copies. The 19th-century **Fontana del Nettuno** at the northern end of the piazza depicts Neptune fighting with a sea monster, surrounded by sea nymphs.

With its stately, yet vibrantly theatrical facade, the **Chiesa di Sant'Agnese in Agone** (📞06 681 92 134; www.santagneseinagone.org; ⏰9.30am-12.30pm & 3.30-7pm Tue-Sat, 9am-1pm & 4-8pm Sun) is typical of Francesco Borromini's baroque style.

NEED TO KNOW
Map p82; 🚌Corso del Rinascimento

Campo De' Fiori & Around

Campo de' Fiori   Market

Map p82 (🚇Corso Vittorio Emanuele II) Noisy and colourful, 'Il Campo' is a major focus of Roman life: by day it hosts a much-loved market, while at night it turns into a raucous open-air pub. For centuries, it was the site of public executions, and in 1600 the philosophising monk Giordano Bruno, immortalised in Ettore Ferrari's sinister statue, was burned at the stake here for heresy.

Palazzo Farnese   Palazzo

Map p82 (📞06 688 92 818; www.ambafrance-it.org in Italian & French; Piazza Farnese; under 15yr not admitted; 🕐tours 3, 4 & 5pm Mon & Thu, by appt only; 🚇Corso Vittorio Emanuele II) Dominating the elegant piazza of the same name, Palazzo Farnese is one of Rome's greatest Renaissance *palazzi*. It was started in 1514 by Antonio da Sangallo the Younger, continued by Michelangelo, who added the cornice and balcony, and finished by Giacomo della Porta. Nowadays, it's the French Embassy and open only to visitors who've booked a place on the bi-weekly guided tour. The 50-minute visits (with commentary in Italian or French) take in the garden, courtyard and Galleria dei Carracci, home to a series of superb frescoes by Annibale Carracci, said by some to rival those of the Sistine Chapel. Booking forms can be downloaded from the website and should be sent one to four months before you want to visit. Photo ID is required for entry.

The twin fountains in the square are enormous granite baths taken from the Terme di Caracalla.

Palazzo Spada   Palazzo

Map p82 (📞06 683 24 09; www.galleriaborghese.it; Via Capo di Ferro 13; adult/reduced €5/2; 🕐8.30am-7.30pm Tue-Sun; 🚇Corso Vittorio Emanuele II) The central attraction of this 16th-century *palazzo* is Francesco Borromini's famous perspective. What appears to be a 25m-long corridor lined with columns leading to a hedge and life-sized statue is, in fact, only 10m long. The sculpture, which was a later addition, is actually hip-height and the columns diminish in size not because of distance but because they actually get shorter. And look closer at that perfect-looking hedge – Borromini didn't trust the gardeners to clip a real hedge precisely enough so he made one of stone.

Upstairs, the four-room **Galleria Spada** houses the Spada family art collection, with works by Andrea del Sarto, Guido Reni, Guercino and Titian.

Chiesa di Sant'Andrea della Valle   Church

Map p82 (Corso Vittorio Emanuele II 6; 🕐7.30am-noon & 4.30-7.30pm Mon-Sat, 7.30am-12.45pm & 4.30-7.45pm Sun; 🚇Corso Vittorio Emanuele II) A must for opera fans, this towering 17th-century church is where Giacomo Puccini set the first act of *Tosca*. Its most obvious feature is Carlo Maderno's soaring dome, the highest in Rome after St Peter's, but its bombastic baroque interior reveals some wonderful frescoes by Mattia Preti, Domenichino and, in the dome, Lanfranco.

Jewish Ghetto

Museo Ebraico di Roma   Synagogue, Museum

Map p88 (Jewish Museum of Rome; 📞06 684 00 661; www.museoebraico.roma.it; Via Catalana; adult/reduced €10/4; 🕐10am-6.15pm Sun-Thu, 10am-3.15pm Fri summer, 10am-4.15pm Sun-Thu, 9am-1.15pm Fri winter; 🚇Lungotevere de' Cenci) The historical, cultural and artistic heritage of Rome's Jewish community is chronicled in this small but engrossing museum. Housed in the city's early 20th-century synagogue, Europe's second largest, it presents harrowing reminders of the hardships experienced by the city's Jewry.

You can also book one-hour guided walking tours of the Ghetto (adult/reduced €8/5) at the museum.

Fontana delle Tartarughe   Monument

Map p88 (Piazza Mattei; 🚇🚌Via Arenula) This playful 16th-century fountain depicts four

KEVIN GEORGE/ALAMY ©

 Don't Miss
Chiesa di San Luigi dei Francesi

Church to Rome's French community since 1589, this opulent baroque church boasts no fewer than three paintings by Caravaggio. In the Cappella Contarelli, to the left of the main altar, crowds gather to admire the *Vocazione di San Matteo* (The Calling of St Matthew), the *Martiro di San Matteo* (The Martyrdom of St Matthew) and *San Matteo e l'angelo* (St Matthew and the Angel), together known as the St Matthew cycle. These are among Caravaggio's earliest religious works, painted between 1599 and 1602, but they are inescapably his, featuring down-to-earth realism and stunning use of chiaroscuro (the bold contrast of light and dark).

PRACTICALITIES

Map p82; Piazza di San Luigi dei Francesi; ⊙10am-12.30pm & 4-7pm, closed Thu afternoon pm; ⊡Corso del Rinascimento

boys gently hoisting tortoises up into a bowl of water. The tortoises were added by Bernini in 1658.

Area Archeologica del Teatro di Marcello e del Portico d'Ottavia
Archaeological Site

Map p82 (Via del Teatro di Marcello 44; ⊙9am-7pm summer, 9am-6pm winter; ⊡Via del Teatro di Marcello) To the east of the ghetto, the **Teatro di Marcello** is the star turn of this dusty archaeological area. Although originally planned by Julius Caesar, the 20,000-seat theatre was completed by Augustus in 11 BC and named after a favourite nephew, Marcellus. In the 16th century, a *palazzo* was built onto the original building, which now houses some exclusive apartments lived in by a few lucky Romans.

Beyond the Teatro di Marcello, the **Portico d'Ottavia** is the oldest *quadriporto* (four-sided porch) in

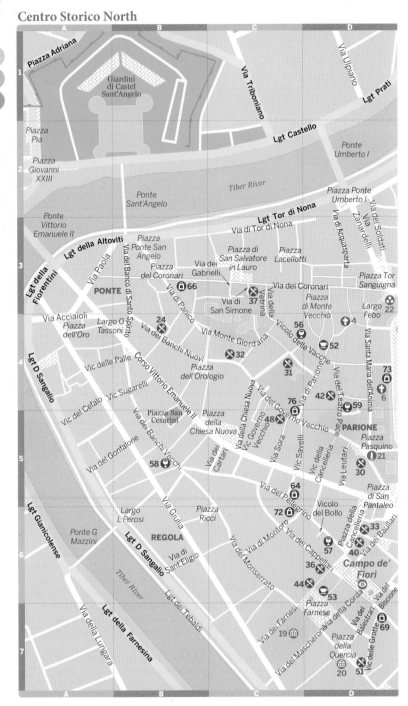

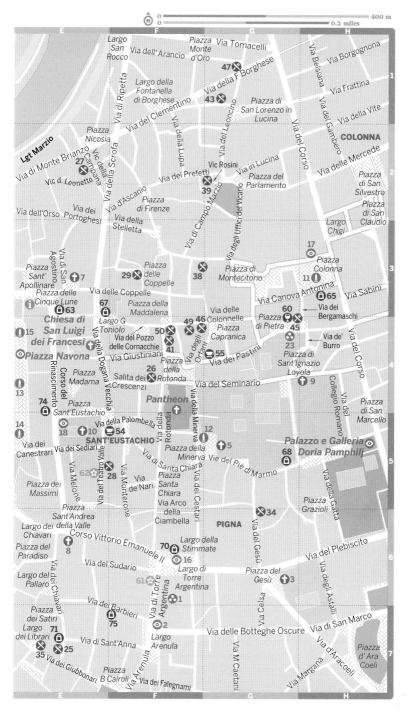

Largo San Rocco
Via dell'Arancio
Piazza Monte d'Oro
Via Tomacelli
Via Borgognona
Via Belsiana
Via della F Borghese
47
Via Frattina
Largo della Fontanella di Borghese
43
Via della Vite
Via del Gambero
Piazza di San Lorenzo in Lucina
Via del Clementino
Via di Ripetta
COLONNA
Piazza Nicosia
Via del Corso
Via di Monte Brianzo
Lgt Marzio
27
Via della Campana
Via della Scrofa
Via della Lupa
Via del Leoncino
Via delle Mercede
Vic. d. Leonetto
Via dei Prefetti
Vic Rosini
Via in Lucina
Piazza di San Silvestro
Via dei Portoghesi
Via d'Ascanio
39
Piazza del Parlamento
Piazza di San Claudio
Via dell'Orso
Piazza di Firenze
Largo Chigi
Via della Stelletta
Via di Campo Marzio
Via degli Uffici del Vicario
17
Piazza Sant' Apollinare
Piazza di Sant'Agostino
7
29
Piazza delle Coppelle
38
Piazza di Montecitorio
Piazza Colonna
11
Piazza delle Cinque Lune
63
67
Piazza della Maddalena
Via delle Coppelle
Via Canova
Via Antonina
65
Via Sabini
Chiesa di San Luigi dei Francesi
Largo G Toniolo
49 46
Via delle Colonnelle
60
Via dei Bergamaschi
15
Via del Pozzo delle Cornacchie
50
Piazza Capranica
Piazza di Pietra
45
Piazza Navona
41
Via degli Orfani
Via de' Burro
Via Giustiniani
55
Via dei Pastini
23
13
26
Piazza della Rotonda
Piazza di Sant'Ignazio Loyola
74
Salita dei Crescenzi
Via del Seminario
9
Piazza Sant'Eustachio
Piazza Madama
Pantheon
Corso del Rinascimento
18
10
54
12
SANT'EUSTACHIO
Via della Palombella
Piazza della Minerva
5
14
Via della Rotonda
Via della Minerva
68
Palazzo e Galleria Doria Pamphilj
Via dei Canestrari
Via dei Sediari
Via di Santa Chiara
Vie del Piè di Marmo
62
28
Via Monterone
Piazza Santa Chiara
Piazza dei Massimi
Via de' Nari
Via Arco della Ciambella
Piazza Grazioli
Via del Collegio Romano
Piazza di San Marcello
Via del Teatro Valle
Via dei Cestari
Via Melone
Piazza Sant'Andrea della Valle
34
Largo dei Chiavari
Via del Plebiscito
PIGNA
Piazza del Paradiso
8
Corso Vittorio Emanuele II
70
Largo della Stimmate
Via del Gesù
Via degli Astalli
Largo del Pallaro
Via del Sudario
16
Piazza del Gesù
3
Largo di Torre Argentina
Via di Torre Argentina
61
1
Via dei Chiavari
Via dei Barbieri
Piazza dei Satiri
75
2
Via Celsa
Via di San Marco
Largo dei Librari
71
35
25
Via di Sant'Anna
Largo Arenula
Via delle Botteghe Oscure
Via d'Aracoeli
Via dei Giubbonari
Piazza B Cairoli
Via Arenula
Via dei Falegnami
Via M Caetani
Via Margana
Piazza d'Ara Coeli

Centro Storico North

Rome. The dilapidated columns and fragmented pediment once formed part of a vast rectangular portico, supported by 300 columns, that measured 132m by 119m. From the Middle Ages until the late 19th century, the portico housed Rome's fish market.

Isola Tiberina

The world's smallest inhabited island, the Isola Tiberina (Tiber Island) has been associated with healing since the 3rd century BC, when the Romans adopted the Greek god of healing Asclepius (aka Aesculapius) as their own and erected a temple to him on the island. Today, the island is home to the Ospedale Fatebenefratelli.

To reach the Isola from the Jewish Ghetto, cross Rome's oldest standing bridge, the 62 BC **Ponte Fabricio**. Visible to the south of the island are the remains of **Ponte Rotto** (Broken Bridge, Map p88), Ancient Rome's first stone bridge, which was all but swept away in a 1598 flood.

Piazza Colonna & Around

Palazzo e Galleria
Doria Pamphilj   Art Gallery, Palazzo
Map p82 (06 679 73 23; adult/reduced €10.50/7.50; ⏱10am-5pm, last admission 4.15pm; 🚌Via del Corso) You wouldn't know it from the grimy exterior but this *palazzo* houses one of Rome's richest private art collections, with works by Raphael, Tintoretto, Brueghel, Titian, Caravaggio, Bernini and Velázquez.

Palazzo Doria Pamphilj dates to the mid-15th century, but its current look was largely the work of the current owners, the Doria Pamphilj family, who acquired it in the 18th century. Masterpieces abound, but look out for Titian's *Salomè con la testa del Battista* (Salome with the Head of John the Baptist) and two early Caravaggios: *Riposo durante la fuga in Egitto* (Rest During the Flight into Egypt) and *Maddalene Penitente* (Penitent Magdalen). The undisputed star is the Velázquez portrait of an implacable Pope Innocent X, who grumbled that it was 'too real'.

Piazza Colonna   Piazza
Map p82 (🚌Via del Corso) Together with Piazza di Montecitorio, this stylish piazza is Rome's political nerve centre. On its northern flank, the 16th-century **Palazzo Chigi** (www.governo.it, in Italian; Piazza Colonna 370; admission free; ⏱guided visits 9am-2pm Sat Sep-Jun, booking obligatory) has been the official residence of Italy's prime minister since 1961.

Rising 30m above the piazza, the **Colonna di Marco Aurelio** was

Bridge to Isola Tiberina

Model church on display in Chiesa di Sant'Ignazio di Loyola

RICHARD I'ANSON/LONELY PLANET IMAGES ©

completed in AD 193 to honour Marcus Aurelius' military victories. In 1589 Marcus was replaced on the top of the column with a bronze statue of St Paul.

South of the piazza, in **Piazza di Pietra**, is the **Tempio di Adriano**. Eleven huge Corinthian columns, now embedded in what used to be Rome's stock exchange, are all that remain of Hadrian's 2nd-century temple.

Chiesa di Sant'Ignazio di Loyola
Church

Map p82 (Piazza Sant'Ignazio; ⊙7.30am-7pm Mon-Sat, 9am-7pm Sun; 🚍Via del Corso) Rome's most important Jesuit church after the Chiesa del Gesù, this lordly building flanks Piazza Sant'Ignazio, an exquisite rococo square laid out in 1727 to resemble a stage set.

The church was built by the Jesuit architect Orazio Grassi in 1626, and boasts a Carlo Maderno facade and a celebrated trompe l'oeil ceiling fresco by Andrea Pozzo (1642–1709), which depicts St Ignatius Loyola being welcomed into paradise by Christ and the Madonna.

 # Eating

Around Piazza Navona, Campo de' Fiori and the Pantheon you'll find an array of eateries, including some of the capital's best restaurants (both contemporary and traditional Roman). The atmospheric Jewish Ghetto is famous for its unique Roman-Jewish cooking.

Pantheon & Around

Casa Coppelle
Mediterranean €€

Map p82 (🕿06 688 91 707; www.casacoppelle.it; Piazza delle Coppelle 49; meals €35; 🚍🚊Largo di Torre Argentina) Intimate and elegant with wonderful French-inspired food and a warm, attractive buzz, this is a great find. Kick off with *millefoglie di bufala e melanzane,* a vibrant mix of pungent buffalo mozzarella and sliced aubergine, before moving onto the main event, superbly cooked steak with delicious, thinly sliced potato crisps.

La Rosetta
Seafood €€€

Map p82 (🕿06 686 10 02; www.larosetta.com; Via della Rosetta 8; lunch menu €50, tasting menu €140; ⊙closed Sun lunch & 3 weeks Aug; 🚍🚊Largo di Torre Argentina) Run by

Roman super-chef Massimo Riccioli, La Rosetta is one of the capital's oldest and best-known seafood restaurants. The menu, which makes no compromises for vegetarians or meat-eaters, features classic fish dishes alongside more elaborate creations such as scallops with cream of artichoke and mint. Bookings are essential, and it's more affordable at lunchtime.

Armando al Pantheon   Trattoria €€

Map p82 (☎06 688 03 034; www.armando alpantheon.it; Salita dei Crescenzi 31; meals €40; ⏾closed Sat dinner & Aug; 🔁🚇Largo di Torre Argentina) A family-run trattoria, Armando's is a wood-panelled, inviting, authentic institution close to the Pantheon. It specialises in traditional Roman fare but you can also branch out on dishes like guinea fowl with porcini mushrooms and black beer and spaghetti with truffles. Book ahead.

Osteria Sostegno   Trattoria €€

Map p82 (☎06 679 38 42; www.ilsostegno.it; Via delle Colonnelle 5; meals €35-40; ⏾Tue-Sun; 🔁🚇Largo di Torre Argentina) Follow the green neon arrow to the end of a narrow alley and you'll find this well-kept secret. It's intimate, a favourite of journalists and politicians, with excellent dishes such as *caprese* (tomato and buffalo mozzarella salad) and *ravioli di ricotta e spinaci con limone e zafferano* (ricotta and spinach ravioli with lemon and saffron). Nearby, the **Ristorante Settimio** (Map p82; ☎06 678 96 51; Via delle Colonnelle 14; meals €35-40) is run by the same family.

Enoteca Corsi   Osteria €

Map p82 (☎06 679 08 21; Via del Gesù 87; meals €20-25; ⏾lunch Mon-Sat; 🔁🚇Largo di Torre Argentina) Merrily worse for wear, family-run Corsi is a genuine old-style

Roman eatery. The look is rustic – bare wooden tables, paper tablecloths, wine bottles – and the atmosphere one of controlled mayhem. The menu, chalked up on a blackboard, offers no surprises, just honest, homey fare like *melanzane parmigiana* or roast chicken with potatoes.

San Crispino   Ice Cream €€

Map p82 (Piazza della Maddalena 3; tubs about €3; ⏾midday-12.30pm Sun-Thu, midday-1.30am Fri & Sat; 🚇Largo di Torre Argentina) A branch of the celebrated Roman gelateria that dishes up what many claim is the best ice cream in town. Flavours such as *pompelmo e rum* (grapefruit and rum) or *limone e pistacchio* (lemon and pistachio) are based on fresh natural ingredients and served in tubs only.

Piazza Navona & Around

Pizzeria da Baffetto   Pizzeria €

Map p82 (☎06 686 16 17; Via del Governo Vecchio 114; pizzas €6-9; ⏾6.30pm-1am; 🚇Corso Vittorio Emanuele II) For the full-on Roman pizza experience get down to this local institution. Meals here are raucous, chaotic

Wood-fired pizza

Centro Storico South

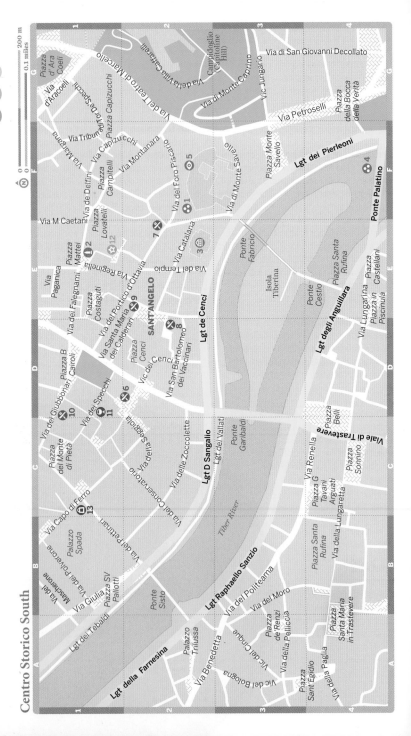

0 — 200 m
0 — 0.1 miles

Centro Storico South

and fast, but the thin-crust pizzas are spot on and the vibe is fun. To partake, join the queue and wait to be squeezed in wherever there's room.

Casa Bleve
Wine Bar, Gastronomic €€€

Map p82 (☎ 06 686 59 70; www.casableve.it; Via del Teatro Valle 48-49; meals €60; ⊙ Tue-Sat, closed Aug; ☒ ☒ Largo di Torre Argentina) This gorgeous, stately wine bar is a gourmet delight. Its wine collection is one of the best in town; the dining hall is a picture, set in a column-lined courtyard capped by stained glass; and the food is top class.

Campana
Trattoria €€

Map p82 (☎ 06 687 52 73; Vicolo della Campana 18; meals €35; ⊙ Tue-Sun; ☒ ☒ Largo di Torre Argentina) Caravaggio, Goethe and Federico Fellini are among the luminaries who have dined at what is said to be Rome's oldest trattoria, dating back to around 1518. Nowadays, local families crowd its two dining rooms to dine on fresh fish and traditional Roman cuisine served by proficient, black-waistcoated waiters.

Lo Zozzone
Sandwich Shop €

Map p82 (☎ 06 688 08 575; Via del Teatro Pace 32; panini from €6; ⊙ Mon-Sat; ☒ Corso del Rinascimento) With a few inside tables and a mile-long menu of *panini,* the affectionally named 'dirty one' is a top spot for a cheap lunchtime bite. The filling, delicious *panini* are made with *pizza bianca* and combinations of cured meats, cold cuts, cheeses and vegetables.

Cul de Sac
Wine Bar, Trattoria €€

Map p82 (☎ 06 688 01 094; www.enoteca culdesac.com; Piazza Pasquino 73; meals €30; ⊙ noon-4pm & 6pm-12.30am daily; ☒ Corso Vittorio Emanuele II) A popular little wine bar, just off Piazza Navona, with an always busy terrace and narrow, bottle-lined interior. Choose from the encyclopedic wine list and ample menu of Gallic-inspired cold cuts, pates, cheeses and main courses. Book ahead in the evening.

Gelateria del Teatro
Gelateria €

Map p82 (Via di San Simone 70; cones €2; ☒ Corso del Rinascimento) In a cute alleyway just off pedestrian Via dei Coronari, this lovely little gelateria offers up to 40 flavours. The standouts are the Sicilian-inspired flavours like *cannolo siciliano* (based on Sicily's signature ricotta pastry tubes) and *pistachio* (with nuts from the Sicilian town of Bronte).

Da Tonino
Trattoria €

Map p82 (Via del Governo Vecchio 18; meals €20; ⊙ Mon-Sat; ☒ Corso Vittorio Emanuele II) Unsigned Tonino's might be defiantly low-key with its simple wooden tables and yellowing pictures, but it's almost always packed. There's no menu: the waiter will reel off the choices of rib-sticking Roman staples, such as hearty *pasta alla gricia.*

Alfredo e Ada
Trattoria €

Map p82 (☎ 06 687 88 42; Via dei Banchi Nuovi 14; meals €20; ⊙ Mon-Fri; ☒ Corso Vittorio Emanuele II) For a taste of a authentic Roman cooking, head to this much-loved place with its wood panelling and spindly marble-topped tables. It's distinctly no-frills – the wine list consists of two choices, red or white – but the food, whatever is put in front of you (there's no menu), is filling and warming, just like your Italian *nonna* would have cooked it.

Gelateria Giolitti   Gelateria €
Map p82 (Via degli Uffici del Vicario 40; 🚇Corso del Rinascimento) Rome's most famous gelateria started as a dairy in 1900 and still keeps the hordes happy with succulent sorbets and creamy combinations. Gregory Peck and Audrey Hepburn swung by in *Roman Holiday* and it used to deliver marron glacé to Pope John Paul II.

Da Francesco   Trattoria, Pizzeria €€
Map p82 (📞06 686 40 09; Piazza del Fico 29; pizzas €6-9, meals €30; 🕐closed Tue; 🚇Corso Vittorio Emanuele II) Gingham, paper tablecloths, frazzled waiters, groaning plateloads of pasta, tasty pizza: this quintessential Roman kitchen has character coming out of its ears, and tables and chairs spilling onto the pretty piazza. Rock up early or queue. No credit cards.

Campo de' Fiori & Around

Forno di Campo de' Fiori   Bakery, Pizza al Taglio €
Map p82 (Campo de' Fiori 22; pizza slices about €3; 🕐7.30am-2.30pm & 4.45-8pm Mon-Sat; 🚇Corso Vittorio Emanuele II) This is one of Rome's best takeaway joints, serving bread, *panini* and delicious straight-from-the-oven pizza *al taglio* (by the slice). Aficionados recommend the pizza *bianca* (white pizza with olive oil, rosemary and salt) but the *panini* and pizza *rossa* ('red' pizza, with olive oil, tomato and oregano) are just as good.

Ditirambo   Modern Italian €€
Map p82 (📞06 687 16 26; www.ristorante ditirambo.it; Piazza della Cancelleria 72; meals €35-40; 🕐closed Mon lunch; 🚇Corso Vittorio Emanuele II; 🖊) This hugely popular new-wave trattoria offers a laid-back, unpretentious atmosphere and innovative, organic cooking. The menu changes according to what's good at the market

but the focus is on a fresh, creative approach. Book ahead.

Grappolo D'oro   Modern Italian €€
Map p82 (📞06 689 70 80; Piazza della Cancelleria 80; meals €35-40; 🕐closed Tue-Fri lunch; 🚇Corso Vittorio Emanuele II) More contemporary looking than nearby Ditirambo, this informal, stylish eatery stands out among the sometimes lacklustre options around Campo de' Fiori. The food is creative without being over-designed, and includes old favourites such as *spaghetti alla carbonara* (among the best in Rome, according to local foodie bible *Gambero Rosso*).

Vineria Roscioli Salumeria   Gastronomic, Delicatessen €€€
Map p82 (📞06 687 52 87; Via dei Giubbonari 21; meals from €50; 🕐Mon-Sat; 🚇Via Arenula) This deli-cum-wine bar-cum-restaurant is a foodie paradise. Out back in the chic restaurant, you can dine on sophisticated Italian food accompanied by some truly outstanding wines – the wine list, which runs to some 1100 labels, contains some truly superlative Italian and French vintages. Reservations recommended.

Antico Forno Roscioli   Bakery, Pizza al Taglio €
Map p82 (Via dei Chiavari 34; pizza slice from €2; 🕐7.30am-8pm Mon-Fri, 7.30am-2.30pm Sat; 🚇Via Arenula) Not the Roscioli's renowned delicatessen and wine bar, but its brother bakery around the corner. Join the lunchtime crowds for a slice of delicious pizza (the *pizza bianca* is legendary) or a freshly baked pastry. There's also a counter serving hot pastas and vegetable side dishes.

Osteria ar Galletto   Osteria €€
Map p82 (📞06 686 17 14; www.ristorantear gallettoroma.com; Piazza Farnese 102; meals €35-40; 🕐Mon-Sat; 🚇Corso Vittorio Emanuele II) You wouldn't expect there to be anywhere reasonably priced on Piazza Farnese, one of Rome's most refined piazzas, but this long-running *osteria* is the real thing, with good, honest Roman

food, a warm local atmosphere and dazzlingly set exterior tables.

Sergio alle Grotte
Traditional Italian €€

Map p82 (📞06 686 42 93; Vicolo delle Grotte 27; meals €30-35; 🕐12.30-3.30pm & 6.30pm-1am Mon-Sat; 🚇Via Arenula) A flower's throw from the Campo, Sergio alle Grotte is a textbook Roman trattoria: chequered tablecloths, dodgy wall murals, bustling waiters and steaming plateloads of delicious pasta. In the summer there are tables outside on the cobbled, ivy-hung lane.

Jewish Ghetto

Giggetto al Portico d'Ottavia
Traditional Italian €€

Map p88 (📞06 686 11 05; www.giggettoalportico.it; Via del Portico d'Ottavia 21a; meals €40; 🕐Tue-Sun; 🚇🚇Piazza B Cairoli) An atmospheric setting in the Ghetto, rustic interiors, white-jacketed waiters, *fabuloso* Roman–Jewish cooking – this is a quintessential Roman restaurant. Celebrate all things fried by tucking into the marvellous *carciofi alla giudia, fiore di zucca* (zucchini or squash flowers)

and *baccalà* (cod) and follow on with a *zuppa di pesce* (fish soup) or *rigatoni alla gricia.*

Piperno
Traditional Italian €€€

Map p88 (📞06 688 06 629; www.ristorante piperno.it; Via Monte de' Cenci 9; meals €55; 🕐closed Mon & Sun dinner; 🚇🚇Via Arenula) This Roman-Jewish institution is tucked away in a quiet corner of the Ghetto. It's formal without being stuffy, a wood-panelled restaurant of the old school, where white-clad waiters serve wonderful deep-fried *filetti di baccalà* (cod fillets) and *tagliolini alla pescatora* (long ribbon pasta with seafood). Booking is essential for Sunday.

Alberto Pica
Gelateria €

Map p88 (Via della Seggiola; cones/tubs from €1.50; 🚇🚇Via Arenula) This is a historic Roman gelateria, open since 1960. In summer, it offers flavours such as *fragoline di bosco* (wild strawberry) and *petali di rosa* (rose petal), but rice flavours are specialities year-round (resembling frozen rice pudding – yum).

Restaurant menu in the Jewish Ghetto

Sora Margherita Trattoria €€
Map p88 (☎06 687 42 16; Piazza delle Cinque Scole 30; meals €30; ⏲closed dinner Mon-Thu, all day Sun; 🚊🚌Via Arenula) No-frills Sora Margherita started as a cheap kitchen for hungry locals, but word has spread and it's now a popular lunchtime haunt of slumming uptowners. Expect dog-eat-dog queues, a rowdy Roman atmosphere and classic Roman-Jewish dishes such as *carciofi alla giudia* (fried artichoke).

Piazza Colonna & Around

Matricianella Traditional Italian €€
Map p82 (☎06 683 21 00; www.matricianella.it; Via del Leone 2/4; meals €40; ⏲Mon-Sat; 🚌Via del Corso) With its gingham tablecloths and chintzy murals, this popular trattoria is loved for its traditional Roman cuisine. You'll find all the usual menu stalwarts as well as some great Roman-Jewish dishes. Booking is essential.

Pizzeria al Leoncino Pizzeria €
Map p82 (☎06 686 77 57; Via del Leoncino 28; pizzas €6-8.50; ⏲closed Wed; 🚌Via del Corso) Some places just never change and fortunately for us, this boisterous neighbourhood pizzeria is one of them. A bastion of budget eating in an otherwise expensive area, it has a wood-fired oven, two small rooms, cheerful decor and gruff but efficient waiters who will serve you an excellent Roman-style pizza and ice-cold beer faster than you can say '*delizioso*'.

Gino Trattoria €€
Map p82 (☎06 687 34 34; Vicolo Rosini 4; meals €30; ⏲Mon-Sat; 🚌Via del Corso) Hidden away down a narrow lane close to parliament, Gino's is perennially packed with gossiping politicians. Join the right honourables for well-executed staples such as *rigatoni alla gricia* (pasta with cured pig's cheek) and meatballs, served under hanging garlic and gaudily painted vines. No credit cards.

🍷 Drinking & Nightlife

The *centro storico* is home to a couple of nightlife centres: the area around Piazza Navona, with a number of elegant bars and clubs catering to the beautiful, rich and stylish (and sometimes all three); and the rowdier area around Campo de' Fiori, where the crowd is younger and the drinking is heavier.

Pantheon & Around

Caffè Sant'Eustachio   Cafe
Map p82 (Piazza Sant'Eustachio 82; ⏰8.30-1am Sun-Thu, to 1.30am Fri, to 2am Sat; 🚇Corso del Rinascimento) This small unassuming cafe, generally three-deep at the bar, serves Rome's best coffee. The famous *gran caffè* is created by beating the first drops of espresso and several teaspoons of sugar into a frothy paste, then adding the rest of the coffee on top. It's superbly smooth and guaranteed to put zing into your sightseeing.

Caffè Tazza d'Oro   Cafe
Map p82 (Via degli Orfani 84; ⏰Mon-Sat; 🚇Via del Corso) A busy, stand-up bar with burnished wood and brass fittings, this place serves superb coffee. Its espresso hits the mark perfectly and there's a range of delicious coffee concoctions, such as *granita di caffè*, a crushed-ice coffee with a big dollop of cream, and *parfait di caffè*, a €3 coffee mousse.

Piazza Navona & Around

Etablì   Bar
Map p82 (📞06 97 616 694; www.etabli.it; Vicolo delle Vacche 9a; ⏰6pm-2am Tue-Sun, restaurant 7.30pm-midnight; 🚇Corso del Rinascimento) Housed in an airy 17th-century *palazzo*, Etablì is a fab rustic-chic lounge bar-cum-restaurant where Roman lovelies float in to have a drink, read the paper, indulge in *aperitivo* and use the wifi. Restaurant meals average about €35.

Bar della Pace
Bar

Map p82 (Via della Pace 5; ⊙9am-3am Tue-Sun, 4pm-3am Mon; 🚇Corso Vittorio Emanuele II) The quintessential *dolce vita* cafe. Inside it's all gilded baroque, polished surfaces and mismatched wooden tables; outside locals and tourists strike poses over their Camparis against a backdrop of ivy. The perfect people-watching spot.

La Maison
Nightclub

Map p82 (www.lamaisonroma.it; Vicolo dei Granari 4; 🚇Corso Vittorio Emanuele II) Chandeliers and long, low banquettes provide a sexy backdrop for a see-and-be-seen crowd, who flirt and frolic to a soundtrack of poppy tunes and commercial house. It's smooth, mainstream and exclusive, yet more fun than you might expect. Entrance is free, if you can get past the door police, but drinks are about €15 a throw.

Campo de' Fiori & Around

Open Baladin
Bar

Map p88 (www.openbaladin.com; Via degli Specchi 6; ⊙12.30pm-2am; 🚇Corso Vittorio Emanuele II) A designer beer bar near Campo de' Fiori, Open Baladin is leading the way in the recent beer trend that is sweeping the city. It's a slick, stylish place with more than 40 beers on tap and up to 100 bottled beers, many produced by Italian artisanal breweries.

Femme
Bar

Map p82 (Via del Pellegrino 14; ⊙6pm-2am Tue-Sun 🚇Corso Vittorio Emanuele II) Entering this bar, with its funky sounds and silver-seated modernist look, is like wandering into a Calvin Klein advert. The cocktails (€6) are the business and the splendid *aperitivo* is almost worth losing one's cool over.

Caffè Farnese
Cafe

Map p82 (Via dei Baullari 106; ⊙7am-2am; 🚇Corso Vittorio Emanuele II) We're with Goethe, who thought Piazza Farnese one of the world's most beautiful squares. Judge for yourself from the vantage point of this unassuming cafe. Try the *caffè alla casa* (house coffee) – made to a secret recipe.

Il Goccetto
Wine Bar

Map p82 (Via dei Banchi Vecchi 14; ⊙11.30am-2pm & 6.30pm-midnight Mon-Sat, closed Aug; 🚇Corso Vittorio Emanuele II) Draw up a chair and join the cast of loquacious regulars at this old-style *vino e olio* (wine and oil) shop to imbibe delicious drops by the glass (there are more than 800 labels to choose from), snack on tasty cheese and salami, and get to grips with all the neighbourhood banter.

Piazza Colonna & Around

Salotto 42
Bar

Map p82 (www.salotto42.it; Piazza di Pietra 42; ⊙10am-2am Tue-Sat, to midnight Sun & Mon; 🚇Via del Corso) On a picturesque piazza, facing the columns of the Tempio di Adriano, this is a hip, glamorous lounge bar, complete with an ivy-clad facade, vintage armchairs, sleek sofas and a collection of heavy, coffee-table design books. Run by an Italian-Swedish couple, it has an excellent *aperitivo* spread and serves a Sunday brunch (€15).

⭐ Entertainment

Rialtosantambrogio
Cultural Centre

Map p88 (📞06 68133 640; www.rialto.roma.it; Via di San'Ambrogio 4; 🚇🚇Via Arenula) This ancient courtyard-centred building is Rome's most central *centro sociale* (social centre), with an art-school vibe and an edgy programme of theatre, exhibitions and art-house cinema. It also stages seriously kicking club nights and central Rome's best gigs – check the website for upcoming events.

Teatro Argentina
Theatre

Map p82 (📞06 684 00 01; www.teatrodiroma.net; Largo di Torre Argentina 52; tickets €12-27; 🚇🚇Largo di Torre Argentina) Rome's top theatre is one of the two official homes of the Teatro di Roma; the other is the Teatro India. Founded in 1732, it retains its original frescoed ceiling and a grand gilt-and-velvet auditorium. Rossini's *Barber of Seville* premiered here and today it stages a wide-ranging programme of drama (mostly in Italian) and high-profile dance performances.

Teatro Valle — Theatre
Map p82 (📞06 688 03 794; www.teatro valle.it; Via del Teatro Valle 21; tickets €16-31; 🚌🚊Largo di Torre Argentina) Another of Rome's historic stages, this perfectly proportioned 18th-century theatre is like a pocket opera house, with three levels of red-and-gold private boxes. Its interesting programme spans everything from old classics to ballet, rock opera and recitals. English-language works are sometimes performed in English with Italian subtitles.

 Shopping

Pantheon & Around

Spazio Sette — Home & Garden
Map p82 (www.spaziosette.it, in Italian; Via dei Barbieri 7; 🚌🚊Largo di Torre Argentina) Even if you don't buy any of the designer homeware at Spazio Sette, it's worth popping in to see sharp modern furniture set against 17th-century frescoes. Formerly home to a cardinal, the *palazzo* now houses a three-floor shop full of quality furniture, kitchenware, tableware and gifts.

Feltrinelli — Bookstore
Map p82 (www.lafeltrinelli.it, in Italian; Largo di Torre Argentina 11; 🕗9am-8pm Mon-Fri, 9am-10pm Sat, 10am-9pm Sun; 🚌🚊Largo di Torre Argentina) Italy's most famous bookseller (and publisher) has shops across the capital. This one has a wide range of books (in Italian) on art, photography, cinema and history, as well as an extensive selection of Italian litera-

ture and travel guides in various languages, including English.

Piazza Navona & Around

Officina Profumo Farmaceutica di Santa Maria Novella — Cosmetics
Map p82 (Corso del Rinascimento 47; 🚊Corso del Rinascimento) Step in for the scent of the place, if nothing else. This bewitching shop – the Roman branch of one of Italy's oldest pharmacies – stocks natural perfumes and cosmetics as well as herbal infusions, teas and pot pourri, all carefully shelved in wooden cabinets under a giant Murano-glass chandelier.

Nardecchia — Antiques
Map p82 (Piazza Navona 25; 🚊Corso del Rinascimento) You'll be inviting people to see your etchings after a visit to this historic Piazza Navona shop, famed for its antique prints. Nardecchia sells everything from 18th-century etchings by Giovanni Battista Piranesi to more affordable 19th-century panoramas. Bank on about €120 for a small framed print.

Piazza della Rotonda (p73)
GEOFF STRINGER/LONELY PLANET IMAGES ©

Vestiti Usati Cinzia Fashion

Map p82 (Via del Governo Vecchio 45; 🚍Corso Vittorio Emanuele II) Vestiti Usati Cinzia, owned by a former costume designer, remains one of the best vintage shops on Via del Governo Vecchio. There are jackets (in leather, denim, corduroy and linen), slouchy boots, screen-printed T-shirts, retro skirts and suede coats, and you can snap up vintage designer sunglasses.

Ai Monasteri Cosmetics

Map p82 (www.monasteri.it; Corso del Rinascimento 72; ⏱4.30-7.30pm Mon, Wed & Fri, 10am-1pm Sat; 🚍Corso del Rinascimento) This apothecary-like, wonderfully scented shop sells herbal essences, spirits, soaps, balms and liqueurs, all created by monks and beautifully packaged. You can stock up on everything from sage toothpaste to rose shampoo, cherry brandy and a mysterious-sounding elixir of love, though quite why monks are expert at this is anyone's guess.

Casali Art

Map p82 (Via dei Coronari 115; 🚍Corso del Rinascimento) On Via dei Coronari, a lovely pedestrian street known for its antique furniture shops, Casali deals in antique prints, many delicately hand-coloured. The shop is small but the choice is not, ranging from 16th-century botanical manuscripts to €3 postcard prints of Rome.

Città del Sole Toys

Map p82 (www.cittadelsole.it; Via della Scrofa 65; ⏱10am-7.30pm, closed Mon morning & Sun; 🚍Corso del Rinascimento) Città del Sole is a parent's dream, a treasure-trove of imaginative toys created to stretch the growing mind rather than numb it. From well-crafted wooden trains to insect investigation kits, here you'll find toys to (with any luck) keep your children occupied for hours.

Campo De' Fiori & Around

Ibiz – Artigianato in Cuoio Accessories

Map p82 (Via dei Chiavari 39; 🚍Corso Vittorio Emanuele II) In this pint-sized workshop, Elisa Nepi and her father craft exquisite, well-priced leather goods, including wallets, bags, belts and sandals, in simple but classy designs and myriad colours.

Campo de' Fiori market (p80)

With €40 you should be able to pick up a wallet, purse or pair of sandals.

Arsenale
Fashion

Map p82 (www.patriziapieroni.it; Via del Pellegrino 172; 🚊 Corso Vittorio Emanuele II) Arsenale is a watchword with fashion-conscious Roman women and the virgin-white shop marries urban minimalism with heavy, rustic fittings to create a clean, contemporary look. Roman designer Patrizia Pieroni started Arsenale over 15 years ago, but it still feels cutting edge with its interestingly structured clothes in rich, luscious fabrics.

Libreria del Viaggiatore
Bookstore

Map p82 (Via del Pellegrino 78; 🚊 Corso Vittorio Emanuele II) If Rome is only a stop on your Grand Tour, this beguiling old-fashioned bookshop is a must. Small but world-encompassing, it's crammed with guides and travel literature in various languages and has a huge range of maps, including hiking maps.

Borini
Shoes

Map p88 (Via dei Pettinari 86-87; 🚊 🚊 Via Arenula) Don't be fooled by the discount, workaday look – those in the know pile into this unglitzy shop, run by the Borinis since 1940, to try on the cool, candy-coloured shoes. Whatever is 'in' this season, Borini will have it, at reasonable prices and in a cover-every-eventuality rainbow palette.

daDADA 52
Fashion

Map p82 (www.dadada.eu; Via dei Giubbonari 52; 🚊 Corso Vittorio Emanuele II) Every young Roman fashionista makes a stop at daDADA, for its funky cocktail dresses, bright print summer frocks and eclectic coats. Prices start at around €100 but most items are north of €200. There's also a second branch at Via del Corso 500.

Piazza Colonna & Around

Confetteria Moriondo & Gariglio
Chocolate

Map p82 (Via del Piè di Marmo 21-22; ⏱9am-7.30pm Mon-Sat; 🚊 🚊 Largo di Torre Argentina) Roman poet Trilussa dedicated several sonnets to this shop, and you can see why. This is no ordinary sweetshop but a veritable temple to bonbons. Moriondo and Gariglio were Torinese cousins who moved to Rome after the unification of Italy, and many of the chocolates are handmade to their original recipes.

AS Roma Store
Sportswear

Map p82 (Piazza Colonna 360; 🚊 Via del Corso) An official club store of AS Roma, one of Rome's two top-flight football teams. The club has been through the mill in recent times, so help boost the team's coffers by buying a replica shirt or keyring, or indeed anything from the selection of branded clothes and trinkets. You can also buy match tickets here.

Tridente, Trevi & the Quirinale

Tridente, Rome's most glamorous district, is full of designer boutiques, swish hotels and some breathtaking architectural and artistic sights. These include the splendid neoclassical showpiece Piazza del Popolo, numerous glittering churches, the rococo Spanish Steps and the Museo dell'Ara Pacis – the controversial modern museum designed by US architect Richard Meier. The district is easily walkable – it's a short stroll from the Centro Storico or Piazza Venezia – and accessible from Spagna and Flaminio Metro stations.

The Quirinale, one of Rome's hills, is home to the extraordinary Trevi Fountain and the imposing presidential Palazzo del Quirinale, as well as important churches designed by the masters of Roman baroque – Gian Lorenzo Bernini and Francesco Borromini. Other artistic hotspots in the area include the lavish Galleria Colonna and the sumptuous Galleria Nazionale d'Arte Antica – Palazzo Barberini. The principal gateway to the Trevi and Quirinale is the Barberini Metro stop.

Trevi Fountain (p109)
WILL SALTER/LONELY PLANET IMAGES ©

Tridente, Trevi & the Quirinale Highlights

Spanish Steps (p106)

It's a quintessential Roman experience to while away time on this rococo flight of steps, people-watching, chattering, photo-snapping and dreaming, with a view down designer-store-lined Via Condotti – the glittering backbone of the Tridente district. This is where Dickens watched artists' models tout for work on 19th-century mornings and where Keats lived, in a small apartment overlooking the steps.

Chiesa di Santa Maria del Popolo (p105)

This remarkable Renaissance church was partly designed by Bramante and Bernini, and contains works by Raphael and Pinturicchio, as well as Rome's earliest stained-glass windows. What dazzles beyond everything else, however, are the arresting Caravaggio masterpieces in the Chigi Chapel – ferociously dramatic works that use light and shade to create tangible atmosphere and depth.

Trevi Fountain (p109)

Almost filling an entire piazza, this foaming fountain is an exuberant, thrilling vision – a remarkable surprise approached via narrow streets in the city centre. It's almost always thronged with people, tossing coins over their shoulders into the waters to ensure a return visit to Rome. If you want to see it with less company, try late in the evening when the crowds have ebbed away.

Palazzo del Quirinale (p107)

If you're in Rome on a Sunday morning between June and September, visit the imposing presidential palace, the Palazzo del Quirinale. Not only will you have the rare chance to explore the building that Napoleon envisaged as Rome's Versailles, but you will also have the amazing opportunity to hear a classical concert in the Carlo Moderno–designed chapel at the end of your visit.

Palazzo Barberini (p108)

The majestic Roman seat of the powerful Barberini family is an architectural wonder, with staircases at either side of the building designed by the great baroque rivals Borromini and Bernini. As well as architectural treasures, the gallery is packed with works of genius by Raphael, Fra Angelico, Caravaggio and Holbein, among others, and astounds with its incredible salon ceiling, decorated by Pietro da Cortona.

Tridente, Trevi & the Quirinale Walk

On this walk you'll see some of the greatest hits of Tridente, Trevi and the Quirinale, including Pincio Hill Gardens, Piazza del Popolo, the Spanish Steps and the Trevi Fountain.

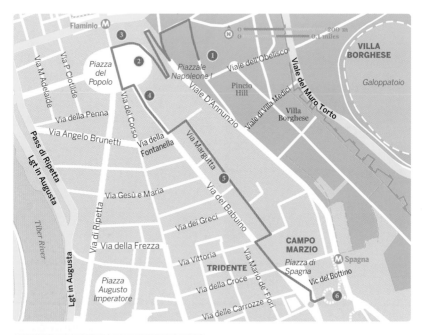

WALK FACTS
- **Start** Pincio Gardens
- **Finish** Keats–Shelley House
- **Distance** 1.5km
- **Duration** Two hours

1 Pincio Hill Gardens

Begin your walk in **Pincio Hill Gardens** (p104), which are adjacent to the Villa Borghese park, and have a balcony offering sublime views over the dramatic disc of Piazza del Popolo and the rooftops and domes of Rome. These gardens are where Henry James' Daisy Miller walked with Winterborne

in *Daisy Miller,* attracting attention for her prettiness.

2 Piazza del Popolo

From the Pincio Hill Gardens, zigzag your way downhill to **Piazza del Popolo** (p104). This impressive 16th-century piazza was once the first glimpse of Rome that visitors coming from the north would see as they entered through the grand Porta del Popolo. It's centred on an ancient Egyptian obelisk and surrounded by three beautiful churches. The twin **Chiesa di Santa Maria dei Miracoli** and **Chiesa di Santa Maria in Montesanto** are cleverly constructed to appear identical, though they in fact occupy different footprints.

③ Chiesa di Santa Maria del Popolo

The several churches that surround the piazza include the **Chiesa di Santa Maria del Popolo** (p105), which contains several mesmerising paintings by Caravaggio, as well as the Raphael-designed Cappella Chigi, which was completed by Bernini. The apse of the church was designed by Bramante and decorated by Pinturicchio.

④ Hotel de Russie

From the church, cross the piazza to Via del Babuino (Street of the Baboon) and the **Hotel de Russie** (p263), favoured by the artistic avant garde in the early 20th century. Jean Cocteau stayed here with Picasso when they were both working with the Ballets Russes, and wrote a letter home in which he described plucking oranges from outside his window. Its courtyard **Stravinkij Bar** (p115) is a lovely place to stop for a drink.

⑤ Via Margutta

Running parallel to Via Babuino is **Via Margutta**. Famous for its artistic and cinematic connections, this picturesque cobbled street was where Truman Capote settled when he visited Rome – the short story 'Lola' was set in his Via Margutta apartment. Picasso and Stravinsky worked in studios on this street; Gregory Peck's fictional character in *Roman Holiday* had an apartment here, and Fellini lived on Via Margutta for many years.

⑥ Spanish Steps

A short walk and you're almost at the **Spanish Steps** (p106), which Dickens described in his *Pictures from Italy* with some amusement, noting the characterful artists' models waiting to be hired here. Just south of the steps, and overlooking them, is the apartment where Keats died of tuberculosis, aged just 25. The **Keats–Shelley House** (p106) is now a fascinating small museum and the ideal place to end your tour.

 The Best…

PLACES TO EAT

Palatium Contemporary wine bar that showcases the best in Lazio produce, with delicious food and tipples. (p113)

Dal Bolognese Glamorous restaurant on the edge of Piazza del Popolo. (p108)

Colline Emiliane Another Emilia-Romagna specialist, with glorious ragù, delicate pastas and slow-roasted meats. (p114)

PLACES TO DRINK

Salotto Locarno Chic art deco bar with summer courtyard, ideal for cocktail sipping. (p115)

Stravinkij Bar Purring elegance, overlooked by terraced gardens. (p115)

Canova Tadolini Unique cafe housed in sculptor Antonio Canova's former studio. (p115)

CHURCHES

Chiesa di Santa Maria del Popolo Splendid Renaissance church designed and decorated by Bramante, Bernini, Caravaggio, Bernini and Raphael. (p105)

Chiesa di Sant'Andrea al Quirinale See how Bernini created a sense of grandeur out of limited space. (p107)

Chiesa di San Carlo alle Quattro Fontane Borromini's baroque masterpiece, a 17th-century architectural marvel. (p108)

View from the Pincio Hill Gardens
JEAN-PIERRE LESCOURRET/LONELY PLANET IMAGES ©

Discover Tridente, Trevi & the Quirinale

⟨⊕⟩ Getting There & Away

○ **Metro** The Trevi and Quirinale areas are closest to Barberini Metro stop, while Spagna and Flaminio stations are perfectly placed for Tridente. All three stops are on line A.

○ **Bus** Numerous buses run down to Piazza Barberini or along Via Veneto, and many end up at Piazza San Silvestro, ideal for a foray into Tridente.

◉ Sights

The Piazza del Popolo, the Spanish Steps, the Trevi Fountain, Rome's most designer district, Palazzo Barberini and a sprinkling of Caravaggios, all a hop and a skip from Villa Borghese (see p211) when you're in need of a breather: this area is one of Rome's wealthiest, in terms of cuisine, art and culture, as well as hard cash, and offers an embarrassment of riches for the visitor.

Piazza del Popolo & Around

Piazza del Popolo　　　　　Piazza
Map p110 (M Flaminio) For centuries the site of public executions, this elegant neoclassical piazza is a superb people-watching spot. It was originally laid out in 1538 to provide a grandiose entrance to the city – at the time, and for centuries before, it was the main northern gateway into the city. Since then it has been extensively altered, most recently by Giuseppe Valadier in 1823. Guarding its southern entrance are Carlo Rainaldi's twin 17th-century baroque churches, **Chiesa di Santa Maria dei Miracoli** and **Chiesa di Santa Maria in Montesanto**. Over on the northern flank of the piazza is the **Porta del Popolo**, created by Bernini in 1655.

Pincio Hill Gardens　　　　Park
Map p110 (M Flaminio) Overlooking Piazza del Popolo, the 19th-century Pincio Hill Gardens are named after the Pinci family, who owned this part of Rome in the 4th century. It's quite a climb up from the

Piazza del Popolo
COTO ELIZONDO/ DIGITAL VISION/GETTYIMAGES ©

MIREK HEJNICKI/SHUTTERSTOCK ©

 Don't Miss
Chiesa di Santa Maria del Popolo

The first chapel was built here in 1099, over the tombs of the Domiti family, to exorcise the ghost of Nero, who was secretly buried on this spot and whose malicious spirit was thought to haunt the area. Some 400 years later, in 1472, it was given a major overhaul by Pope Sixtus IV. Pinturicchio was called in to decorate the pope's family chapel, the Cappella delle Rovere, and to paint a series of frescoes on the apse, itself designed by Bramante. Also in the apse are Rome's first stained-glass windows, crafted by Frenchman Guillaume de Marcillat in the early 16th century. The altar houses the 13th-century painting Madonna del Popolo, and the altarpiece of the Assumption is by Annibale Carracci.

Raphael designed the Cappella Chigi, dedicated to his patron Agostino Chigi, but never lived to see it completed. Bernini finished the job for him more than a hundred years later, contributing statues of Daniel and Habakkuk to the altarpiece, which was built by Sebastiano del Piombo.

The church's absolute highlight, however, is the Cappella Cerasi with its two Caravaggios: the Conversione di San Paolo (Conversion of St Paul) and the Crocifissione di San Pietro (Crucifixion of St Peter).

NEED TO KNOW

Map p110; admission free; ⊘7am-noon & 4-7pm Mon-Sat, 8am-1.30pm & 4.30-7.30pm Sun; Ⓜ Flaminio, Spagna

piazza, but at the top you're rewarded with lovely views over to St Peter's and the Gianicolo hill.

Museo dell'Ara Pacis   Museum

Map p110 (☎ 06 820 59 127; www.arapacis.it; Lungotevere in Augusta; adult/reduced €9/7; ⊘9am-7pm Tue-Sun; 🚌 Lungotevere in Augusta) The first modern construction in Rome's historic centre since WWII, Richard Meier's minimalist glass-and-marble pavilion echoes the surrounding Fascist architecture.

Inside is the Ara Pacis Augustae (Altar of Peace), Augustus' great monument to peace. One of the most important works of ancient Roman sculpture, the vast marble altar (it measures 11.6m by 10.6m by 3.6m) was completed in 13 BC and positioned near Piazza San Lorenzo in Lucina, slightly to the southeast of its current site.

Mausoleo di Augusto   Monument
Map p110 (Piazza Augusto Imperatore; 🚇 Piazza Augusto Imperatore) Once one of Ancient Rome's most imposing monuments, this is now an unkempt mound of earth, overgrown with weeds and surrounded by unsightly fences. Plans for a revamp have been on the table for some years, but there's still no sign of activity.

The mausoleum, which was built in 28 BC, is the last resting place of Augustus, who was buried here in AD 14, and his favourite nephew and heir Marcellus. Mussolini had it restored in 1936 with an eye to being buried here himself.

Piazza di Spagna & Around
Piazza di Spagna & the Spanish Steps   Piazza, Monument
Map p110 (admission free; Ⓜ Spagna, Flaminio) The Piazza di Spagna was named after the Spanish Embassy to the Holy See, although the staircase, designed by the Italian Francesco de Sanctis and built in 1725 with a legacy from the French, leads to the French Chiesa della Trinità dei Monti. In the late 1700s the area was much loved by English visitors on the Grand Tour and was known to locals as *er ghetto de l'inglesi* (the English ghetto). Keats lived for a short time in an apartment overlooking the Spanish Steps, and died here of tuberculosis at the age of 25. The rooms are now a museum (see p106) devoted to the Romantics, especially Keats.

At the foot of the steps, the fountain of a sinking boat, the **Barcaccia** (1627), is believed to be by Pietro Bernini, father of the more famous Gian Lorenzo.

Keats–Shelley House   Museum
Map p110 (📞 06 678 42 35; www.keats-shelley -house.org; Piazza di Spagna 26; adult/reduced €4.50/3.50; 🕐 10am-1pm & 2-6pm Mon-Fri,

Piazza di Spagna and the Spanish Steps

TRIDENTE, TREVI & THE QUIRINALE SIGHTS

11am-2pm & 3-6pm Sat; **M**Spagna) Next to the Spanish Steps, the Keats–Shelley House is where Romantic poet John Keats died of TB in February 1821. The house is now a small museum crammed with memorabilia relating to the poets and their colleagues Mary Shelley and Lord Byron.

Chiesa della Trinità dei Monti
Church

Map p110 (☎06 679 41 79; Piazza Trinità dei Monti; ⏱7am-1pm & 3-7pm Tue-Sun; **M**Spagna) Looming over the Spanish Steps, this landmark church was commissioned by King Louis XII of France and consecrated in 1585. Apart from the great views from outside, it has some wonderful frescoes by Daniele da Volterra. If you don't fancy climbing the steep steps, there's a lift up from Spagna metro station.

Trevi Fountain to the Quirinale

Palazzo del Quirinale
Palazzo

Map p110 (☎06 4 69 91; www.quirinale.it; Piazza del Quirinale; adult €5; ⏱8.30am-noon Sun mid-Sep–mid-Jun; **M**Barberini) Overlooking the high-up Piazza del Quirinale is the imposing presidential palace, formerly the papal summer residence, open to the public on Sundays.

The immense Palazzo del Quirinale served as the papal summer residence for almost three centuries until the keys were begrudgingly handed over to Italy's new king in 1870. Since 1948, it has been home of the Presidente della Repubblica, Italy's head of state.

Pope Gregory XIII (r 1572–85) originally chose the site and over the next 150 years the top architects of the day worked on it, including Bernini, Domenico Fontana and Carlo Maderno.

Piazza del Quirinale
Piazza

Map p110 (**M**Barbarini) A wonderful spot to enjoy a glowing Roman sunset, this piazza marks the summit of the Quirinale hill. The central **obelisk** was moved here from the Mausoleo di Augusto in 1786 and is flanked by 5.5m statues of **Castor** and **Pollux** reining in a couple of rearing horses.

If you're in the neighbourhood on a Sunday you can catch the weekly changing of the guard (6pm in summer, 4pm the rest of the year).

Chiesa di Santa Maria della Vittoria
Church

Map p110 (☎06 482 61 90; Via XX Settembre 17; ⏱8.30am-noon & 3.30-6pm Mon-Sat, 3.30-6pm Sun; **M**Repubblica) On a busy road junction, this modest church is an unlikely setting for one of the great works of European art – Bernini's extravagant and sexually charged *Santa Teresa traffita dall'amore di Dio* (Ecstasy of St Teresa).

Galleria Colonna
Gallery

Map p110 (☎06 225 82 493; www.galleria colonna.it; Via della Pilotta 17; adult/reduced €10/8; ⏱9am-1.15pm Sat, daily private tours on request, closed Aug; ☐Via IV Novembre) The only part of Palazzo Colonna open to the public, this incredibly opulent gallery houses the Colonna family's small but stunning private art collection.

The only part of the palace open to the public is the purpose-built gallery (constructed by Antonio del Grande from 1654 to 1665). Its six rooms are crowned by fantastical ceiling frescoes, all dedicated to Marcantonio Colonna, the family's greatest ancestor, who defeated the Turks at the naval Battle of Lepanto in 1571. Note also the cannonball lodged in the gallery's marble stairs, a vivid reminder of the 1849 siege of Rome.

The art on display features a fine array of 16th- to 18th- century paintings, the highlight of which is Annibale *Carracci's* vivid *Mangiafagioli* (The Bean Eater).

Chiesa di Sant'Andrea al Quirinale
Church

Map p110 (☎06 474 08 07; Via del Quirinale 29; ⏱8.30am-noon & 3.30-7pm Mon-Sat, 9am-noon & 4-7pm Sun; ☐Via Nazionale) It's said that in his old age Bernini liked to come and enjoy the peace of this late-17th-century church, regarded by many as one of his greatest creations. Faced with severe space limitations, he managed to produce a sense of grandeur by designing an elliptical floor plan with a series of chapels opening onto the central area.

Chiesa di San Carlo alle Quattro Fontane · Church

Map p110 (📞 06 488 31 09; Via del Quirinale 23; ⏱ 10am-1pm & 3-6pm Mon-Fri, 10am-1pm Sat, noon-1pm Sun; 🚇 Via Nazionale) It might not look it, with its filthy facade and unappealing location, but this tiny church is a masterpiece of Roman baroque. The elegant curves of the facade, the play of convex and concave surfaces, the dome illuminated by hidden windows, all combine to transform a minuscule space into a light, airy interior.

Time Elevator · Cinema

Map p110 (📞 06 977 46 243; www.time-elevator .it; Via dei Santissimi Apostoli 20; adult/reduced €12/9; ⏱ 10.30am-7.30pm; 🚇 Piazza Venezia) Just off Via del Corso, the Time Elevator cinema is ideal for armchair sightseers. There are three programmes, but the one to see is *Time Elevator Rome,* a 45-minute trip through 3000 years of Roman history. Note that children under five aren't admitted and anyone who suffers from motion sickness should probably give it a miss.

Piazza Barberini & Via Veneto

Piazza Barberini · Piazza

Map p110 (Ⓜ Barberini) More a traffic thoroughfare than a place to linger, this noisy square is named after the Barberini family, one of Rome's great dynastic clans. In the centre, the Bernini-designed **Fontana del Tritone** (Fountain of the Triton) depicts the sea-god Triton blowing a stream of water from a conch while seated in a large scallop shell supported by four dolphins. Bernini also crafted the **Fontana delle Api** (Fountain of the Bees) in the northeastern corner, again for the Barberini family, whose crest featured three bees in flight.

Galleria Nazionale d'Arte Antica – Palazzo Barberini · Gallery

Map p110 (📞 06 225 82 493; www.galleriaborg hese.it; Via delle Quattro Fontane 13; adult/reduced €5/2.50; ⏱ 9am-7.30pm Tue-Sun, ticket office closes 7pm; Ⓜ Barberini) The Palazzo Barberini was commissioned by Urban VIII to celebrate the Barberini family's rise to papal power. Many high-profile baroque architects worked on it, including Carlo Moderno and rivals Bernini and Borromini. The palace houses part of the Galleria Nazionale d'Arte Antica. Besides works by Raphael, Caravaggio, Guido Reni, Bernini, Filippo Lippi, Holbein, Titian and Tintoretto, there is the mesmerising ceiling of the main salon, the *Triumph of Divine Providence* (1632–39) by Pietro da Cortona.

Chiesa di Santa Maria della Concezione · Church

Map p110 (📞 06 487 11 85; Via Vittorio Veneto 27; admission by donation; ⏱ 9am-noon & 3-6pm Fri-Wed; Ⓜ Barberini) There's nothing special about this 17th-century church but dip into the **Capuchin cemetery** below and you'll be gobsmacked. Everything from the picture frames to the light fittings is made of human bones. Between 1528 and 1870 the resident Capuchin monks used the bones of 4000 of their departed brothers to create the mesmerising and macabre display.

⚔ Eating

Rome's designer shopping district may be fashionista heaven, but it retains a neighbourhood feel, albeit a wealthy one. Lots of classy eateries are sandwiched between the boutiques.

Piazza del Popolo & Around

Dal Bolognese · Traditional Italian €€€

Map p110 (📞 06 361 14 26; Piazza del Popolo 1; meals €70; ⏱ Tue-Sun, closed Aug; Ⓜ Flaminio) Dine inside surrounded by wood

RICHARD I'ANSON/LONELY PLANET IMAGES ©

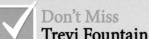

Don't Miss
Trevi Fountain

Rome's most famous fountain, Fontana di Trevi, is a baroque extravaganza that almost fills an entire piazza. The foaming masterpiece is famous as the place where Anita Ekberg waded in a gown for Fellini's *La Dolce Vita* (1960).

The flamboyant baroque ensemble was designed by Nicola Salvi in 1732 and depicts Neptune's chariot being led by Tritons with sea horses – one wild, one docile – representing the moods of the sea. The water still comes from the aqua virgo, an underground aqueduct that is over 2000 years old, built by General Agrippa under Augustus and that brings water from the Salone springs around 19 kilometres away. The name Trevi refers to the *tre vie* (three roads) that converge at the fountain.

The famous tradition is to toss a coin into the fountain, thus ensuring your return. Around €3000 is thrown into the Trevi on an average day.

NEED TO KNOW
Map p110; admission free; **M** Barberini

panelling and exotic flowers, or outside, people-watching with views over Piazza del Popolo. As the name suggests, Emilia-Romagna dishes are the name of the game; everything is good, but try the tortellini in soup, tagliatelle with ragú, or the damn fine fillet steak.

Babette   Italian €€€
Map p110 (☎ 06 321 15 59; Via Margutta 1; meals €55; ☼ closed Jan & Aug; **M** Spagna or Flaminio; ☞) You're in for a feast at Babette's, which has a chic yet unpretentious brasserie-style interior of exposed brick walls and vintage painted signs. Food is delicious, with a sophisticated, creative, French twist (think *tortiglioni* with courgette and

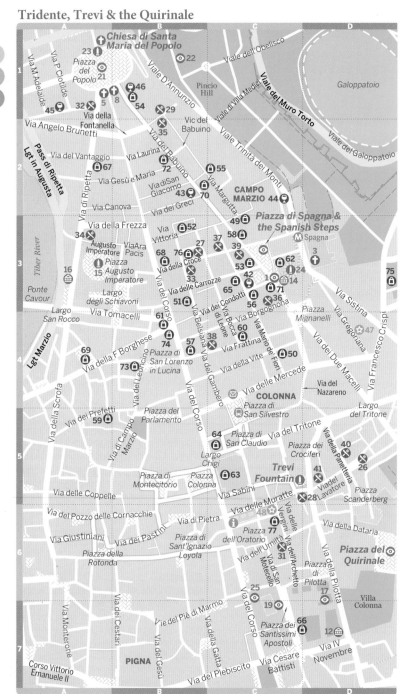

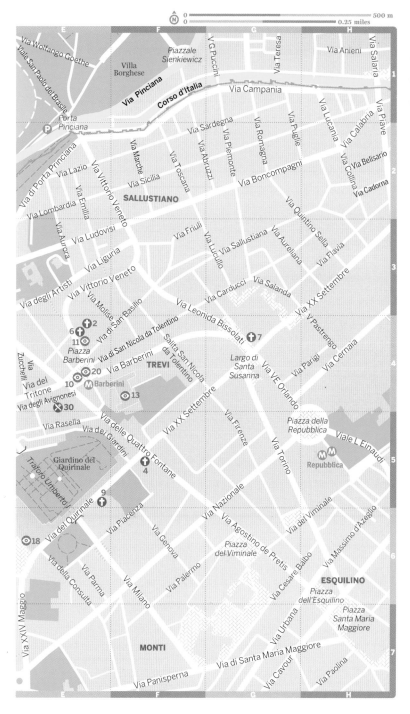

0
0.25 miles
500 m

Via Wolfango Goethe
Viale San Paolo del Brasile
Villa Borghese
Piazzale Sienkiewicz
V G Puccini
Via Teresa
Via Anieni
Via Salaria

Via Pinciana
Corso d'Italia
Via Campania
Via Lucania
Via Calabria
Via Piave

Porta Pinciana
Via di Porta Pinciana
Via Lazio
Via Marche
Via Sardegna
Via Abruzzi
Via Piemonte
Via Romagna
Via Puglie
Via Collina
Via Belisario
Via Cadorna

Via Vittorio Veneto
Via Sicilia
Via Toscana
Via Boncompagni

Via Lombardia
Via Emilia
SALLUSTIANO
Via Quintino Sella
Via Flavia

Via Aurora
Via Ludovisi
Via Friuli
Via Luculo
Via Sallustiana
Via Aureliana

Via degli Artisti
Via Liguria
Via Vittorio Veneto
Via Carducci
Via Salanda
Via XX Settembre

Via Molise
Via Leonida Bissolati
V Pastrengo
Via Cernaia

Via di San Basilio
6 ⊕2
11 ◎
Piazza Barberini
Via di San Nicola da Tolentino
Salita San Nicola da Tolentino
⊕7
Largo di Santa Susanna
Via Parigi

Via Zucchelli
◎◎20
Via Barberini
TREVI
Via VE Orlando

Via del Tritone
10 Ⓜ Barberini
◎13

Via degli Avignonesi
✕30

Via Rasella
Via delle Quattro Fontane
Via XX Settembre
Via Frenze
Piazza della Repubblica
Viale L Einaudi

Via dei Giardini
Via Torino
ⓂⓂ Repubblica

Giardino del Quirinale
⊕4

Trattorio Umberto I
⊕9
Via Piacenza
Via Nazionale
Via del Viminale

◎18
Via del Quirinale
Via Genova
Via Agostino de Pretis
Piazza del Viminale
Via Massimo d'Azeglio

Via della Consulta
Via Parma
Via Palermo
ESQUILINO
Piazza dell'Esquilino
Piazza Santa Maria Maggiore

Via XXIV Maggio
MONTI
Via Cesare Balbo
Via Urbana

Via Panisperna
Via di Santa Maria Maggiore
Via Cavour
Via Paolina

Tridente, Trevi & the Quirinale

pistachio pesto), and the wine list is short but super. There's a daily buffet (€10 Tuesday to Friday, €25 weekends).

'Gusto
Pizzeria €

Map p110 (📞06 322 62 73; Piazza Augusto Imperatore 9; pizza €6-9.50; 🚇Piazza Augusto Imperatore) This mould-breaking warehouse-style gastronomic complex, all exposed brickwork and industrial chic, is still buzzing after all these years. It's a great place to sit on the terrace and eat Neapolitan-style pizzas (rather than the upmarket restaurant fare, which receives mixed reports). There's live music on Tuesday and Thursday evenings.

Margutta Ristorante
Vegetarian €€

Map p110 (📞06 678 60 33; Via Margutta 118; meals €50; 🚇Spagna or Flaminio; 🖋) Vegetarian restaurants in Rome are rarer than parking spaces, and this airy art gallery–restaurant is an unusually chic way to eat your greens. Best value is the Saturday/Sunday buffet brunch (€15/25). It also offers a four-course vegan menu (€32).

Piazza di Spagna & Around

Palatium
Wine Bar €€

Map p110 (📞06 692 02 132; Via Frattina 94; meals €40; 🕐11am-11pm Mon-Sat, closed Aug; 🚇Via del Corso) Conceived as a showcase of Lazio's bounty, this sleek wine bar close to the Spanish Steps serves excellent local specialities, such as *porchetta* (pork roasted with herbs), artisan cheese and delicious salami, as well as an impressive array of Lazio wines (try lesser-known drops such as Aleatico). *Aperitivo* is a good bet too.

Nino
Tuscan €€

Map p110 (📞06 679 5676; Via Borgognona 11; meals €60; 🕐lunch & dinner Mon-Sat; 🚇Spagna) With a look of wrought-iron chandeliers, polished dark wood and white tablecloths, which is surely pretty unchanged since it opened in 1934, Nino is enduringly popular with the rich and famous. Waiters can be brusque if you're not on the A-list, but the food is good hearty fare, including memorable steaks and Tuscan bean soup.

Achilli Enoteca al Parlamento
Roman €€€

Map p110 (📞06 687 3446; Via dei Prefetti 15; meals €75; 🕐Tue-Sat, closed Aug; 🚇Spagna) This new, intimate temple of gastronomy, part of a historic wine bar, specialises in Roman cuisine such as *amatriciana* (pasta with tomato and pancetta sauce), *cacio e pepe* (pasta with Pecorino cheese and black pepper) and carbonara, as well as elegant combinations of seasonal ingredients such as pumpkin and truffles.

Fiaschetteria Beltramme
Trattoria €€

Map p110 (Via della Croce 39; meals €45; 🚇Spagna) With a tiny dark interior whose walls are covered in paintings and sketches right up to the high ceilings, Fiaschetteria (meaning 'wine-sellers') is a discreet, intimate, stuck-in-time place with a short menu and no telephone. Expect fashionistas with appetites digging into traditional Roman dishes (*pasta e ceci* and so on).

Pasticcio
Fast Food €

Map p110 (Via della Croce; pasta dish €4; 🕐1-3pm Mon-Sat; 🚇Spagna) A great find in this pricey 'hood. Pasticcio is a pasta shop that serves up around two choices of pasta at lunch time. It's fast food, Italian style – great fresh pasta with tasty sauces.

Otello alla Concordia
Trattoria €€

Map p110 (📞06 679 11 78; Via della Croce 81; meals €40; 🕐lunch & dinner Mon-Sat; 🚇Spagna) A perennial favourite with both tourists and locals, Otello is a haven near the Spanish Steps. Outside dining is in the vine-covered courtyard of an 18th-century *palazzo* where, if you're lucky, you can dine in the shadow of the wisteria-covered pergola.

Antica Enoteca
Wine Bar €€

Map p110 (📞06 679 08 96; Via della Croce 76b; meals €35; 🕐11am-1am; 🚇Spagna) Near the Spanish Steps, locals and tourists alike prop up the 19th-century wooden bar, or sit at outside tables or those in the back room, sampling wines by the glass, snacking on antipasti, and ordering well-priced soul food such as pasta or polenta.

Trevi Fountain to the Quirinale

Da Michele
Pizza al Taglio €

Map p110 (📞 349 252 53 47; Via dell'Umiltà 31; pizza slices from €2; ⏰ 8am-5pm Mon-Fri, to 8pm summer; 🚇 Via del Corso) A handy address in Spagna district: buy your fresh, light and crispy *pizza al taglio,* and you'll have a delicious fast lunch.

Vineria Chianti
Wine Bar €€

Map p110 (📞 06 678 75 50; Via del Lavatore 81-82; meals €35; 🚇 Via del Tritone) This pretty ivy-clad wine bar is bottle-lined inside, with watch-the-world-go-by streetside seating in summer. Cuisine is Tuscan, so the beef is particularly good, but it also serves up imaginative salads, and pizza in the evenings.

Al Presidente
Seafood €€€

Map p110 (📞 06 679 73 42; Via Arcione 95; meals €75; ⏰ Tue-Sun, closed Jan & Aug; 🚇 Via del Tritone) Al Presidente is a discreet, greenery-shrouded place, under the walls of the presidential palace and which also has outdoor seating in summer. Innovative dishes include *baccalà* whisked into polenta and grilled, and *trippa di coda di rospo* (tripe of angler-fish tail), but it also does a lipsmacking *pasta all'amatriciana.*

Antico Forno
Fast Food €

Map p110 (📞 06 679 28 66; Via delle Muratte 8; panini €3; ⏰ 7am-9pm; 🚇 Via del Tritone) A mini-supermarket opposite the Trevi Fountain, this busy place has a well-stocked deli counter where you can choose a filling for your freshly baked *panino* or *pizza bianca,* plus an impressive selection of focaccia and pizza.

Piazza Barberini & Via Veneto

Colline Emiliane
Emilia-Romagna €€

Map p110 (📞 06 481 75 38; Via degli Avignonesi 22; meals €45; ⏰ Tue-Sat, Sun lunch, closed Aug; Ⓜ Barberini) This welcoming, tucked-away restaurant just off Piazza Barberini flies the flag for Emilia-Romagna, the well-fed Italian province that has given Parmesan, balsamic vinegar, bolognese sauce and Parma ham to the world. On offer here are delicious meats, home-made pasta, rich *ragùs,* and desserts worthy of a moment's silence.

Palazzo del Quirinale (p107)

San Crispino
Ice Cream €

Map p110 (📞06 679 39 24; Via della Panetteria 42; ⏱midday-12.30pm Sun-Thu, midday-1.30am Fri & Sat) Possibly the best gelato in Rome. What? You want a cone? The delicate, strictly natural and seasonal flavours are served only in tubs (cones would detract from the taste).

Drinking & Nightlife

Piazza del Popolo & Around

Salotto Locarno
Bar

Map p110 (Via della Penna 22; ⏱noon-3am; MFlaminio) Sister to city-centre venue Salotto 42 and summer-only Salotto Gianicolo, this attracts a similar mix of fashionistas and stylish Romans. As part of the art deco Hotel Locarno, it's got a lovely Agatha Christie–era feel, and a greenery-shaded outdoor terrace in summer.

Stravinkij Bar – Hotel de Russie
Bar

Map p110 (📞06 328 88 70; Via del Babuino 9; MFlaminio) Can't afford to stay at the celeb-magnet Hotel de Russie? Then splash out on a drink at its enchanting bar, set in the courtyard, with sunshaded tables overlooked by terraced gardens. Impossibly romantic in the best *dolce vita* style, it's perfect for a cocktail and some posh snacks.

Piazza di Spagna & Around

Caffè Greco
Cafe

Map p110 (📞06 679 17 00; Via dei Condotti 86; ⏱9am-8pm; MSpagna) Caffè Greco opened in 1760 and retains the look: penguin waiters, red flock and gilt mirrors. Casanova, Goethe, Wagner, Keats, Byron, Shelley and Baudelaire were all regulars. Now there are fewer artists and lovers and more shoppers and tourists.

Canova Tadolini
Cafe

Map p110 (📞06 321 10 702; Via del Babuino 150a/b; ⏱9am-10.30pm Mon-Sat; MSpagna) In 1818 sculptor Canova signed a contract for this studio that agreed it would be forever preserved for sculpture. The place is still stuffed with statues, and it's a unique experience to sit among the great maquettes and sup an upmarket tea or knock back some wine and snacks.

Ciampini 2
Cafe

Map p110 (📞06 681 35 108; Viale Trinità dei Monti; ⏱8am-9pm May-Oct; MSpagna) Hidden away a short walk from the top of the Spanish Steps towards the Pincio, this graceful cafe has a garden-party vibe, with green wooden latticework surrounding the outside tables. There are lovely views over the backstreets behind Spagna, and the ice cream is renowned (particularly the truffle).

Entertainment

Gregory's
Live Music

Map p110 (📞06 679 63 86; www.gregorysjazz.com; Via Gregoriana 54d; ⏱7pm-2am Tue-Sun Sep-Jun; MBarberini/Spagna) If it were a voice tone, it'd be husky: unwind in the downstairs bar then unwind some more on squashy sofas upstairs to some slinky live jazz, with quality local performers. Gregory's is a popular hang-out for local musicians.

Teatro Quirino
Theatre

Map p110 (📞06 679 45 85; www.teatroquirino.it, in Italian; Via delle Vergini 7; 🚌Via del Tritone) Within splashing distance of the Trevi Fountain, this grand 19th-century theatre produces the odd new work and a stream of well-known classics – expect to see works (in Italian) by Arthur Miller, Tennessee Williams, Shakespeare, Seneca and Luigi Pirandello.

Shopping

Piazza del Popolo & Around

Vertecchi
Art

Map p110 (☎Via della Croce 70; ⏰3.30am-7.30pm Mon, 10am-7.30pm Tue-Sat; Ⓜ Spagna) Ideal for last-minute gift-buying, this large paperware and art shop has beautiful printed paper, and an amazing choice of notebooks, art stuff and trinkets.

Danielle
Shoes

Map p110 (☎06 6792467; Via Frattina 85a; Ⓜ Spagna) If you're female and in need of an Italian shoe fix, this is an essential stop on your itinerary, for both classic and fashionable styles – foxy heels, boots and ballet pumps – made in soft leather, in myriad colours and at extremely reasonable prices.

Armando Rioda
Artisanal

Map p110 (☎06 6992 4406; Via Belsiana 90; Ⓜ Spagna) Climb the well-worn stairs to this workshop, choose from a swatch of the softest leathers, and you can shortly be the proud owner of a handmade, designer-style bag, wallet, belt or brief-case. If you have a bag specially made, you're looking at around €200 to €250.

TAD
Department Store

Map p110 (☎06 326 95 131; Via del Babuino 155a; Ⓜ Flaminio/Spagna) TAD is a cutting-edge conceptual department store that sells an entire lifestyle. Here you can buy clothes by Chloë, Balenciaga and more, have a haircut, buy scent and flowers, and furnish your apartment with wooden daybeds and Perspex dining chairs. Don't forget to pick up soundtracks to your perfect life from the CD rack.

Mycupoftea
Artisanal

Map p110 (☎06 3265 1061; Via del Babuino 61; Ⓜ Spagna) This is a creative open-plan space, run by women, that showcases the work of two or three designers or artists at a time, selling interesting, individual and affordable jewellery, art and design.

Borsalino
Accessories

Map p110 (☎06 326 50 838; Piazza del Popolo 20; Ⓜ Flaminio) Italians really cut a dash in a hat, but don't fret, you can learn. Borsalino is *the* Italian hatmaker, favoured by 1920s criminal Al Capone, Japanese Emperor Hirohito and Humphrey Bogart. Think fedoras, pork-pie styles, felt cloches and woven straw caps.

Alinari
Antiques, Bookstore

Map p110 (☎06 679 29 23; Via Alibert 16; Ⓜ Spagna) The Florentine Alinari brothers founded their enterprise in 1852, and produced more than a million plate-glass negatives in their lifetimes. At their Rome shop you can buy beautiful prints of their work depicting the city in the 19th century, as well as some meaty coffee-table books on photography.

Mercato delle Stampe
Market

Map p110 (Largo della Fontanella di Borghese; ⏰7am-1pm Mon-Sat; 🚌Piazza Augusto Imperatore) The Mercato delle Stampe (Print Market) is well worth a look if you're a fan of vintage books and old prints. Squirrel through the permanent stalls and among the tired posters and dusty back editions, and you might turn up some interesting music scores, architectural engravings or chromolithographs of Rome.

L'Olfattorio
Perfume

Map p110 (☎06 361 23 25; Via di Ripetta 34; ⏰10.30am-1.30pm & 2.30-7.30pm Tue-Sat; Ⓜ Flaminio) Like a bar, but with perfume instead of drinks, with scents made by names such as Artisan Parfumeur, Diptyque, Les Parfums de Rosine and Coudray. The bartender will guide you through different combinations of scents to work out your ideal fragrance. Smellings are free but you should book ahead.

Tod's
Shoes

Map p110 (☎06 682 10 066; Via della Fontanella di Borghese 56; 🚌Via del Corso) The trademark of Tod's is its rubber-studded loafers (the idea was to reduce those pesky driving scuffs), perfect weekend footwear for kicking back at your country estate.

ATLANTIDE PHOTOTRAVEL/CORBIS ©

Piazza di Spagna & Around

Bottega di Marmoraro
Artisanal

Map p110 (Via Margutta 53b; **M** Flaminio) A particularly charismatic hole-in-the-wall shop, lined with marble carvings, where you can get marble tablets engraved with any inscription you like (€15). Peer inside at lunchtime and you might see the *marmoraro* cooking a pot of tripe for his lunch on the open log fire.

Artigiani Pellettieri – Marco Pelle/Di Clemente
Artisanal

Map p110 (✆ 06 361 34 02; Via Vittoria 15, int 2; **M** Spagna) Ring the bell at this unassuming doorway and hurry up flights of stairs to a family-run leather workshop that feels like it hasn't changed for decades. The elderly artisans create belts (€70 to €100), watch straps (€40 to €90), bags, picture frames, travel cases and other such elegant stuff.

AVC by Adriana V Campanile
Shoes

Map p110 (✆ 06 699 22 355; Piazza di Spagna 88; **M** Spagna) Designer Campanile started with a small shop in Parioli, and nowadays her heels stalk the city. You can see why:

AVC shoes and boots are covetably wearable, stunningly chic and practical – and not insanely priced.

Eleonora
Clothing

Map p110 (✆ 06 6919 0554; Via del Babuino 97; ◷ 10am-7.30pm Mon-Sat, 11am-7.30pm Sun; **M** Spagna) The brash exterior disguises a Tardis of a shop; venture inside this Tridente hotspot and you'll find that its finger is on the pulse, with a very classy selection of designers, including Dolce & Gabbana, Fendi, Missoni, Marc Jacobs and Sergio Rossi.

Furla
Accessories

Map p110 (✆ 06 692 00 363; Piazza di Spagna 22; **M** Spagna) Simple, good-quality bags in soft leather and a brilliant array of colours is why the handbagging hordes keep flocking to Furla, where all sorts of accessories, from sunglasses to shoes, are made.

Sermoneta
Accessories

Map p110 (✆ 06 679 19 60; Piazza di Spagna 61; **M** Spagna) Buying leather gloves in Rome is a rite of passage for some, and its most famous glove-seller is the place to do it. Choose from a kaleidoscopic range of quality leather and suede gloves lined with silk and cashmere. An expert assistant will size up your hand in a glance. Just don't expect them to smile.

Teichner   Food
Map p110 (📞06 687 14 49; Piazza San Lorenzo in Lucina; 🚇Via del Corso) This is one of Rome's many temples to food, so wander in, inhale the delicious scents and select from cheese, hams, pickles, pestos and so on. There are also a select few ready dishes, such as aubergine (eggplant) *parmigiana*.

Enoteca al Parlamento   Wine
Map p110 (📞06 687 34 46; Via dei Prefetti 15; 🚇Via del Corso) A delectable mingling of scents – wine, chocolate, fine meats and cheeses – greets you as you enter this stately, old-fashioned shop, an empire of taste, walled with wine. Try some caviar tartines, sample the wines, consult the helpful staff, and even dine at the restaurant (see p113).

Anglo-American Bookshop   Bookstore
Map p110 (📞06 679 52 22; Via della Vite 102; 🚇Spagna) Particularly good for university reference books, the Anglo-American is well stocked and well known. It has an excellent range of literature, travel guides, children's books and maps, and if it hasn't got a book you want, you can order it.

Fendi   Clothing
Map p110 (📞06 69 66 61; Largo Goldoni 420; 🚇Spagna) A temple to subtly blinging accessories, this multi-storey art deco building is the Fendi mothership. The look is old-style glamour, with beauty and distinction.

Mada   Shoes
Map p110 (📞06 679 86 60; Via della Croce 57; 🚇Spagna) Blink-and-you'll-miss-it Mada is one of those shops that transcends fashion, supplying supremely elegant, beautifully made shoes (€210 to €380) to discerning Italian women of all ages. Pure old-school Italian quality.

Bulgari   Jewellery
Map p110 (📞06 679 38 76; Via dei Condotti 10; 🚇Spagna) If you have to ask the price, you can't afford it. Sumptuous window displays mean you can admire the world's finest jewellery without spending a *centesimo*.

Fausto Santini   Shoes
Map p110 (📞06 678 41 14; Via Frattina 120; 🚇Spagna) Rome's best-known shoe designer, Fausto Santini is famous for his beguilingly simple, architectural shoe designs. Colours are beautiful, quality impeccable.

Via dei Condotti
RICHARD I'ANSON/LONELY PLANET IMAGES ©

Trevi Fountain to the Quirinale

Lucia Odescalchi Jewellery
Map p110 (☎06 699 25506; Palazzo Odescalchi, Piazza Santissimi Apostoli 81; Ⓜ Spagna) If you're looking for a unique piece of statement jewellery that will make an outfit, this shop, housed in the evocative archives of the family palazzo, is the place to head. The avant-garde pieces often have an almost medieval beauty, and run from incredible polished steel and chain mail to pieces created out of pearls and fossils. Prices start at around €140.

Vignano Accessories
Map p110 (☎06 679 51 47; Via Marco Minghetti; Ⓠ Via del Corso) Piled high with head candy, Vignano opened in 1873 and sells top hats, bowlers and deerstalkers, as well as hacking jackets, to a princely clientele, as if nothing much has changed since it first opened its doors. The hours are exhilaratingly Roman – they open when they feel like it.

Libreria Giunti al Punto Bookstore
Map p110 (☎06 699 41 045; Piazza dei Santissimi Apostoli 59-65; ⏱10am-8pm Mon-Sat May-Oct, 9.30am-7.30pm Mon-Sat Nov-Apr, 10.30am-1pm & 4-7.30pm Sun year-round; Ⓠ Piazza Venezia) The 'Straight to the Point' children's bookshop is an ideal place to distract your kids. Large, colourful and well stocked, it has thousands of titles in Italian and a selection of books in French,
Spanish, German and English, as well as a good range of toys, from Play Doh to puzzles.

La Rinascente Department Store
Map p110 (☎06 679 76 91; Largo Chigi 20; Ⓠ Via del Corso) La Rinascente is a stately, upmarket department store, with a particularly buzzing cosmetics department, amid art nouveau interiors.

Galleria Alberto Sordi Shopping Centre
Map p110 (Piazza Colonna; ⏱10am-10pm; Ⓠ Via del Corso) This elegant stained-glass arcade appeared in Alberto Sordi's 1973 classic, *Polvere di Stelle,* and has since been renamed for Rome's favourite actor, who died in 2003. It's a serene place to browse stores such as Zara, AVC, Feltrinelli, Coccinelle, Gusella and the Bridge, and there's an airy cafe ideal for a quick coffee break.

Piazza Barberini & Via Veneto

Underground Market
Map p110 (☎06 360 05 345; Ludovisi underground car park, Via Francesco Crispi 96; ⏱3-8pm Sat & 10.30am-7.30pm Sun 2nd weekend of the month Sep-Jun; Ⓜ Barberini) Monthly market held underground, in a subterranean car park near Villa Borghese. There are more than 150 stalls selling everything from antiques and collectables to clothes and toys.

Monti, Esquilino & San Lorenzo

The Esquilino area, which encompasses Rome's main train station, is scruffy in parts but has countless gems to explore. There's the marvellous Museo Nazionale Romano – Palazzo Massimo alle Terme, which displays unparalleled Roman frescoes, and the gloriously decorative Basilica di Santa Maria Maggiore.

Downhill from the Esquilino, Monti was once the ancient city's notorious Suburra slum – a red-light district and the childhood home of Julius Caesar – but is now an increasingly charming neighbourhood of inviting eateries, shops and *enoteche* (wine bars).

To the east of Termini lies the scruffy student district of San Lorenzo, with plenty of character and some excellent restaurants.

A quick tram ride southeast, Pigneto is even more bohemian – the Roman equivalent of London's Shoreditch. It's still fashionably edgy, although house prices are rising, and its bars and funky offbeat shops attract a regular crowd of artists and fashion-conscious urbanites.

Basilica di Santa Maria Maggiore (p129)

Monti, Esquilino & San Lorenzo Highlights

Museo Nazionale Romano – Palazzo Massimo alle Terme (p135)

Housing part of the Museo Nazionale Romano collection, this is one of Rome's finest museums. It has a virtuoso collection of classical carving, but the absolute highlight is its incredible ancient Roman frescoes, including the decoration for entire rooms. The collection has recently been given a new layout to mimic the frescoes' original settings.

Monti (p133)

The bohemian, chic neighbourhood of Monti has a charming, village-like feel. It's just a few streets between Via Cavour and Via Nazionale, and is full of bijou clothing and jewellery shops, characterful restaurants, and inviting *enoteche* (wine bars). It's an ideal stop for a lazy coffee and a browse during the day, or to dine and drink after dark.

PAOLO CORDELLI/LONELY PLANET IMAGES ©

VITO ARCOMANO/ALAMY ©

Basilica di Santa Maria Maggiore (p129) ③

The glorious church of Santa Maria Maggiore dates from the 5th century and its glittering nave mosaics are original. In its entirety, the basilica is beautifully harmonious despite having been much altered over the years: the 75m belfry (the highest in Rome) is from the 14th century, Ferdinand Fuga's façade is baroque, and the swirling Cosmati paving of the interior dates from the 12th century.

④ Pigneto (p139)

Pigneto, in the southeast of Rome, is the iconic working-class district immortalised by neo-realist filmmaker Pier Pasolini in the 1960s. It has a small-town feel – its streets of low-rise, dilapidated housing running down to the railway tracks. In recent years the area has become the favoured nightlife hangout for Rome's artistic and wannabe bohemian crowd, and the main drag, Via del Pigneto, is lined with busy pavement bars, cafes and restaurants. Necci (p139)

⑤ San Lorenzo (p132)

The scrubby, down-at-heel student zone not far from Termini station is a popular place for student nightlife, but also harbours some trendy, popular restaurants serving inspirational cuisine. These range from long-standing *trattorie*, favoured by film directors and football stars, to chic new restaurants popular with artistic crowds. It's well worth heading here for dinner to see a different side of Rome and eat out as the Romans do.

Monti, Esquilino & San Lorenzo Walk

This route around these busy districts – home to embassies, museums, parliamentary buildings and Rome's most important transport hub, Termini – takes in the major sights of the Esquilino hill as well as the charming area of Monti.

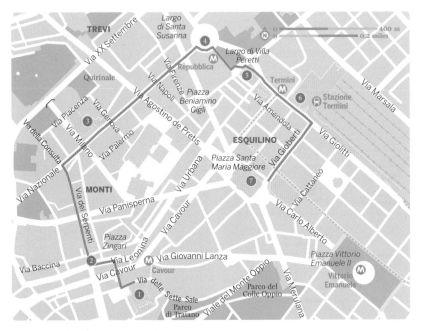

① Basilica di San Pietro in Vincoli

Start your walk around the highlights of this art-filled area at the church of **'St Peter in Chains'** (p126). The basilica dates from the 5th century and contains the star attractions of Michelangelo's statue of Moses and the chains that are believed to have bound St Peter when he was incarcerated.

② Piazza Madonna dei Monti

Walk down the steps to Via Cavour. Cross the busy road and take another flight of steps down to the charming Monti district. Walk about 200m west along Via Leonina and turn right into Via dei Serpenti, which runs uphill. You'll shortly arrive at the charming, small **Piazza Madonna dei Monti**, centred on a stepped fountain and served by a couple of cafes with pavement tables.

③ Palazzo delle Esposizioni

Carry on up Via dei Serpenti, with its restaurants, boutiques and wine bars, until you reach the junction with Via Nazionale. Across the road to your right, you'll see the grandiose **Palazzo delle Esposizioni** (p128). The palazzo houses temporary exhibitions of artists that have ranged from Marc Rothko to Aleksandr Rodčenko, and has an excellent bookshop and cafe. Its restaurant, **Open Colonna** (p135), is an ideal place to stop for a bargain lunch under a dramatic plate-glass ceiling.

4 Piazza della Republica

From the Palazzo delle Esposizioni, walk up the busy thoroughfare of Via Nazionale, lined with shops, to reach the equally busy **Piazza della Republica** (p132). The piazza contains monumental architecture, laid out post unification, and is centred on the 1901 sculpture of the **Fontana delle Naiadi**.

5 Museo Nazionale Romano – Palazzo Nazionale alle Terme

Taking the exit that leads towards Termini station, you'll find yourself facing the **Palazzo Nazionale alle Terme** (p135), a pale pink, 19th-century neo-Renaissance building that houses some incredibly exquisite ancient Roman frescoes and sculpture.

6 Termini Station

Around the corner, just east of Palazzo Nazionale alle Terme, is the modernist **Termini station**, which was completed in 1950. Termini is a busy transport hub, and worth a look for its monumentalist architecture: there's something sublime about its long, clean concrete lines. Inside is a busy mall with a wide range of shops selling everything from books to clothing.

7 Basilica di Santa Maria Maggiore

From Termini, take Via Gioberti (which leads off Via Gioletti, the road running alongside the station) southwest for 200m and you'll arrive at **Basilica di Santa Maria Maggiore** (p129), which sits atop the Esquilino. One of Rome's four patriarchal basilicas, the mighty church has beautiful mosaics on its façade and interior, and an exquisite kaleidoscopic Cosmati floor.

 The Best...

PLACES TO EAT

L'Asino d'Oro Pure class at reasonable prices, this Umbrian import offers memorable cooking using a delectable mix of flavours. (p133)

Trattoria Monti Wonderful regional cuisine from the Marches region at this sophisticated, long-standing family-run place. (p134)

Agata e Romeo Upmarket creative cuisine at a Roman gastronomic institution, with an illustrious wine cellar. (p134)

PLACES TO DRINK

Ai Tre Scalini Monti's most popular wine bar. (p137)

La Bottega del Caffè Perfect for people-watching, with seats on a pretty piazza. (p137)

WORKS OF ART

Frescoes at Palazzo Massimo alle Terme Amazing wall paintings: top-of-the-range home decor from over 2000 years ago. (p135)

Michelangelo's colossal Moses Masterful sculpture housed in the Basilica di San Pietro in Vincoli. (p126)

5th-century interior and 13th-century facade The sumptuous mosaics of Santa Maria Maggiore (p129)

Palazzo delle Esposizioni
VITO ARCOMANO/ALAMY ©

Discover Monti, Esquilino & San Lorenzo

🔀 Getting There & Away

- **Metro** Cavour Metro stop is most convenient for Monti, while Termini, Castro Pretorio and Vittorio Emanuele stations are useful for Esquilino.

- **Bus** Termini is the city's main bus hub, connected to places all over the city; Monti is accessible by buses stopping on Via Nazionale or Via Cavour. San Lorenzo (buses 71, 140 and 492) and Pigneto (buses 81, 810 and 105, and night bus N12) are best reached by bus or tram.

- **Tram** This is an easy way to access San Lorenzo (tram 3) or Pigneto (trams 5, 14 or 19).

⊙ Sights

The sometimes scruffy district of Esquilino is lined with grand 19th-century buildings. It might not be Rome's prettiest district, but it's studded with some stupendous art and museums, including one of Rome's finest patriarchal basilicas in Santa Maria Maggiore and two outposts of the Museo Nazionale Romano, containing a staggering array of treasures.

Esquilino

Basilica di San Pietro in Vincoli   Church

Map p130 (☎ 06 488 28 65; Piazza di San Pietro in Vincoli 4a; ◷ 8am-12.30pm & 3.30-7pm Apr-Sep, 8am-12.30pm & 3-6pm Oct-Mar; Ⓜ Cavour) Pilgrims and art lovers flock to this 5th-century church for two reasons: to marvel at Michelangelo's macho sculpture of Moses and to see the chains that bound St Peter when he was imprisoned in the Carcere Mamertino.

The church was built in the 5th century especially to house these shackles, which had been sent to Constantinople after the saint's death but were later returned as relics. They arrived in two pieces and legend has it that when they were reunited they miraculously joined together.

To the right of the altar, Michelangelo's colossal Moses (1505) forms the centrepiece of Pope Julius II's unfinished tomb. Moses, who sports a magnificent waist-length beard and two small horns sticking out of his head, has been studied for centuries, most famously by Sigmund Freud in a 1914

Basilica di San Pietro in Vincoli
JUERGEN SCHONNOP/DREAMSTIME.COM ©

essay, *The Moses of Michelangelo*. The horns were inspired by a mistranslation of a biblical passage: where the original said that rays of light issued from Moses' face, the translator wrote 'horns'. Michelangelo was aware of the mistake, but he gave Moses horns anyway.

Despite the tomb's imposing scale, it was never completed – Michelangelo originally envisaged 40 statues but he got sidetracked by the Sistine Chapel, and Pope Julius was buried in St Peter's Basilica.

Domus Aurea
Site

Map p130 (06 399 67 700; www.pierreci.itt; Viale della Domus Aurea; adult/reduced €6/3; closed for restoration; Colosseo) A monumental exercise in vanity, the Domus Aurea (Golden House) was Nero's great gift to himself. Built after the fire of AD 64 and named after the gold that covered its facade, it was a huge complex covering up to a third of the city.

It's estimated that only around 20% remains of the original complex. It has frequently had to be closed for repairs

following flooding and was last open in 2010.

During the Renaissance, artists (including Ghirlandaio, Perugino and Raphael) lowered themselves into the ruins in order to study the frescoed grottoes and to doodle on the walls. All of them later used motifs from the Domus Aurea frescoes in their work.

Museo Nazionale d'Arte Orientale
Museum

Map p130 (06 469 74 832; www.museoori entale.it; Via Merulana 248; adult/reduced €6/3; 9am-2pm Tue, Wed & Fri, 9am-7.30pm Thu, Sat & Sun; Vittorio Emanuele) Rome's little-known but impressive National Museum of Oriental Art is housed in the 19th-century Palazzo Brancaccio. The collection starts on a high with some exquisite items from Iran and Central Asia, such as Iranian glassware dating from the 5th to 6th century BC, and goes on to encompass fascinating items from the ancient settlement of Swat in Pakistan, 12th-century homewares from Afghanistan, engraved ritual vessels from China dating 800 to 900 years before Christ, and Ming porcelain figures.

Chiesa di Santa Croce in Gerusalemme   Church
Map p136 (📞06 701 47 69; Piazza di Santa Croce in Gerusalemme 12; 🕐7am-1pm & 2-7.30pm; 🚇Piazza di Porta Maggiore) One of Rome's seven pilgrimage churches, the Chiesa di Santa Croce in Gerusalemme was founded in 320 by St Helena, mother of Emperor Constantine, in the grounds of her palace. It takes its name from the Christian relics, including a piece of Christ's cross and St Thomas' doubting finger, that St Helena brought to Rome from Jerusalem. The relics are housed in a chapel at the end of the left-hand aisle.

Of particular note are the lovely 15th-century Renaissance apse frescoes representing the legends of the Cross.

Chiesa di Santa Pudenziana   Church
Map p130 (📞06 481 46 22; Via Urbana 160; 🕐8.30am-noon & 3-6pm; 🚇Cavour) This, the church of Rome's Filipino community, boasts a sparkling 4th-century apse mosaic, the oldest of its kind in Rome. An enthroned Christ is flanked by two female figures who are crowning St Peter and St Paul; on either side of them are the apostles dressed as Roman senators.

Piazza della Repubblica & Around

Museo Nazionale Romano – Terme di Diocleziano   Museum
Map p130 (📞06 399 67 700; www.pierreci.it; Viale Enrico de Nicola 78; adult/reduced €7/3.50, valid for three days for all four Museo Nazionale Romano, audioguide €5; 🕐9am-7.45pm Tue-Sun; 🚇Termini) Over the road from Piazza dei Cinquecento are the remains of the Terme di Diocleziano (Diocletian's Baths), Ancient Rome's largest baths complex, which covered about 13 hectares and could hold up to 3000 people. It was completed in the early 4th century but fell into disrepair after invaders destroyed the feeder aqueduct in about 536.

Through memorial inscriptions and other artefacts the museum supplies a fascinating insight into the structure of Roman society, with exhibits relating to cults and the development of Christianity and Judaism. Upstairs delves into even more ancient history, with tomb objects dating from the 9th to 11th centuries BC, including jewellery and amphorae.

Outside, the vast, elegant cloister was constructed from drawings by Michelangelo.

Chiesa di Santa Maria degli Angeli   Church
Map p130 (📞06 488 08 12; www.santamaria degliangeliroma.it; Piazza della Repubblica; 🕐7am-6.30pm Mon-Sat, 7am-7.30pm Sun; 🚇Repubblica) This hulking basilica occupies what was once the central hall of Diocletian's baths complex. It was originally designed by Michelangelo, but only the great vaulted ceiling remains from his plans. Today the chief attraction is the 18th-century double meridian in the transept, one tracing the polar star and the other telling the precise time of the sun's zenith (sunlight enters through a hole to the right of the window above the entrance to the church's right wing). Until 1846, this sundial was used to regulate all Rome's clocks.

Chiesa di San Paolo entro le Mura   Church
Map p130 (📞06 488 33 39; www.stpaulsrome .it; cnr Via Nazionale & Via Napoli; 🕐9.30am-4.30pm Mon-Fri; 🚇Via Nazionale) With its stripy neo-Gothic exterior and prominent position, Rome's American Episcopal church is something of a landmark in this city. Inside, the unusual 19th-century mosaics, designed by the Birmingham-born artist and designer Edward Burne-Jones, feature the faces of his famous contemporaries. In his representation of The Church on Earth, St Ambrose (on the extreme right of the centre group) has JP Morgan's face, and General Garibaldi and Abraham Lincoln (wearing a green tunic) are among the warriors.

Palazzo delle Esposizioni   Gallery
Map p130 (📞06 399 67 500; www.palazzo esposizioni.it, in Italian; Via Nazionale 194; 🕐depends on exhibition; 🚇Via Nazionale)

WILL SALTER/LONELY PLANET IMAGES ©

 Don't Miss
Basilica di Santa Maria Maggiore

Santa Maria Maggiore was built on the summit of the Esquilino in the 5th century. Outside, the 18.78m-high column in the Piazza di Santa Maria Maggiore came from the basilica of Massenzio in the Roman Forum, and the church exterior is decorated with glimmering 13th-century mosaics, protected by a baroque porch with five openings, designed by Ferdinando Fuga in 1741. The 75m belfry, the highest in Rome, is 14th-century Romanesque.

The great interior retains its original 5th-century structure despite the basilica having been much altered over the centuries. The nave floor is a fine example of 12th-century Cosmati paving. Particularly spectacular are the 5th-century mosaics in the triumphal arch and nave, depicting Old Testament scenes.

A plaque to the right of the altar marks the spot where Gianlorenzo Bernini and his father Pietro are buried. Steps lead down to the confessio (a crypt in which relics are placed), where a statue of Pope Pius IX kneels before a reliquary containing a fragment of Jesus' manger.

NEED TO KNOW

Map p130; ☑06 698 86 800; Piazza Santa Maria Maggiore; audioguide €5; ☉7am-7pm; Ⓜ Spagna, Flaminio

This huge neoclassical palace was built in 1882 as an exhibition centre. After a dazzling five-year makeover, it emerged in 2007 as a splendid cultural hub, with cathedral-scale exhibition spaces and sleekly designed art labs, bookshop, cafe and top-notch, glass-roofed restaurant (see p135) that's also an excellent place for a laid-back lunch.

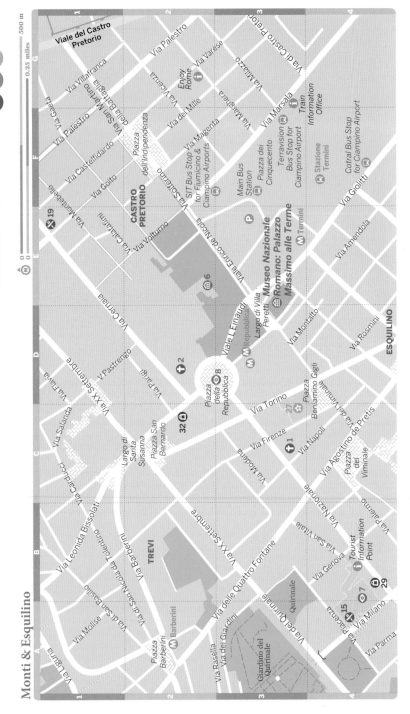

Monti & Esquilino

MONTI, ESQUILINO & SAN LORENZO

500 m
0.25 miles

Viale del Castro Pretorio

Row G
Viale del Castro Pretorio
Via Palestro
Via Villafranca
Via Gaeta
Via San Martino della Battaglia
Via Vicenza
Via Varese
Via Milazzo
Via di Castro Pretorio

Row F
Via Palestro
Via Castelfidardo
Via Goito
Piazza dell'Indipendenza
Via dei Mille
Via Magenta
Via Marghera
Via Marsala
Enjoy Rome
Train Information Office

Row E
Via Montebello
Via Calatafimi
Via Volturno
Via Solferino
Viale Enrico de Nicola
19
CASTRO PRETORIO
6
Piazza dei Cinquecento
Terravision Bus Stop for Ciampino Airport
Main Bus Station
Stazione Termini
Cotral Bus Stop for Ciampino Airport
Via Giolitti

Row D
Via Flavia
Via XX Settembre
Via Salanda
Via Cernaia
Via Pastrengo
Via Parigi
2
Viale L Einaudi
Largo di Villa Peretti
M Repubblica
Museo Nazionale Romano: Palazzo Massimo alle Terme
P
M Termini
Via Montalto
Via Amendola
Via Rosmini
ESQUILINO

Row C
Via Carducci
Largo di Santa Susanna
Piazza San Bernardo
32
Piazza della Repubblica
8
Via Torino
Via Firenze
Via Modena
Via Napoli
27
Piazza Beniamino Gigli
1
Via Nazionale
Via Agostino de Pretis
Piazza del Viminale

Row B
Via Leonida Bissolati
Via Barberini
TREVI
Via XX Settembre
Via delle Quattro Fontane
Via San Vitale
Via Genova
Tourist Information Point
Via Palermo

Row A
Via Liguria
Via Molise
Via di San Basilio
Via di San Nicola da Tolentino
M Barberini
Piazza Barberini
Via Rasella
Via dei Giardini
Quirinale
Giardino del Quirinale
Via del Quirinale
Via Piacenza
15
7
29
Via Milano
Via Parma

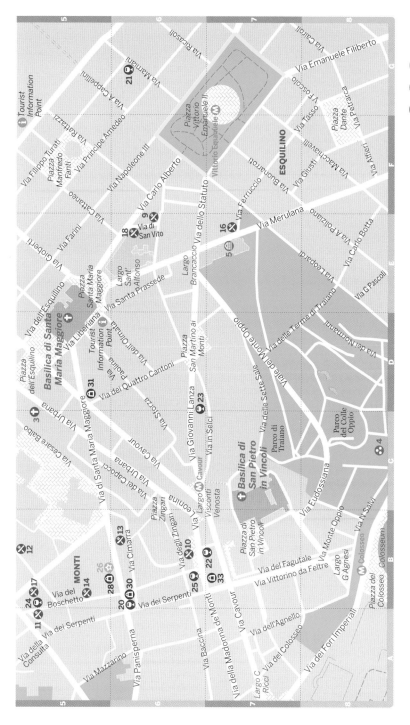

Monti & Esquilino

Piazza della Repubblica   Piazza

Map p130 (Ⓜ Repubblica) Flanked by grand 19th-century neoclassical colonnades, this landmark piazza was laid out as part of Rome's post-unification makeover. It follows the lines of the semicircular *exedra* (benched portico) of Diocletian's baths complex and was originally known as Piazza Esedra. In the centre, the **Fontana delle Naiadi** aroused puritanical ire when it was unveiled by architect Mario Rutelli in 1901. The nudity of the four naiads or water nymphs, who surround the central figure of Glaucus wrestling a fish, was considered too provocative – how Italy has changed. Each reclines on a creature symbolising water in a different form: a water snake (rivers), a swan (lakes), a lizard (streams) and a sea-horse (oceans).

San Lorenzo & Beyond

Basilica di San Lorenzo Fuori le Mura   Church

Map p136 (🗐 06 49 15 11; Piazzale San Lorenzo; ⊙8am-noon & 4-6.30pm; 🚇Piazzale del

Verano) St Lawrence Outside the Walls is one of Rome's four patriarchal basilicas, and is an atmospheric, tranquil edifice that's starker than many of the city's grand churches, a fact that only adds to its breathtaking beauty. It was the only one of Rome's major churches to have suffered bomb damage in WWII, and is a hotchpotch of rebuilds and restorations, yet still has the serenity of a harmonious whole.

St Lawrence was burned to death in AD 258, and Constantine had the original basilica constructed in the 4th century over his burial place, but it was rebuilt 200 years later. Subsequently a nearby 5th-century church dedicated to the Virgin Mary was incorporated into the building, resulting in the church you see today. The nave, portico and much of the decoration date to the 13th century.

Chiesa di Dio Padre Misericordioso   Church

(🗐 06 231 58 33; www.diopadremisericordioso .it; Via Francesco Tovaglieri 147; ⊙9am-6pm Mon-Fri, 7.30am-12.30pm & 3.30-7.30pm daily;

Via Francesco Tovaglieri) Rome's first minimalist church, this beautiful white Richard Meier creation has a remarkable and appropriate purity, and for lovers of contemporary architecture, it is well worth the trek out to the suburbs to see it. Built out of white concrete, stucco, gleaming travertine and 976 sq m of glass, it is an exercise in dazzling lightness and white, making use of the play of light both inside and out.

🍴 Eating

Monti, conveniently just north of the Colosseum if you're looking for somewhere nearby, has some wonderful choices. An ancient slum, it's one of Rome's most interesting up-and-coming districts, with intimate bars, wine bars, restaurants and boutiques. In the busy, hotel-packed district around Stazione Termini it's harder to find a good eaterie, but there are some notable classic trattorie, restaurants and *artisanal gelaterie,* and this area contains Rome's best ethnic eats.

Monti

L'Asino d'Oro   Modern Italian €€

Map p130 (☎06 4891 3832; Via del Boschetto 73; meals €40; ⓜCavour) This fabulous restaurant has been transplanted from Orvieto and its Umbrian origins resonate in Lucio Sforza's delicious, exceptional cooking. It's unfussy yet innovative, with dishes featuring lots of flavourful contrasts, such as slow-roasted rabbit in a rich berry sauce and desserts that linger in the memory.

La Carbonara   Trattoria €€

Map p130 (☎06 482 51 76; Via Panisperna 214; meals €35; ⓐMon-Sat; ⓜCavour) On the go since 1906, this busy restaurant was favoured by the infamous Ragazzi di Panisperna (named after the street), the group of young physicists, including Enrico Fermi, who constructed the first atomic bomb. The waiters are brusque, it crackles with energy and the interior is covered in graffiti – tradition dictates that diners should leave their mark in a message on the wall.

Cafe in Monti

VITO ARCOMANO/ALAMY ©

Ciuri Ciuri
Pasticceria €

Map p130 (📞06 454 44 548; Via Leonina 18; snacks around €2.50; ⏱10am-midnight; 🚇Cavour) A Sicilian ice cream and pastry shop where you can pop by (and eat in) for delectable homemade sweets such as *cannoli* (a type of pastry), cassata and *pasticini di mandorla* (almond pastries), all available in moreish bite-sized versions, and created using the freshest of ingredients. There are rib-sticking *arancini* (fried rice balls), and they also have the best ice cream in the neighbourhood.

Da Valentino
Trattoria €€

Map p130 (📞06 4880 643; Via del Boschetto; meals €30; ⏱Mon-Sat; 🚇Cavour) The vintage 1930s sign outside says 'Birra Peroni', and inside the lovely old-fashioned feel indicates that not much has changed here for years, with black-and-white photographs on the walls, white tablecloths and tiled floors. Come here when you're in the mood for grilled *scamorza* (a type of Italian cheese, similar to mozzarella), as this is the main focus of the menu, with myriad variations: served with tomato and rocket, tomato and gorgonzola, cheese and artichokes, grilled meats, hamburgers and so on.

Sweety Rome
Cafe €

Map p130 (📞06 4891 3713; Via Milano 48; cupcakes from €3; 🚇Cavour) This is an unusual proposition in Rome: delectable cupcakes (including irresistible red velvet options), all topped with a swirl of beautiful creamy icing. Sweety Rome also proffers a great Sunday brunch (€8), plus excellent breakfasts to those who are tiring of the cafe-*cornetto* combination, featuring pancakes, eggs and muffins.

Esquilino

Agata e Romeo
Modern Italian €€€

Map p130 (📞06 446 61 15; Via Carlo Alberto 45; meals €120; ⏱Mon-Fri; 🚇Vittorio Emanuele) This elegant, restrained place was one of Rome's gastronomic pioneers, and still holds its own as one of the city's most gourmet takes on Roman cuisine. Chef Agata Parisella designs and cooks menus, offering creative uses of Roman traditions; husband Romeo curates the wine cellar; and daughter Maria Antonietta chooses the cheeses. Bookings essential.

Trattoria Monti
Trattoria €€

Map p130 (📞06 446 65 73; Via di San Vito 13a; meals €45; ⏱lunch & dinner Tue-Sat, lunch Sun; 🚇Vittorio Emanuele) The Camerucci family runs this elegant, intimate, brick-arched place, where the air of contentment is palpable as you enter – a reflection of the top-notch traditional cooking from the Marches region, with an unusual menu that includes lots of daily specials.

Panella l'Arte del Pane
Fast Food €

Map p130 (📞06 487 24 35; Via Merulana 54; pizza slices €2.50-5; ⏱8am-11pm Mon-Thu, 8am-midnight Fri & Sat, 8.30am-4pm Sun; 🚇Vittorio Emanuele) With a sumptuous array of *pizza al taglio, supplì* (fried rice balls), focaccia and fried croquettes, this is a sublime express lunch stop, where you can sip a glass of chilled *prosecco* while eyeing up the array gastronomic souvenirs on display in the deli.

Palazzo del Freddo di Giovanni Fassi
Ice Cream €

Map p136 (📞06 446 47 40; Via Principe Eugenio 65; from €2; ⏱noon-12.30am Sat, 10am-midnight Sun, noon-midnight Tue-Thu; 🚇Vittorio Emanuele) A great back-in-time barn of a place, sprinkled with marble tabletops and vintage gelato-making machinery, Fassi offers fantastic classic flavours, such as riso (rice), pistachio and nocciola (hazelnut).

Trimani
Wine Bar €€

Map p130 (📞06 446 96 30; Via Cernaia 37b; meals €45; ⏱Mon-Sat; 🚆🚇Termini) Part of the Trimani family's wine empire (their shop just round the corner stocks about 4000 international labels), this is an unpretentious yet highly professional *enoteca,* with knowledgeable, multilingual staff. It's Rome's biggest wine bar and has a vast selection of Italian regional wines as well as an ever-changing food menu – tuck into local salami and cheese or fresh oysters.

MAURITIUS IMAGES GMBH/ALAMY ©

Don't Miss
Museo Nazionale Romano – Palazzo Massimo alle Terme

This light-filled museum, packed with spectacular classical art, is one of Rome's finest.

The ground and 1st floors are devoted to sculptural masterpieces, including the mesmerising *Boxer*, a crouching Aphrodite from Villa Adriana (p222), the softly contoured, 2nd-century BC *Sleeping Hermaphrodite*, and the ideal vision of the Discus Thrower.

However, the sensational frescoes on the 2nd floor blow everything else away. Lighting brings out the colours of the frescoes, which include scenes from nature, mythology, domestic and sensual life in the intimate cubicula (bedrooms), and delicate landscapes from the winter triclinium (dining room).

The showstopping highlight is the room (30 BC to 20 BC) from Villa Livia, one of the homes of Augustus' wife Livia Drusilla. The frescoes depict realistic yet paradisiacal garden full of roses, pomegranates, iris and camomile, and once decorated a summer triclinium, a living room built half underground as an escape from the heat. Detail of Portonaccio sarcophagus

NEED TO KNOW
Map p130; ☑ 06 399 67 700; www.pierreci.it; Largo di Villa Peretti 1; adult/reduced €7/3.50; audioguide €4; ☺9am-7.45pm Tue-Sun; ☑ Ⓜ Termini

Piazza della Republica & Around

Open Colonna Modern Italian €€€
Map p130 (☑ 06 478 22 641; Via Milano 9a;

meals €20-80; ☺noon-midnight Tue-Sat & Sun lunch; ☑Via Nazionale; ❋) Spectacularly set at the back of Palazzo delle Esposizioni, superchef Antonello Colonna's superb, chic restaurant is tucked onto a

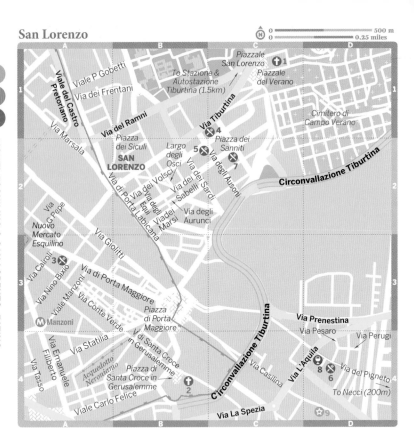

mezzanine floor under an extraordinary glass roof. The cuisine is new Roman: innovative takes on traditional dishes, cooked with wit and flair. The best thing? There's a more basic but still delectable fixed two-course lunch or buffet for €15, and Saturday and Sunday brunch at €28, served in the dramatic, glass-ceilinged hall, with a terrace for sunny days.

Doozo   Japanese €€

Map p130 (☏ 06 481 56 55; Via Palermo 51; sushi €6-10, dishes & sets €12-30; ☺dinner Tue-Sun, lunch Tue-Sat; 🚇Via Nazionale) Doozo (meaning 'welcome') is a spacious, Zen restaurant, bookshop and gallery that offers tofu, sushi, *soba* (buckwheat noodle) soup and other Japanese delicacies, plus beer and green tea in wonderfully serene surroundings.

San Lorenzo & Beyond

Tram Tram
Trattoria €€

Map p136 (📞06 49 04 16; Via dei Reti 44; meals €45; 🕐Tue-Sun; 🚃🚋Via Tiburtina) This trendy, yet old-style, lace-curtained trattoria takes its name from the trams that rattle past outside. It offers tasty traditional dishes, such as *involtini di pesce spada con patate* (rolls of swordfish with potato). Book ahead.

Pommidoro
Trattoria €€

Map p136 (📞06 445 26 92; Piazza dei Sanniti 44; meals €50; 🕐Mon-Sat, closed Aug; 🚋Via Tiburtina, 🚃Via dei Reti) Throughout San Lorenzo's metamorphosis from down-at-heel working-class district to down-at-heel bohemian enclave, Pommidoro has remained the same. A much-loved local institution, it's a century-old trattoria, with high star-vaulted ceilings, a huge fireplace and outdoor conservatory seating.

Pastificio San Lorenzo
Modern Italian €€€

Map p136 (📞06 972 7 3519; Via Tiburtina 135; meals €50; 🕐from 7pm; 🚋Via Tiburtina, 🚃Via dei Reti) The place is packed, the vibe is 'this is where it's at', and the food.... is fine – nothing to shout about, but perfectly scrumptious old favourites with pappadelle and *ragù,* served up in a stylish fashion with equivalent prices.

🍸 Drinking & Nightlife

The Monti area, north of the Colosseum, is splendid for *aperitivo,* a meal or after-dark drinks, with lots of charming candlelit wine bars and even a couple of bar-clubs to lengthen your evening.

Monti

Ai Tre Scalini
Wine Bar

Map p130 (Via Panisperna 251; 🕐12.30pm-1am Mon-Fri, 6pm-1am Sat & Sun; Ⓜ Cavour) The Three Steps is always packed, with crowds spilling out into the street. Apart from a tasty choice of wines, it sells the damn fine Menabrea beer, brewed in

northern Italy. You can also tuck into a heart-warming array of cheeses, salami and dishes such as *porchetta di Ariccia con patate al forno* (roasted Ariccia pork with roast potatoes).

La Bottega del Caffè
Cafe

Map p130 (Piazza Madonna dei Monti 5; 🕐8am-2am; Ⓜ Cavour) Ideal for frittering away any balmy section of the day, this appealing cafe-bar has greenery-screened tables out on the captivatingly pretty Piazza Madonna dei Monti with its fountain.

La Barrique
Wine Bar

Map p130 (Via del Boschetto 41b; 🕐1-3pm & 7pm-1.30am Mon-Fri, 7pm-1.30am Sat; Ⓜ Cavour) A dark and cool, softly lit, bottle-lined wine bar, La Barrique offers excellent French and Italian wines – including many by the glass – and 120 types of Champagne, divinely accompanied by *bruchettine* (little bruschettas) and *crostone.*

Esquilino

Bar Zest at the Radisson Blu
Bar

Map p130 (Via Filippo Turati 171; 🕐10.30am-1am; 🚋Via Cavour) In need of a cocktail in the Termini district? Then pop up to the 7th-floor bar at the slinkily designed Radisson Blu. Waiters are cute, chairs are by Jasper Morrison, views are through plate-glass, and there's a sexy rooftop pool.

Finnegans
Pub

Map p130 (Via Leonina 66; Ⓜ Cavour) At first glance this seems like an Irish pub anywhere in the world, but look closer and it has some Italian twists – the clientele are well-groomed expats and fresh-faced Romans, and you can order Bellinis as well as Guinness. It's Irish-run and shows all the big football and rugby games, and there's occasional live music.

Hangar
Nightclub

Map p130 (Via in Selci 69; 🕐10.30pm-2.30am Wed-Mon, closed 3 weeks Aug; Ⓜ Cavour) A gay landmark since 1984, Hangar is friendly and welcoming, with a cruisey vibe, and attracts locals and out-of-towners, with porn nights on Monday and strippers on Thursday. Feeling frisky? Head to the dark room.

★ Entertainment

Teatro dell'Opera di Roma
Opera, Ballet

Map p130 (IUC; ☎06 481 601; www.operaroma.it; Piazza Beniamino Gigli; Ⓜ Repubblica) It is functional and Fascist-era outside, but the interior of Rome's premier opera house – all plush red and gilt – is a stunning surprise. It's also home to Rome's official ballet company; tickets for the ballet cost anywhere between €13 and €65; for the opera you'll be forking out between €12 and €80. From July to mid-August, performances of both opera and ballet shift outdoors in the monumental setting of the old Roman baths, the Terme di Caracalla (p151).

Charity Café
Live Music

Map p130 (☎06 478 25 881; www.charitycafe .it; Via Panisperna 68; ☽ usually 6pm-2am; Ⓜ Cavour) Think narrow space, spindly tables, dim lighting and a laidback vibe: this is a place to snuggle down and listen to some slinky live jazz. Supremely civilised, relaxed, untouristy and very Monti.

🔒 Shopping

Monti

La Bottega del Cioccolato
Food

Map p130 (☎06 482 14 73; Via Leonina 82; ☽9.30am-7.30pm Oct-Aug; Ⓜ Cavour) Run by the younger generation of Moriondo & Gariglio (see p97) is a magical world of scarlet walls and old-fashioned glass cabinets set into black wood, with irresistible smells wafting in from the kitchen and rows of lovingly homemade chocolates on display.

Fabio Piccioni
Jewellery

Map p130 (☎06 474 16 97; Via del Boschetto 148; ☽10.30am-1pm Tue-Sat, 2-8pm Mon-Sat; Ⓜ Cavour) A sparkling Aladdin's Cave of decadent one-of-a-kind costume jewellery; artisan Fabio Piccioni recycles old trinkets to create remarkable art deco–inspired jewellery.

Abito
Clothing

Map p130 (☎06 4881 017; Via Panisperna 61; Ⓜ Cavour) Wilma Silvestre designs elegant clothes with a difference. Choose from the draped, chic, laid-back styles on the rack, and you can have one made up just for you in a day or just a few hours – choose the fabric and the colour.

Fausto Santini Outlet
Shoes

Map p130 (☎06 488 09 34; Via Cavour 106; Ⓜ Cavour) Close to the Basilica di Santa Maria Maggiore, this store is named after Fausto Santini's father, Giacomo. It sells end-of-line and sale Fausto Santini boots, shoes and bags, and is well worth a look for a bargain for his signature architectural designs in butter-soft leather at a fraction of the retail price.

Via dei Serpenti
VITO ARCOMANO/ALAMYS ©

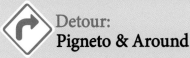

Detour:
Pigneto & Around

Pigneto is emerging as Rome's nuovo-hip district, a rapid metamorphosis from the working-class quarter it has been for decades.

Primo (Map p136; ☎06 701 3827; Via del Pigneto 46; 🚋 Circonvallazione Casilina; 📶) Flagship of the Pigneto scene, Primo is still buzzing after several years, with lots of outdoor tables and a vaguely industrial-brasserie-style interior.

Vini e Olii (Map p136; Via del Pigneto 18; 🚋 Circonvallazione Casilina) Forget the other bars that line Pigneto's main pedestrianised drag, with their scattered outside tables and styled interiors. *This* is where the locals head.

Necci (off Map p136; ☎06 976 01 552; Via Fanfulla da Lodi 68; 🚋 Circonvallazione Casilina; 📶) To start your exploration of this bar-studded area, try the iconic Necci, opened as an ice-cream parlour in 1924.

Circolo degli Artisti (Map p136; ☎06 703 05 684; www.circoloartisti.it; Via Casilina Vecchia 42; ⏲various; 🚋 Via Casilina) For the sound of the underground, Circolo is one of Rome's best nights out, serving up a fine menu of fun: there's Screamadelica, with Italy's alternative music oracle Fabio Luzzietti; Friday cracks open the electronica and house for gay night Omogenic.

Esquilino

Bookàbar   Bookstore
Map p130 (☎06 489 13 361; Via Milano 15-17; ⏲10am-8pm Mon-Thu, 10am-10.30pm Fri & Sat, 10am-8pm Sun; 🚋Via Nazionale) In Firouz Galdo–designed, cool, gleaming white rooms, Bookàbar – the bookshop attached to Palazzo delle Esposizioni – is just made for browsing. There are books on art, architecture and photography, DVDs, CDs, vinyl, children's books and gifts for the design-lover in your life.

Piazza della Repubblica & Around

Feltrinelli International   Bookstore
Map p130 (☎06 482 78 78; Via VE Orlando 84; Ⓜ Repubblica) The international branch of Italy's ubiquitous bookseller has a splendid collection of books in English, plus Spanish, French, German and Portuguese. You'll find everything from recent-release bestsellers to dictionaries, travel guides, DVDs and an excellent assortment of maps.

San Giovanni to Testaccio

Extending to the south and east of the Colosseum, this area encompasses some remarkable sights. There's the majestic cathedral of San Giovanni in Laterano, the thrillingly multilayered church of San Clemente, and the monumental ruins of the Terme di Caracalla, a huge complex of Roman baths.

Further west, on the banks of the Tiber, the traditional working-class area of Testaccio is a bastion of old-school Roman cuisine, with a number of excellent trattorias and a popular nightlife district. Rising above it, the Aventino boasts wonderful medieval churches, including the magnificent Basilica di Santa Sabina. Up here you'll also find one of Rome's great curiosities – the famous keyhole view of St Peter's dome.

All these areas are easily accessible by metro and bus. It's easiest to divide sightseeing into two separate patches: San Giovanni and the Celio, and Aventino and Testaccio.

Basilica di San Giovanni in Laterano (p146)

San Giovanni to Testaccio Highlights

Basilica di San Giovanni in Laterano (p146)

You'll feel very small as you explore the echoing baroque interior of Rome's oldest Christian basilica, which was the most important church in Christendom for over a thousand years. Rome's cathedral is a sumptuous and imposing display of the glories of the Church, with an 18th-century façade designed by Alessandro Galilei and interior styled by Borromini.

WILL SALTER/LONELY PLANET IMAGES ©

Basilica di San Clemente (p149)

The Basilica di San Clemente offers the opportunity to explore the multiple layers of Roman history. The 12th-century church itself is beautiful, but it is particularly extraordinary because a 4th-century church lies beneath it, decorated by faded 11th-century frescoes. Descend yet another layer and you will discover some 1st-century housing and a pagan temple.

CHRISTIAN HANDL/IMAGEBROKER ©

Terme di Caracalla (p151)

The towering ruins of this 3rd-century Roman bath complex are almost inconceivably huge. The vast leisure centre had capacity for up to 1600 people, and was undercut by 9km of tunnels, where slaves kept the mechanics of the hot and cold rooms going. The baths were in use until AD 537, when the Visigoths sacked Rome. Dramatically lit, it's used as a spectacular backdrop for opera performances in the summer.

3

4

Basilica di Santa Sabina (p148)

Atop Aventino hill, in a serene, leafy and covetable residential neighbourhood, lies the church of Santa Sabina, a tranquil escape from the city and a beautifully harmonious space. It's notable among Rome's churches for the restraint of its design, and is lined by 24 Corinthian columns that were custom made rather than plundered from elsewhere. It lies alongside the orange groves of Parco Savello, with lovely views over Rome.

5

Priorato dei Cavalieri di Malta (p151)

Close to Santa Sabina is a mysterious, small piazza that has something very *Alice in Wonderland* about it – decorated by symbols and dominated by a building with an oversized, firmly locked door. This is the doorway to Priorato dei Cavalieri di Malta – the priory of the Knights of Malta. Although closed to the public, it contains a storybook-worthy surprise: look through the peephole in the door to see.

San Giovanni to Testaccio Walk

Discover the highlights of San Giovanni, Celio and Aventino districts, including the mighty Basilica of San Giovanni, the fascinating underworld of the church of San Clemente, and the culinary delights of Testaccio.

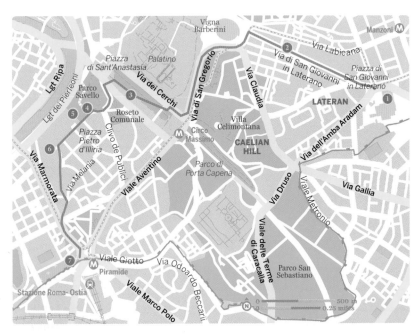

WALK FACTS

- **Start** San Giovanni in Laterano
- **Finish** Cimitero Acattolico per gli Stranieri
- **Distance** 3km
- **Duration** Three hours

1 Basilica di San Giovanni in Laterano

Start your walk at this awe-inspiring **church** (p146), topped by the imposing, gesticulating 7m-high figures of Christ and his apostles. The broad piazza it faces hosts the annual May Day free concert, for which huge crowds gather. Almost opposite is the **Scala Santa** (p148), the staircase Jesus is said to have walked in Pontius Pilate's house.

2 Basilica di San Clemente

From San Giovanni, take Via di San Giovanni in Laterano northwest. You will pass the **Basilica di San Clemente** (p149), whose plain exterior hides wonders on the inside: the ground-level, 12th-century church has some beautiful medieval mosaics; on the level below lies a 4th-century church; and deeper underground still is a 1st-century pagan temple. San Clemente, and the excavations of **Ludus Magnus**, the former gladiatorial school at the end of the street, are a glimpse of the many levels that lie beneath the modern city.

3 Circo Massimo

Continue descending the slight incline, skirting around the **Colosseum**, and walk on to **Circo Massimo** (p58). This was ancient Rome's largest stadium, with a 600m racetrack and a capacity of up to 250,000 people. Chariot races and battle re-creations were held here while the Roman emperors looked down from their palaces on the nearby **Palatino**.

4 Parco Savello

From Circo Massimo you can walk up Clivo dei Publici, passing the **Roseto Publico** (Rome's rose garden) on your left, to a small but beautiful **park** (p149) on the top of the Aventino hill. Known as the **Giardino delgi Aranci** (Orange Garden), it's a lovely, perfumed place to hang out and enjoy views over the Tiber to St Peter's Basilica.

5 Basilica di Santa Sabina

Beside Parco Savello is this august Dominican **church** (p148), which dates from the 5th century. The great carved doors are part of the original church, and bear one of the oldest known depictions of the crucifixion – without the cross.

6 Piazza dei Cavalieri di Malta

At the southern end of Via di Santa Sabina, this ornamental neoclassical **piazza** (p151) was designed by master engraver Piranesi, and looks like a drawing sprung to life. Look through the keyhole of the **Priorato dei Cavalieri di Malta** and you'll see the dome of St Peter's, perfectly positioned at the end of two perfect rows of hedges.

7 Cimitero Accattolico per gli Stranieri

From the piazza, walk downhill until you meet the busy Via Marmorata, then turn left to reach Rome's **Protestant Cemetery** (p151). Overlooking a 1st-century-BC pyramid and a 21st-century road junction, it is a surprisingly tranquil and relaxing place, and appropriately romantic – poets Keats and Shelley, both of whom died in Italy, are buried here.

 The Best…

PLACES TO EAT

Il Bocconcino Simple neighbourhood restaurant with gingham tablecloths and homecooked food, close to San Giovanni and the Colosseum. (p152)

Trattoria da Bucatino Buzzy neighbourhood place serving traditional favourites in Testaccio. (p152)

Checchino dal 1887 A historic, classy restaurant in Testaccio, specialising in cooking the fifth quarter – Rome's traditional offal dishes. (p152)

PLACES TO DRINK

L'Oasi della Birra This rustic subterranean bar has an amazing range of beers, plus excellent accompaniments such as cheeses, salami and main dishes. (p153)

Aroma Fantastic, flower-framed views complement a sundowner at the Hotel dei Gladiatori terrace bar. (p153)

BURIED TREASURES

Basilica di San Clemente It's an extraordinary experience to descend through layers of Roman history at this beautiful church. (p149)

Cimitero Accattolico per gli Stranieri An idyllic and tranquil place of rest, with a romantic air that seems to reflect its buried alumni: Keats and Shelley, among others. (p151)

Grave at Cimitero Accattolico per gli Stranieri
AFP/GETTY IMAGES ©

Don't Miss
Basilica di San Giovanni in Laterano

For a thousand years this monumental cathedral was the most important church in Christendom. Founded by the Emperor Constantine in the fourth century, it was the first Christian basilica to be built in Rome and, until the 14th century, was the pope's main place of worship. The Vatican still has extraterritorial authority over it, despite it being Rome's official cathedral and the pope's seat as Bishop of Rome.

Map p150

Piazza di San Giovanni in Laterano 4

audioguide €5

⏰ 7am-6.30pm

Ⓜ San Giovanni

History

The oldest of Rome's four papal basilicas (the others are St Peter's, the Basilica di San Paolo Fuori le Mura and the Basilica di Santa Maria Maggiore), it was constructed during the building boom that followed Constantine's accession to power in 312, and consecrated by Pope Sylvester I in 324. From then until 1309, when the papacy moved to Avignon, it was the principal pontifical church, and the adjacent Palazzo Laterano was the pope's official residence. Both buildings fell into disrepair during the papacy's French interlude, and when Pope Gregory XI returned to Rome in 1377 he preferred to decamp to the fortified Vatican rather than stay in the official papal digs.

Over the course of its long history, the basilica has been vandalised by invading barbarians and twice destroyed by fire. It was rebuilt each time and the basilica you see today is a culmination of several comprehensive makeovers.

Facade

Surmounted by fifteen 7m-high statues – Christ with St John the Baptist, John the Evangelist and the 12 Apostles – Alessandro Galilei's monumental white facade is a mid-18th-century work of late-baroque classicism, designed to convey the infinite authority of the Church. Behind the colossal columns, the portico gives onto five sets of doors. The central **bronze doors** were moved here from the Curia in the Roman Forum while, to their right, the wooden **Holy Door** is opened only in jubilee years.

Interior

The interior has been revamped on numerous occasions, although it owes much of its present look to Francesco Borromini, who was called in by Pope Innocent X to decorate it for the 1650 jubilee. Divided into a central nave and four minor aisles, it's a breathtaking sight, measuring 130m (length) by 55.6m (width) by 30m (height). Beneath your feet, the beautiful inlaid mosaic **floor** was laid down by Pope Martin V in 1425.

The central nave is lined with 18th-century sculptures of the apostles, each 4.6m high and each set in a heroic pose in its own dramatic niche. At the head of the nave, the pointed Gothic **baldachin** that rises over the papal altar is one of the few features that survived Borromini's 17th-century facelift. Up top, behind a grill are the remaining relics of the heads of St Peter and St Paul. In front of the altar, a double staircase leads to the **confessio,** which houses the Renaissance tomb of Pope Martin V.

Behind the altar, the massive apse is decorated with sparkling mosaics, parts of which date to the 4th century, but most of which was added in the 19th century.

Cloister

To the left of the altar, the beautiful **cloister** (admission €2; ⊙9am-6pm) was built by the Vassalletto family in the 13th century. It's a lovely, peaceful place with graceful Cosmatesque twisted columns set around a central garden. These columns were once completely covered with inlaid marble mosaics, remnants of which can still be seen. Lining the ambulatories are marble fragments of the original basilica, including the remains of a 5th-century papal throne and inscriptions of a couple of papal bulls.

Basilica Legends

There are various legends associated with the basilica. Inside, on the first pilaster in the right-hand nave you'll see traces of a fresco by Giotto depicting Pope Boniface VIII declaring the first jubilee in 1300. While admiring this, cock your ear towards the next pilaster, where a monument to Pope Sylvester II (r 999–1003) is said to sweat and creak when the death of a pope is imminent. Outside on the western side of the cloister, four columns support a slab of marble that medieval Christians believed represented the height of Jesus.

Discover San Giovanni to Testaccio

Getting There & Away

Bus Useful bus routes include 85 and 87, which stop near the Basilica di San Giovanni in Laterano; 714, which serves San Giovanni and the Terme di Caracalla; and 175, which runs to the Aventino,

Metro San Giovanni is accessible by metro line A. For Testaccio take line B to Piramide. The Aventino is walkable from Testaccio and Circo Massimo (line B).

◉ Sights

San Giovanni

Basilica di San Giovanni in Laterano — Church

See p146.

Scala Santa & Sancta Sanctorum — Church

Map p150 (Piazza di San Giovanni in Laterano 14; Scala/Sancta free/€3.50; ☺ Scala 6.15am-noon & 3.30-6.45pm summer, 6.15am-noon & 3-6.15pm winter, Sancta Sanctorum 10.30-11.30am & 3-4pm, closed Wed am & Sun year-round; Ⓜ San Giovanni) The Scala Santa is said to be the staircase that Jesus walked up in Pontius Pilate's palace in Jerusalem. It was brought to Rome by St Helena in the 4th century, and is considered so sacred that you can climb it only on your knees, saying a prayer on each of the 28 steps. At the top of the stairs, and accessible by two side staircases if you don't fancy the knee-climb, is the Sancta Sanctorum (Holy of Holies), once the pope's private chapel.

Aventino & Around

Basilica di Santa Sabina — Church

Map p150 (Piazza Pietro d'Illiria 1; ☺ 8.15am-12.30pm & 3.30-6pm; 🚌 Lungotevere Aventino) This magnificent, solemn basilica was founded by Peter of Illyria in around AD 422. It was enlarged in the 9th century and again in 1216, just before it was given to the newly founded Dominican order – look out for the mosaic tombstone of Muñoz de Zamora, one of the order's founding fathers, in the nave floor.

One of the few surviving 4th-century elements are the basilica's cypress-wood

Organ of the Basilica di San Giovanni in Laterano
MARTIN MOOS/LONELY PLANET IMAGES ©

PINKY77/DREAMSTIME.COM ©

Don't Miss
Basilica di San Clemente

This fascinating basilica provides a vivid glimpse into Rome's multilayered past: a 12th-century basilica built over a 4th-century church, which, in turn, stands over a 2nd-century pagan temple and 1st-century Roman house.

The medieval church features a marvellous 12th-century apse mosaic depicting the *Trionfo della Croce* (Triumph of the Cross), with 12 doves symbolising the apostles and a crowd of bystanders including the Madonna, St John, St John the Baptist and other saints.

Steps lead down to the 4th-century *basilica inferiore,* mostly destroyed by Norman invaders in 1084, but with some faded 11th-century frescoes illustrating the life of San Clemente. Follow down another level and you'll find yourself walking an ancient lane leading to the Roman house and a dark temple of Mithras, which contains an altar depicting the god slaying a bull. Beneath it all, you can hear the eerie sound of a subterranean river, running through a Roman Republic–era drain.

NEED TO KNOW

Map p150; www.basilicasanclemente.com; Via di San Giovanni in Laterano; admission church/excavations free/€5; 9am-12.30pm & 3-6pm Mon-Sat, noon-6pm Sun; M Colosseo

doors. They feature 18 carved panels depicting biblical events, including one of the oldest Crucifixion scenes in existence.

Inside, the three naves are separated by 24 Corinthian columns, which support an arcade decorated with a faded red-and-green frieze.

Parco Savello Garden

Map p150 (Via di Santa Sabina; dawn-dusk; Lungotevere Aventino) Known to Romans as the *Giardino degli Aranci* (Orange Garden), this pocket-sized park is a romantic haven. Grab a perch at the small

San Giovanni to Testaccio

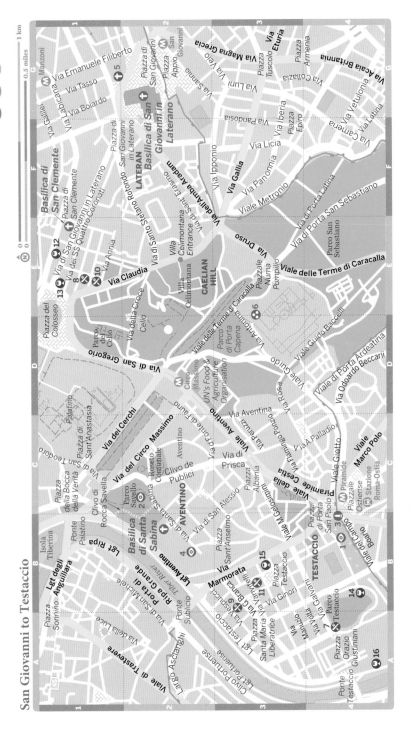

San Giovanni to Testaccio

panoramic terrace and watch the sun set over the Tiber and St Peter's dome.

Piazza dei Cavalieri di Malta
Piazza

Map p150 (Via di Santa Sabina; 🚌Lungotevere Aventino) At the southern end of Via di Santa Sabina, this ornate cypress-shaded square takes its name from the Cavalieri di Malta (Knights of Malta), who have their Roman headquarters here, in the **Priorato dei Cavalieri di Malta**. Although it's closed to the public, the priory offers one of Rome's most charming views: look through the keyhole and you'll see the dome of St Peter's perfectly aligned at the end of a hedge-lined avenue.

Terme di Caracalla
Ruins

Map p150 (🕿 06 399 67 700; Viale delle Terme di Caracalla 52; adult/reduced incl Mausoleo di Cecilia Metella & Villa dei Quintili €6/3, audioguide €5; 🕑9am-1hr before sunset Tue-Sun, 9am-2pm Mon year-round; 🚌Via delle Terme di Caracalla) The remnants of the emperor Caracalla's vast baths complex are among Rome's most awe-inspiring ruins. Inaugurated in 216, the original 10-hectare complex comprised baths, gymnasiums, libraries, shops and gardens. Between 6000 and 8000 people were thought to pass through every day while, underground, hundreds of slaves sweated in 9.5km of tunnels, tending to the plumbing systems. The baths remained in continuous use until 537, when the Visigoths smashed their way into Rome and cut off the city's water supply.

In summer the ruins are used to stage spectacular opera performances.

Testaccio

Cimitero Acattolico per gli Stranieri
Cemetery

Map p150 (Via Caio Cestio 5; voluntary donation €2; 🕑9am-5pm Mon-Sat, 9am-1pm Sun; Ⓜ Piramide) Despite the busy roads that surround it, Rome's 'Non-Catholic Cemetery for Foreigners' (aka the Protestant Cemetery) is a surprisingly restful place. As the traffic thunders past, you can wander the lovingly tended paths contemplating Percy Bysshe Shelley's words: 'It might make one in love with death to think that one should be buried in so sweet a place.' And so he was, along with fellow Romantic poet John Keats and a whole host of luminaries, including Antonio Gramsci, the revered founder of the Italian Communist Party.

Piramide di Caio Cestio
Landmark

Map p150 (Ⓜ Piramide) Sticking out like, well, an Egyptian pyramid, this distinctive landmark stands in the Aurelian Wall at the side of a massive traffic junction. A 36m-high marble-and-brick tomb, it was built for Gaius Cestius, a 1st-century-BC magistrate, and some 200 years later was incorporated into the Aurelian fortification near Porta San Paolo.

Eating

San Giovanni

Il Bocconcino
Trattoria €€

Map p150 (☎ 06 770 791 75; www.ilbocconcino
.com; Via Ostilia 23; meals €30-35; ⏱ Thu-Tue,
closed Aug) Visited the Colosseum and
need lunch in a local trattoria? Try 'the
little mouthful' in the area heading up
towards San Giovanni. Its gingham tablecloths, outdoor seating and cosy interior
look like all the others in this touristy
neighbourhood but it serves excellent
pastas and imaginative meat and fish
mains such as *rombo in impanatura di
agrumi* (turbot with citrus fruit coating).

Taverna dei Quaranta
Trattoria €€

Map p150 (☎ 06 700 05 50; www.tavernadei
quaranta.com; Via Claudia 24; pizzas from €7,
meals €25-30; ⏱ Mon-Sat; Ⓜ Colosseo) Tasty
traditional food, honest prices, near the
Colosseum but off the beaten track –
there's a lot to like about this laid-back,
airy trattoria. There are no great surprises on the menu but daily specials add

variety and all the desserts are homemade – always a good sign.

Testaccio

Trattoria da Bucatino
Trattoria €€

Map p150 (☎ 06 574 68 86; Via Luca della Rob-
bia 84; meals €30; ⏱ Tue-Sun; 🚋 or 🚇 Via
Marmorata) This laid-back neighbourhood
trattoria is hugely popular. Ask for a
table upstairs (with wood panels, Chianti
bottles and a mounted boar's head) and
dig into huge portions of Roman soul
food.

Checchino dal 1887
Traditional Italian €€€

Map p150 (☎ 06 574 63 18; Via di Monte Testaccio 30; meals €60; ⏱ Tue-Sat, closed Aug; 🚋 or
🚇 Via Marmorata) A pig's whisker from the
city's former slaughterhouse, Checchino
is one of the grander restaurants specialising in the *quinto quarto* (fifth quarter –
or insides of the animal). It was here that
the Roman recipe for *coda all vaccinara*
(oxtail stew) was first developed and it's
here that you'll get Rome's best *rigatoni
alla gricia* (pasta tubes with pecorino
cheese, black pepper and pancetta)
according to the local Gambero Rosso
food critics.

Pizzeria Remo
Pizzeria €

Map p150 (☎ 06 574 62 70; Piazza Santa
Maria Liberatrice 44; pizzas from €6;
⏱ 7pm-1am Mon-Sat; 🚋 or 🚇 Via
Marmorata) Not the place for
a romantic dinner, Pizzeria
Remo is one of the city's
most popular pizzerias,
always full of noisy
young Romans. The
pizzas are thin Roman-
style with toppings
loaded onto a crisp,
charred base.

Oxtail stew with salad and wine
TRAVEL DIVISION IMAGES/ALAMY ©

🍷 Drinking & Nightlife

San Giovanni

Aroma
Bar

Map p150 (Hotel Gladiatori, Via Labicana 125; 🕐4pm-midnight; Ⓜ Colosseo) Romance your partner with a drink or two at the gorgeous, flower-ringed rooftop bar of the five-star Hotel Gladiatori. For maximum effect, head up there at sundown for a twilight cocktail and some magical 'marry-me' views over the Colosseum.

Coming Out
Bar

Map p150 (www.comingout.it; Via di San Giovanni in Laterano 8; 🕐10.30am-2am; Ⓜ Colosseo) Spot this easygoing gay bar in the shadow of the Colosseum by the rainbow sign and the mixed, convivial crowds spilling out into the street. It's a popular pre-clubbing stop and features regular drag acts and DJ sets.

Testaccio

L'Oasi della Birra
Bar

Map p150 (🗹 06 574 61 22; Piazza Testaccio 41; 🕐5pm-1am Mon-Thu & Sun, to 2am Fri & Sat; Ⓜ Piramide) Underneath the Palombi wine bar, this rustic watering hole is exactly

what it says it is – an Oasis of Beer. With everything from Teutonic heavyweights to boutique brews, as well as an ample selection of wines and a menu of cheeses, cold cuts, stews and the like, it's ideal for an evening of dedicated eating and drinking.

Contestaccio
Nightclub

Map p150 (www.myspace.com/contestaccio; Via di Monte Testaccio 65b; 🕐8pm-5am Tue-Sun, closed end Jun–mid-Sep; Ⓜ Piramide) With an under-the-stars terrace, restaurant and cool, arched interior, Contestaccio is one of the most popular venues on the Testaccio clubbing strip, serving up a regular menu of DJs and live gigs. Admission is usually free during the week and cocktails are around €8.

Villaggio Globale
Nightclub, Live Music

Map p150 (www.ecn.org/villaggioglobale/joomla; Lungotevere Testaccio 1; Ⓜ Piramide) For a warehouse-party vibe, head to Rome's best-known *centro sociale,* originally a squat, occupying the city's graffiti-sprayed former slaughterhouse. Entrance is usually around €5, beer is cheap, and the music focuses on dancehall, reggae, dubstep and drum 'n' bass.

Southern Rome

Southern Rome harbours Via Appia Antica and trendy Via Ostiense, one of Rome's nightlife centres. The area is quite spread out but public transport connections are good.

Via Appia Antica (the Appian Way) was the 'Queen of Roads' and now runs through a landscape of hulking Roman ruins, pea-green fields and towering umbrella pines. Underlying the area are some 300km of catacombs, used as burial grounds by the early Christians; three of these networks are today open to the public to visit via a guided tour, which is a fascinating experience.

Via Ostiense presents a very different picture. It's an urban wasteland of disused factories and warehouses that increasingly harbour restaurants, pubs, clubs and bars. But it's also home to a couple of gem-like sights: Centrale Montemartini – a great former power plant housing superb classical statuary – and Basilica di San Paolo Fuori le Mura, the world's third-largest church.

Via Appia Antica (p161)

Southern Rome Highlights

Via Appia Antica (p161)

This ancient Roman road now runs through a large area of protected national park, the Parco Regionale dell'Appia Antica, which surrounds the preserved area of the road with lush green countryside. The roadside is dotted by mammoth mausoleums, ruined ancient Roman villas and lavish private houses. It can't help but fire your imagination to walk or cycle along the road, tracing the route of a thousand ancient Roman footsteps.

ATLANTIDE PHOTOTRAVEL/CORBIS ©

❷ Catacombe di San Sebastiano (p160)

The area around the Appia Antica is riddled with underground tunnels, where early Christians buried their dead. Three of the networks are open to the public, the most striking of which is the Catacombe di San Sebastiano. It's extraordinary to walk in the mysterious tunnels, some of which have well-preserved stucco and graffiti dating to the 4th century.

RAIMUND KUTTER/IMAGEBROKER ©

Centrale Montemartini (p164) ③

The genius location for the overflow from the Capitoline Museums is Centrale Montemartini, a former power station in Ostiense. The great halls of the ex-industrial building still gleam with beautiful, silent machinery, and classical statuary is dotted around this polished interior, which forms a wonderfully unlikely but somehow fitting backdrop for the great art of the past.

Clubbing in Ostiense (p165) ④

Ostiense is where Rome's serious club-bers head, and the former industrial area is speckled with clubs and venues making use of the large warehouse and factory spaces of the area. Head to La Saponeria or Goa, Rome's superclub, which pulls in the biggest international DJs and special-ises in keeping the dressed-up hedonistic hordes on the floor.

Basilica di San Paolo Fuori le Mura (p164) ⑤

'St Paul Outside the Walls' is the world's third largest church, but remains surpris-ingly little visited due to its position south of the city centre. It dates from the 4th cen-tury, but what you see today is mostly 19th century. It's well worth the trip: overwhelm-ing in its scale and grandeur, and all the more striking without the crowds.

Southern Rome Walk

This route will take you along a stretch of the Appian Way, which has run through jewel-green countryside for millennia. It's impossible to walk here and not gain a sense of the road's tumultuous and ancient history.

1 Mausoleo di Cecilia Metella

A short walk from the bus stop at the intersection of Via Cecilia Metella and Via Appia Antica brings you to this imposing 1st-century-BC **mausoleum** (p161). Built for the daughter of Quintus Metellus Creticus, it was incorporated into the castle of the Caetani family in the early 14th century.

2 Circo di Massenzio

Just beyond the mausoleum lies the **Circo di Massenzio** (p161). In the 4th century AD, this open area of rolling grass and towering pine trees was a spectacular 10,000-seat arena with a chariot racetrack. In the same complex are the ruins of the **Tomba di Romolo** (p161), built by Emperor Maxentius (AD 306–12) for his son, and the remains of Maxentius' imperial palace.

3 Basilica & Catacombe di San Sebastiano

Continue northwest along the Via Appia, and you'll reach the 4th-century **basilica** (p160) built over the catacombs where apostles Peter and Paul were originally buried, and on the spot where St Sebastian was martyred. The catacombs are fascinating, but don't neglect the impressive church, where you can catch a glimpse of the marble imprint of Jesus's foot.

4 Mausoleo delle Fosse Ardeatine

This is a moving **monument** to the victims of Italy's worst WWII atrocity – on 24 March 1944, 335 people were shot here by the Nazis in reprisal for a partisan attack. To get here, turn left down Via delle Sette Chiese, then left into Via Ardeatina; the mausoleum is about 100m on your right.

WALK FACTS

- **Start** Mausoleo di Cecilia Metella
- **Finish** Porta San Sebastiano
- **Distance** 4.2km
- **Duration** Three hours

⑤ Catacombe di San Callisto

If you're doing this walk on a Sunday, you'll find the Catacombe of San Sebastiano closed. Never fear, though, as on your way back to the Via Appia from the mausoleum, you'll find an entrance to the catacombs of **San Callisto** (p164), off the Via delle Sette Chiese. These – Rome's largest, most famous and busiest catacombs – are a fine alternative. To date archaeologists have unearthed some 500,000 bodies, including seven popes, in 20km of the tunnels.

⑥ Chiesa del Domine Quo Vadis?

This **church** (p164) was built on the spot where St Peter is supposed to have had a vision of Jesus and asked him, 'Domine, quo vadis?' ('Lord, where are you going?') There is a replica of Jesus' footprints in marble (the original is in the Basilica di San Sebastiano) within the church.

⑦ Trattoria Priscilla

Stop for lunch at this small, charming, family-run **restaurant** (p165) built into the walls of the **Tomb of Priscilla**. The restaurant serves up Roman classics, and is a few doors away from the **Appia Antica Park Information office**, which offers maps, brochures, information and bicycle hire.

⑧ Porta San Sebastiano

About 700m beyond Trattoria Priscilla, this 5th-century city **gate** marks the start (or end – all roads lead to Rome, not from it) of Via Appia Antica. The largest and most impressive of the gates in the **Aurelian Wall**, it houses a small museum illustrating the history of the wall.

 The Best…

PLACES TO EAT

Trattoria Priscilla Family-run, intimate neighbourhood restaurant, perfectly placed on the Appian Way. (p165)

Ristorante Cecilia Metella (p165) Smart restaurant on the Appian Way offering Roman favourites.

Doppiozeroo Chic cafe-bar that will suit at any time of day, and is particularly lively around *aperitivo* time (6.30–9pm). (p165)

PLACES TO DRINK

Goa Rome's superclub, featuring big nights out with superstar DJs. (p165)

La Saponeria Gets muso punters in a lather with nu-house, nu-funk hip hop and minimal electronica. (p165)

Doppiozeroo Great for a drink as well as a bit to eat (see above). (p165)

ENTERTAINMENT

La Casa del Jazz Former Mafia boss villa turned atmospheric jazz venue. (p165)

Centrale Montemartini From October to January, Centrale Montemartini opens Saturday nights for 'Sabato Sera nei Musei' featuring gigs and performances. (p164)

Discover
Southern Rome

Getting There & Away

○ **Metro** Metro line B runs to Piramide, Basilica San Paolo, EUR Palasport and EUR Fermi.

○ **Bus** There are bus connections to Porta San Sebastiano (118, 218 and 714), Via Ostiense (23 and 716) and Via Appia Antica (118, 218 and 660).

○ **Archeobus** If you're spending the day here and want to see several sights, the hop-on hop-off Archeobus (€12) departs from Termini every hour.

 ## Sights

The awe-inspiring Appian Way stretches south of Rome, dotted by Roman ruins above and riddled with catacombs underground. Elsewhere Southern Rome offers such treasures as the patriarchal basilica San Paolo Fuori le Mura and the Capitoline Museum collection at Centrale Montemartini. Heading south from Stazione Roma–Ostia, Via Ostiense encompasses converted warehouses, clubs and hidden sights.

Via Appia Antica

Basilica & Catacombe di San Sebastiano
Church, Catacomb

Map p162 (✆ 06 785 03 50; Via Appia Antica 136; adult/reduced €8/4; ⏰ 8.30am-noon & 2-5pm Mon-Sat, closed Nov, to 5.30pm Apr-Sep; 🚌 Via Appia Antica) The Catacombe di San Sebastiano were the first catacombs to be so called, the name deriving from the Greek *kata* (near) and *kymbas* (cavity), because they were located near a cave. During the persecutory reign of Vespasian, they acted as a safe haven for the remains of St Peter and St Paul and became a popular pilgrimage site. There are three perfectly preserved mausoleums and a plastered wall with hundreds of invocations, engraved by worshippers in the 3rd and 4th centuries. The 4th-century basilica (✆ 06 780 00 47; Via Appia Antica 136; ⏰ 8.30am-noon & 2-5pm Mon-Sat, closed Nov, to 5.30pm Apr-Sep), much altered over the years, is dedicated to St Sebastian, who was martyred and buried here in the late 3rd century.

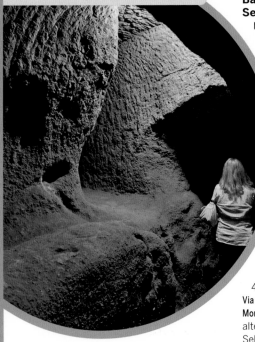

Catacombe di San Sebastiano
RAIMUND KUTTER/IMAGEBROKER ©

GIUSEPPE LANCIA/SHUTTERSTOCK ©

Don't Miss
Via Appia Antica

Heading southeast from Porta San Sebastiano, the Appian Way was known to the Romans as the *regina viarum* (queen of roads). Named after Appius Claudius Caecus, who laid the first 90km section in 312 BC, it was extended in 190 BC to reach Brindisi, some 540km away on the southern Adriatic coast. Flanked by some of the city's most exclusive private villas, as well as Roman tombs, the long cobbled road is a great place for a walk or cycle.

If you're planning on really doing the sights, think about buying the Appia Antica Card (see p274). Near the start of the road, the Appia Antica Regional Park Information Point is very informative. You can buy a map of the park here and hire bikes (per hour/day €3/10).

NEED TO KNOW

Map p162; 📞 06 513 53 16; www.parcoappiaantica.org; Via Appia Antica; 🚇 Via Appia Antica

---

Villa di Massenzio   Ancient Ruins

Map p162 (📞 06 780 13 24; www.villadimassenzio.it; Via Appia Antica 153; adult/reduced €3/2; 🕑 9am-1.30pm Tue-Sat; 🚇 Via Appia Antica) The outstanding feature of Maxentius' enormous 4th-century palace complex is the **Circo di Massenzio,** Rome's best-preserved ancient racetrack – you can still make out the starting stalls used for chariot races.

Near the racetrack, the **Mausoleo di Romolo** (also known as the Tombo di Romolo) was built by Maxentius for his son Romulus.

Mausoleo di Cecilia Metella   Ancient Ruins

Map p162 (📞 06 399 67 700; Via Appia Antica 161; admission incl Terme di Caracalla & Villa dei Quintili adult/reduced €8/4; 🕑 9am-1hr before

Southern Rome

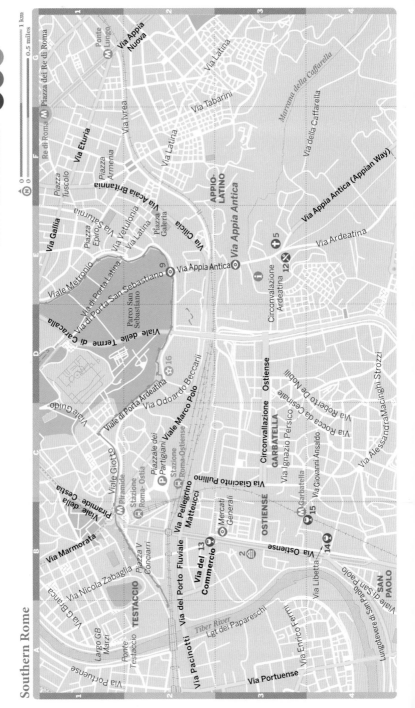

0 0.5 miles
0 1 km

Southern Rome

⦿ Top Sights

⦿ Sights

⊗ Eating

⦿ Drinking & Nightlife

⦿ Entertainment

sunset Tue-Sun; 🚌 Via Appia Antica) Dating to the 1st century BC, this great drum of a mausoleum encloses a burial chamber (built for the daughter of the consul Quintus Metellus Creticus), now roofless. In the 14th century it was converted into a fort by the Caetani family, who used to frighten passing traffic into paying a toll.

Villa dei Quintili   Ancient Ruins

off Map p162 (🗐 06 399 67 700; www.pierreci. it; Via Appia Nuova 1092; adult/reduced incl Terme di Caracalla & Mausoleo di Cecilia Metella €8/4; ⏰ 9am-1hr before sunset Tue-Sun; 🚌 Via Appia Nuova) Set on lush green fields, this vast 2nd-century villa was the luxurious abode of two brothers who were consuls under Emperor Marcus Aurelius. Alas, the villa's splendour was to be the brothers' downfall – in a fit of jealousy, Emperor Commodus had them both killed, taking over the villa for himself.

Catacombe di San Callisto   Catacomb

Map p162 (📞06 513 01 580; www.catacombe.roma.it; Via Appia Antica 110 & 126; adult/reduced €8/4; ⊙8.30am-noon & 2.30-5pm Thu-Tue, closed Feb, to 5.30pm Apr-Sep; 🚌Via Appia Antica) These are the largest and busiest of Rome's catacombs. Founded at the end of the 2nd century and named after Pope Calixtus I, they became the official cemetery of the newly established Roman Church. In the 20km of tunnels explored to date, archaeologists have found the tombs of 500,000 people and seven popes who were martyred in the 3rd century.

Catacombe di Santa Domitilla   Catacomb

Map p162 (📞06 511 03 42; Via delle Sette Chiese 283; adult/reduced €8/4; ⊙9am-noon & 2-5pm Wed-Mon, closed Jan; 🚌Via Appia Antica) Among Rome's largest and oldest, these catacombs stretch for about 17km. They contain Christian wall paintings and the haunting underground **Chiesa di SS Nereus e Achilleus,** a 4th-century

church dedicated to two Roman soldiers martyred by Diocletian.

Chiesa del Domine Quo Vadis?   Church

Map p162 (Via Appia Antica 51; ⊙8am-6pm; 🚌Via Appia Antica) This pint-sized church marks the spot where St Peter, fleeing Rome, met a vision of Jesus going the other way. Reluctantly deciding to join him, Peter tramped back into town where he was arrested and executed. In the aisle are copies of Christ's footprints; the originals are in the Basilica di San Sebastiano (p160).

Ostiense & San Paolo

Basilica di San Paolo Fuori le Mura   Church

Map p162 (📞06 80 800; Via Ostiense 190; ⊙6.45am-6.30pm; Ⓜ San Paolo) The biggest church in Rome after St Peter's (and the world's third largest), the magnificent, little-visited church of St Paul's stands on the site where St Paul was buried after being decapitated in AD 67. Built by Constantine in the 4th century, it was largely destroyed by fire in 1823 and much of what you see today is a 19th-century reconstruction. Not all the ancient church was destroyed in the 19th century fire; many treasures survived, including the 5th-century triumphal arch, with its heavily restored mosaics, and the gothic marble tabernacle over the high altar. The stunning 13th-century Cosmati mosaic work in the **cloisters** (admission free; ⊙9am-1pm & 3-6pm) of the adjacent Benedictine abbey also survived the 1823 fire.

Capitoline Museums at Centrale Montemartini   Museum

Map p162 (📞06 06 08; www.centralemontemartini.org; Via Ostiense 106; adult/

Catacombe di San Callisto

reduced €5.50/4.50, incl Capitoline Museums €14/12, valid 7 days; ⏱9am-7pm Tue-Sun; 🚊Via Ostiense) This fabulous outpost of the Capitoline Museums (Musei Capitolini) is a treat. Housed in a former power station, it boldly juxtaposes classical sculpture against diesel engines and giant furnaces.

Eating

The increasingly fashionable southern neighbourhood of Ostiense features some excellent restaurants. You can also eat well in a rural setting close to Via Appia Antica.

Via Appia Antica & the Catacombs

Ristorante Cecilia Metella   Traditional Italian €€

Map p162 (📞06 511 02 13; Via Appia Antica 125; meals €35; ⏱Tue-Sun; 🚊Via Appia Antica) Near the catacombs of San Callisto, the outside seating at Cecilia Metella is great, set on a low hill under a vine canopy and with glimpses of the jewel-green countryside.

Trattoria Priscilla   Trattoria €€

Map p162 (📞06 513 63 79; Via Appia Antica 68; meals €30; ⏱Mon-Sat, lunch Sun; 🚊Via Appia Antica) Set in a 16th-century former stable, this intimate family-run trattoria has been feeding hungry travellers along the Appian Way for more than a hundred years, serving up traditional *cucina Romana,* so think *carbonara, amatriciana* and *cacio e pepe.*

🍷 Drinking & Nightlife

The ex-industrial area of Ostiense is fertile clubbing land, with its many warehouses, workshops and factories just crying out for a new lease of life as pockets of nightlife nirvana.

Doppiozeroo   Bar

Map p162 (📞06 573 01 961; Via Ostiense 68; ⏱7am-2am Mon-Sat; Ⓜ Piramide) This easygoing bar was once a bakery, hence the name ('double zero' is a type of flour). But today the sleek, modern interior attracts hungry, trendy Romans like bees to honey, especially for the famously lavish, dinner-tastic *aperitivo* between 6.30pm and 9pm.

Goa   Nightclub

Map p162 (📞06 574 82 77; Via Libetta 13; ⏱11pm-4.30am Tue-Sun Oct-May; Ⓜ Garbatella) Rome's serious super-club, with international names (recent guests include Satoshi Tomiie and M.A.N.D.Y.), a fashion-forward crowd, podium dancers and heavies on the door. Lesbian night, Venus Rising (www.venusrising.it), hits Goa the last Sunday of the month.

La Saponeria   Nightclub

Map p162 (📞393 966 1321; Via degli Argonauti 20; ⏱11pm-4.30am Tue-Sun Oct-May; Ⓜ Garbatella) Formerly a soap factory, nowadays La Saponeria lathers up the punters with guest DJs spinning everything from nu-house to nu-funk, minimal techno, dance, hip-hop and R&B. Recent guests include Grandmaster Flash.

⭐ Entertainment

La Casa del Jazz   Live Music

Map p162 (📞06 70 47 31; www.casajazz.it; Viale di Porta Ardeatina 55; admission €10-25; ⏱7pm-midnight; Ⓜ Piramide) In the middle of a 2500-sq-m park in the southern suburbs, the Casa del Jazz (House of Jazz) is housed in a three-storey 1920s villa that belonged to a Mafia boss. When he was caught, the Comune di Roma (Rome Council) converted it into a jazz-tastic complex, including a 150-seat auditorium, rehearsal rooms, cafe and restaurant, and it hosts regular shows by international stars, such as Joan as Policewoman.

Trastevere & Gianicolo

Trastevere is Rome's most vivacious neighbourhood – an outdoor circus of ochre and butterscotch *palazzi*, ivy-clad facades and photogenic cobbled lanes. It's peopled with an eclectic cast of tourists, travellers, students and streetsellers. The name '*tras tevere*' means 'across the Tiber', and there is a real sense that this district stands apart from the rest of the city.

There are also some beautiful sights here: the glittering Basilica di Santa Maria, the country house Villa Farnesina frescoed by Raphael, and Basilica di Santa Cecilia, the last resting place of Santa Cecilia. You can also hike up Gianicolo (Janiculum hill) to be rewarded by some of Rome's most awe-inspiring views and a chance to see Bramante's perfect little Tempietto.

After dark Trastevere really comes into its own. Narrow alleyways heave late into the night, as Romans and tourists flock to the pizzerias, trattorias, bars and cafes that pepper the atmospheric lanes.

Tempietto di Bramante and Chiesa di San Pietro in Montorio (p174)

Trastevere & Gianicolo Highlights

Basilica di Santa Maria in Trastevere (p175)

The best place to start in Trastevere is its buzzing soul – the graceful Piazza di Santa Maria in Trastevere. The piazza is overlooked by its extraordinarily beautiful church, Santa Maria in Trastevere, whose exterior glimmers with exquisite medieval mosaics. The interior doesn't disappoint either – it's burnished by more 12th-century mosaics and lined by recycled Roman columns.

Ombre Rosse (p180)

Although Trastevere is speckled with beautiful churches and some marvellous galleries, one of the district's greatest pleasures is relaxing at a local bar. The classic Ombre Rosse has a long drinks menu, laidback feel, covetable pavement tables alongside a small piazza, and occasional live music. It's the perfect place for watching the world go by.

Cavallini Fresco, Santa Cecilia in Trastevere (p173) ③

Santa Cecilia in Trastevere is another glorious Trastevere church. It contains a Stefano Moderno sculpture of Santa Cecilia, and subterranean excavations of 1st-century Roman houses. The absolute highlight is the Cavallini fresco in the nuns' choir – a beauteous, flamboyant, vibrant work, accessible through a door to the left of the main entrance.

Gianicolo Views (p174) ④

It's a steep haul from Trastevere up Gianicolo (Janiculum Hill), but on the way you'll pass Bramante's perfect little Renaissance Tempietto, and at the top of the hill all your hard work will be repaid. This as close as it gets to soaring like a bird over Rome's rooftops, with stupendous views as far as the eye can see.

Orto Botanico (p174) ⑤

Rome's Botanical Gardens were once the private grounds of Palazzo Corsini, sloping up to the Gianicolo and spreading across 12 rambling, varied hectares. The grounds contain over 8000 plant species – including some of Europe's rarest – with fragrant and medicinal varieties, as well as cacti and a Japanese garden. It's a lovely place to spend a few hours.

Trastevere & Gianicolo Walk

Trastevere is a tangle of buildings hung with ivy and picturesque lines of washing. It's enough to wander and enjoy the street life, but the lanes are also home to some amazing medieval churches, inviting bars and restaurants.

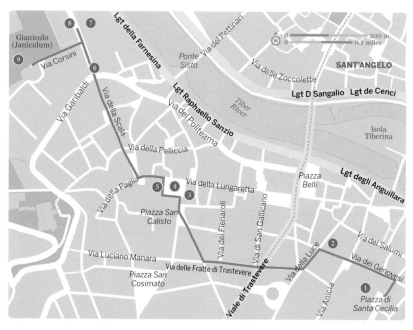

1 Basilica di Santa Cecilia in Trastevere

Start at the **Basilica di Santa Cecilia in Trastevere** (p173), where musicians can pay homage to their patron saint on the very spot where she was martyred in AD 230. St Cecilia is said to have lived and died in a house buried beneath a 5th-century church, on top of which the current basilica now stands.

2 Artigiano Innocenti

From the church, turn left along Via dei Genovesi. Take the third right into Via della Luce to make a stop at this timeless **bakery** (p175), where pinnied ladies chat to the regulars and you can buy delicious biscuits and *crostate* (jam tarts) to eat later or to speed you on your way.

3 Bar San Calisto

Double back along Via della Luce, then turn right into Via delle Fratte in Trastevere, which will take you to another great local institution that's worth a stop. **Bar San Calisto** (p180) plays host to a curious mix of local characters, from *nonni* (grandparents) to punks, clean-cut students to professional stoners.

4 Piazza Santa Maria in Trastevere

Adjoining Piazza San Callisto, this laid-back **piazza** (p174) is a prime people-watching spot, overlooked by its beautiful church. The square's fountain is a 17th-century renovation of a Roman original.

5 Basilica di Santa Maria in Trastevere

Overlooking the piazza, this is said to be the oldest **church** (p175) dedicated to the Virgin Mary in Rome. This gem is Trastevere's most important sight. It was originally built in the 3rd century, but is best known for its stunning gold mosaics, which were added some 900 years later.

6 Porta Settimiana

Take the west exit out of the piazza, then turn north into Via della Scala, which will lead you to **Porta Settimiana**, built in the late 15th century and modified 300 years later in 1798. Leading north from here, Via della Lungara was laid down in the 16th century to connect Trastevere with the Vatican.

7 Villa Farnesina

A short walk north of Porta Settimiana, **Villa Farnesina** (p173) was one of Rome's first great Renaissance palaces. Built in the early 16th century and later bought by the powerful Farnese family, it features some superb frescoes by Raphael. Julius Caesar also once had a country villa on this spot.

8 Galleria Nazionale d'Arte Antica di Palazzo Corsini

On the other side of the street is **Palazzo Corsini** (p174), which contains part of Rome's sumptuous national art collection, including works by Caravaggio and van Dyck.

9 Orto Botanico

Laid out on the slopes of the Gianicolo, Rome's 19th-century **botanical gardens** (p174) is a lovely, low-key place to end your tour and unwind. The entrance is just south of Palazzo Corsini.

 The Best...

PLACES TO EAT

Glass Hostaria Cucina creativa at Trastevere's most sophisticated restaurant. (p178)

Le Mani in Pasta Delish fresh pasta in the quiet side of the district. (p179)

Artigiano Innocenti Made-in-heaven, traditional, tucked-away bakery. (p175)

Sisini Delectable *arancini* (fried rice balls), *pizza al taglio* (by the slice) and fast pasta when you're on the move. (p178)

PLACES TO DRINK

Ma Che Siete Venuti a Fa' Artisanal beers galore. (p179)

Il Barretto Sleek, architecturally striking bar on the way up Gianicolo hill. (p180)

Ombre Rosse Classic, laid-back Trastevere bar that's ideal for people-watching. (p180)

Freni e Frizioni Trastevere's trendiest bar. (p180)

WORKS OF ART

Basilica di Santa Maria in Trastevere Glorious medieval mosaics. (p175)

Cavallini frescoes in Basilica di Santa Cecilia in Trastevere Extraordinary wall paintings in the nuns' choir (p173)

Frescoes in Villa Farnesina How Renaissance papal bankers liked to live, with home decor by Raphael. (p173)

Porta Settimiana
VITO ARCOMANO/ALAMY ©

Discover Trastevere & Gianicolo

🔁 Getting There & Away

○ **Tram** No 8 from Largo di Torre Argentina runs to the main drag of Viale Trastevere.

○ **Bus** From Termini, bus H runs to Viale di Trastevere. For Gianicolo, if you don't fancy the steep steps from Via G Mameli, take bus 870 from Piazza delle Rovere.

Villa Farnesina
VITO ARCOMANO / ALAMY ©

◉ Sights

Trastevere is dotted with exquisite churches, but some of its most wonderful sights are picturesque glimpses down narrow, ochre-and-orange-shaded lanes that will make you catch your breath. The Gianicolo is a superb viewpoint with sweeping panoramas over Rome's rooftops, and has several summer-only bars that are blessed with thrilling views.

East of Viale di Trastevere

Chiesa di San Francesco d'Assisi a Ripa   Church

Map p176 (📞 06 581 90 20; Piazza San Francesco d'Assisi 88; ⏰ 7am-noon & 4-7pm Mon-Sat, 7am-1pm & 4-7.30pm Sun; 🚌 or 🚊 Viale di Trastevere) The 17th-century church of St Francis contains the impressive 18th-century Rospigliosi and Pallavici sculptural monuments, but the overriding reason to visit is to gasp at one of Bernini's most daring works, in the Paluzzi-Albertoni chapel. The *Beata Ludovica Albertoni* (Blessed Ludovica Albertoni; 1674) is a work of highly charged sexual ambiguity showing Ludovica, a Franciscan nun, in a state of rapture as she reclines, eyes shut, mouth open, one hand touching her breast.

St Francis of Assisi is said to have stayed on this spot for a period in the 13th century and you can still see the rock that he used as a pillow and his crucifix, in his cell – the church was later entirely rebuilt several times, its current incarnation dating from the 1680s.

ANNA SERRANO/SIME/4CORNERS ©

Don't Miss
Basilica di Santa Cecilia in Trastevere

This church, with its serene courtyard, remarkable frescoes by Pietro Cavallini, and ancient Roman excavations beneath the building, is the last resting place of St Cecilia, the patron saint of music, who was martyred on this site in AD 230. You can visit the network of excavated houses that lie beneath the church. Below the altar, Stefano Moderno's delicate sculpture shows exactly how her miraculously preserved body was found when it was unearthed in the Catacombe di San Callisto (p161) in 1599. In the apse, look out for the dazzling depiction of Christ and his mother flanked by various saints and, on the far left, Pope Innocent II holding a model of the church. Beneath this is a series of six mosaics by Pietro Cavallini (c 1291) illustrating the life of the Virgin. But the basilica's pride and joy is the spectacular 13th-century fresco, also by Cavallini, in the nuns' choir.

NEED TO KNOW

Map p176; ☑06 589 92 89; Piazza di Santa Cecilia 22; basilica/fresco/crypt free/€2.50/2.50; ⊗basilica & crypt 9.30am-12.30pm, 4-6.30pm, fresco 10am-12.30pm Mon-Sat; ☐ or ☐Viale di Trastevere

West of Viale di Trastevere
Villa Farnesina   Villa
Map p176 (☑06 680 27 397; Via della Lungara 230; adult/reduced €5/4; ⊗9am-1pm Mon-Sat, tours by reservation only; ☐or ☐Viale di Trastevere) Villa Farnesina was built in the early 16th century for Agostino Chigi, the immensely wealthy papal banker. The house was bought by Cardinal Alessando Farnese in 1577, hence its name.

This 16th-century villa is a classic Renaissance design, a symmetrical construction with two wings that features some awe-inspiring frescoes by Sebastiano del Piombo, Raphael and the villa's original architect, Baldassare Peruzzi, who had formerly worked as Bramante's assistant.

The most famous frescoes are in the Loggia of Cupid and Psyche on the ground floor, which are attributed to Raphael, who also painted the Trionfo di Galatea (Triumph of Galatea), depicting a beautiful sea nymph, in the room of the same name. On the 1st floor, Peruzzi's dazzling frescoes in the Salone delle Prospettive are a superb illusionary perspective of a marble colonnade and panorama of 16th-century Rome.

Galleria Nazionale d'Arte Antica di Palazzo Corsini   Gallery
Map p176 (06 688 02 323; www.galleriaborgh ese.it; Via della Lungara 10; adult/child €4/2; 8.30am-7.30pm Tue-Sun; Lungotevere della Farnesina, Piazza Trilussa) Housing part of Italy's national art collection (the rest is in Palazzo Barberini, p108), 16th-century Palazzo Corsini has a distinguished history. Michelangelo, Erasmus and Bramante stayed here but the palazzo is most associated with Queen Christina of Sweden, who took up residencey in 1662, turning it into a centre of artistic life in Rome, and entertaining a steady stream of lovers in her richly frescoed bedroom. She lived here until her death in 1689.

Gallery highlights include Van Dyck's superb, intimate Madonna della Paglia (Madonna of the Straw) in room 3, Rubens' haunting San Sebastiano Liberato dagli Angeli (St Sebastian Liberated by the Angels), Poussin's Triumph of David in room 2, and a fantastic Caravaggio, San Giovanni Battista (St John the Baptist), full of glowering menace, in Room 7.

Piazza Santa Maria in Trastevere   Piazza
Map p176 (or Viale di Trastevere) Traste-vere's focal square is a prime people-watching spot. The octagonal fountain in the centre of the square is of Roman origin and was restored by Carlo Fontana in 1692.

Gianicolo
Orto Botanico   Botanical Garden
Map p176 (06 499 17 107; Largo Cristina di Svezia 24; adult/reduced €4/2; 9am-6.30pm Mon-Sat Apr–mid-Oct, 9.30am-5.30pm Mon-Sat mid-Oct–Mar; Lungotevere della Farnesina, Piazza Trilussa) Formerly the private grounds of Palazzo Corsini (p174), Rome's 12-hectare botanical gardens are a little-known gem and the perfect place to unwind in a lush green, tree-shaded expanse covering the steep slopes of the Giancolo.

Tempietto di Bramante & Chiesa di San Pietro in Montorio   Church
Map p176 (06 581 39 40; www.sanpietroin montorio.it; Piazza San Pietro in Montorio 2; church 8.30am-noon & 3-4pm Mon-Fri, tempi-etto 9.30am-12.30pm & 4-6pm Tue-Sun Apr-Sep, 9.30am-12.30pm & 2-4pm Tue-Sun Oct-Mar; Via Garibaldi) Considered the first great build-ing of the High Renaissance, Bramante's sublime Tempietto (Little Temple; 1508) stands in the courtyard of the Chiesa di San Pietro in Montorio, on the spot where St Peter is said to have been crucified. More than a century later, in 1628, Bernini added a staircase. Bernini also contributed a chapel to the adjacent church, the last resting place of Beatrice Cenci.

It's quite a climb uphill, but you're rewarded by the views. To cheat, take bus 870 from Via Paola just off Corso Vittorio Emanuele II near the Tiber.

⚔ Eating

Traditionally working-class and poor, now chic and pricey, picturesque Traste-vere has a huge number of restaurants, trattorias, cafes and pizzerias.

East of Viale di Trastevere
La Gensola   Sicilian €€
Map p176 (06 581 63 12; Piazza della Gensola 15; meals €50; closed Sun mid-Jun–mid-Sep; or Viale di Trastevere) Tucked away in Trastevere, this tranquil, classy yet unpretentious trattoria thrills foodies with delicious food that has a Sicilian slant

JEAN-PIERRE LESCOURRET/LONELY PLANET IMAGES ©

 Don't Miss
Basilica di Santa Maria in Trastevere

This exquisitely glittering church is said to be the oldest church in Rome dedicated to the Virgin Mary. Its facade is decorated with a beautiful medieval mosaic that depicts Mary feeding Jesus surrounded by 10 women bearing lamps.

The church was first constructed in the early 3rd century over the spot where, according to legend, a fountain of oil miraculously sprang from the ground. Its current Romanesque form is the result of a 12th-century revamp. The portico came later, added by Carlo Fontana in 1702, with its balustrade decorated by four popes.

Inside it's the golden 12th-century mosaics that stand out. Other features to note include the 21 Roman columns, some plundered from the Terme di Caracalla, the wooden ceiling designed in 1617 by Domenichino; and, on the right of the altar, a spiralling Cosmati candlestick, placed on the exact spot where the oil fountain is said to have sprung.

NEED TO KNOW
Map p176; ☏06 581 48 02; Piazza Santa Maria in Trastevere; ⏱7.30am-9pm; 🚌or 🚋Viale di Trastevere

and emphasis on seafood, including an excellent tuna tartare, linguine with fresh anchovies and divine *zuccherini* (tiny fish) with fresh mint. The set menu costs €41.

Artigiano Innocenti Bakery €
Map p176 (☏06 580 39 26; Via delle Luce 21; ⏱8am-8pm Mon-Sat, 9.30am-2pm Sun; 🚌 or

🚋Viale di Trastevere) It's at reassuring spots like this that you can feel the world never changes. This is a stuck-in-time bakery where the staff chat to the regulars, and you can buy light-as-air *crostate* and stock up on biscuits such as *brutti ma buoni* (ugly but good).

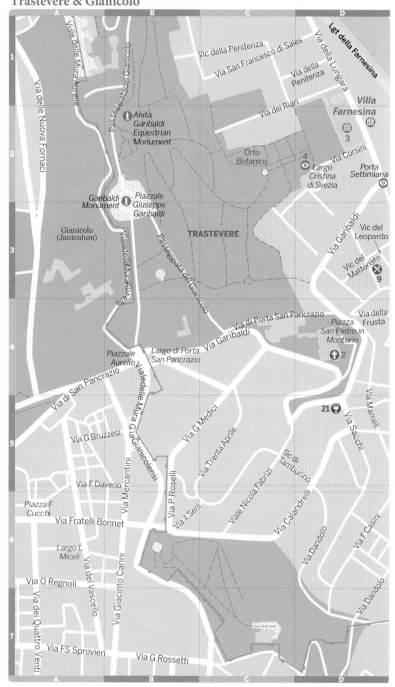

Vic della Penitenza

Via San Francesco di Sales

Via della Penitenza

Lgt della Farnesina

Via della Lungara

Via dei Riari

Villa Farnesina

3

Orto Botanico

4

Via Corsini

Largo Cristina di Svezia

Porta Settimiana

Passeggiata del Gianicolo

Anita Garibaldi Equestrian Monument

Via Garibaldi

Vic del Leopardo

Garibaldi Monument

Piazzale Giuseppe Garibaldi

TRASTEVERE

Vic del Mattonato

9

Gianicolo (Janiculum)

Viale delle Mura Aurelie

Passeggiata del Gianicolo

Via di Porta San Pancrazio

Piazza San Pietro in Montorio

Via della Frusta

Via Garibaldi

2

Piazzale Aurelio

Largo di Porta San Pancrazio

21

Via Mameli

Via di San Pancrazio

Viale delle Mura Gianicolensi

Via G Medici

Via Sacchi

Via G Bruzzesi

Via Mercantini

Via Trenta Aprile

Sc di Tamburino

Via F Daverio

Via P Roselli

Via Il Seni

Viale Nicola Fabrizi

Via Calandrelli

Via F Casini

Piazza F Cucchi

Via Fratelli Bonnet

Via Dandolo

Largo L Miceli

Via del Vascello

Via Giacinto Carini

Via O Regnoli

Via Dandolo

Via dei Quattro Venti

Via FS Sprovieri

Via G Rossetti

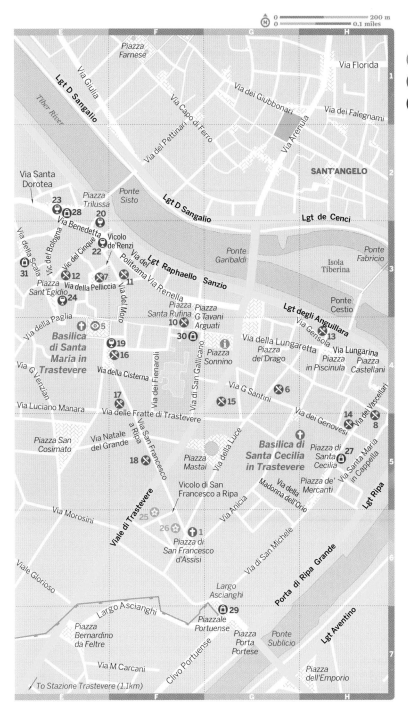

0   200 m
0   0.1 miles

Via Florida

Via Giulia

Lgt D Sangalio

Tiber River

Via Capo di Ferro

Via dei Giubbonari

Via dei Falegnami

Via dei Pettinari

Via Arenula

SANT'ANGELO

Via Santa Dorotea

Piazza Farnese

Piazza Trilussa

Ponte Sisto

23

28

20

Via Benedetta

Lgt D Sangalio

Lgt de Cenci

Vicolo de'Renzi

Via della Scala

Vic de Bologna

Vic del Cinque

22

Via del Politeama

Via Renella

Lgt Raphaello Sanzio

Ponte Garibaldi

Ponte Fabricio

Isola Tiberina

Ponte Cestio

31

12

7

11

Piazza Sant'Egidio

Via della Pelliccia

24

Via del Moro

Piazza Santa Rufina

Piazza G Tavani Arguati

Lgt degli Anguillara

Via Gensola

Ponte Cestio

13

Via della Paglia

5

Basilica di Santa Maria in Trastevere

Via G Venzian

19

16

Via della Cisterna

Via dei Fienaroli

Piazza Sonnino

Via della Lungaretta

Piazza del'Drago

Via Lungarina

Piazza in Piscinula

Piazza Castellani

10

30

Via di San Gallicano

Via G Santini

6

Via Luciano Manara

17

Via delle Fratte di Trastevere

15

Via dei Genovesi

14

8

Via dei Vascellari

Piazza San Cosimato

Via Natale del Grande

Via San Francesco a Ripa

18

Piazza Mastai

Via della Luce

Basilica di Santa Cecilia in Trastevere

Piazza di Santa Cecilia

27

Via Santa Maria in Cappella

Lgt Ripa

Via Morosini

Viale di Trastevere

25

Vicolo di San Francesco a Ripa

Via Anicia

Piazza de' Mercanti

Via della Madonna dell'Orio

26

1

Piazza di San Francesco d'Assisi

Via di San Michele

Porta di Ripa Grande

Viale Glorioso

Largo Ascianghi

Largo Ascianghi

29

Piazza Bernardino da Feltre

Piazzale Portuense

Piazza Porta Portese

Ponte Sublicio

Lgt Aventino

Via M Carcani

Clivo Portuense

Piazza dell'Emporio

To Stazione Trastevere (1.1km)

Trastevere & Gianicolo

Da Enzo
Trattoria €

Map p176 (⌨06 581 83 55; Via dei Vascellari 29; meals €25; ☺Mon-Sat; 🚌Piazza Sonnino) This snug dining room with rough yellow walls and lots of character serves up great, seasonally based Roman meals, such as spaghetti with clams and mussels or grilled lamb cutlets. There's a tiny terrace on the quintessential Trastevere cobbled street.

Panattoni
Pizzeria €

Map p176 (⌨06 580 09 19; Viale di Trastevere 53; pizzas €6.50-9; ☺6.30pm-1am Thu-Tue; 🚌 or 🚋Viale di Trastevere) Panattoni is nicknamed *l'obitorio* (the morgue) because of its marble-slab tabletops. Thankfully the similarity stops there. This is one of Trastevere's liveliest pizzerias, with paper-thin pizzas, a clattering buzz, testy waiters, streetside seating and fried starters (specialities are *supplì* and *baccalà*).

Fior di Luna
Ice Cream €

Map p176 (⌨06 645 61314; Via della Lungaretta 96; from €2; ☺noon-2am Tue-Sun; 🚌 or 🚋Vi-ale di Trastevere) Perfectly placed for picking up an artisanal ice cream to accompany you on your Trastevere meanderings, this busy little hub serves up handmade ice cream and sorbet – it's made in small batches and only uses natural, seasonal ingredients, such as hazelnuts from Tonda and pistachios from Bronte.

Sisini
Pizzeria €

Map p176 (Via di San Francesco a Ripa 137; pizza & pasta from €2; ☺9am-10.30pm Mon-Sat, closed Aug; 🚌 or 🚋Viale di Trastevere) Locals love this fast-food joint (the sign outside says 'Supplì'), serving up fresh *pizza al taglio* and different pasta and risotto dishes served in plastic boxes – there's one small table where you can eat standing up, or you can take away.

West of Viale di Trastevere

Glass Hostaria
Creative Italian €€€

Map p176 (⌨06 583 35 903; Vicolo del Cinque 58; meals €70; ☺dinner Tue-Sun; 🚌Piazza Trilussa) Trastevere's foremost foodie address, the Glass Hostaria is a breath of fresh air in the neighbourhood, a modernist, sophisticated setting with cooking to match. Chef Cristina creates inventive, delicate dishes that combine with fresh ingredients and traditional elements to delight and surprise the palate.

Paris   Roman-Jewish €€

Map p176 (☎ 06 581 53 78; Piazza San Calisto 7; meals €45; ⊙Tue-Sat, lunch Sun, closed 3 weeks Aug; ☒ or ☒Viale di Trastevere) Nothing to do with Paris (it's the name of the founder), this is an elegant, old-school Roman restaurant set in a 17th-century building, and it's the best place outside the Ghetto to sample Roman-Jewish cuisine, such as delicate *fritto misto con baccalà* (deep-fried vegetables with salt cod) and *carciofi alla giudia* (Jewish-style artichokes), as well as Roman dishes such as just-right *rigatoni alla carbonara* (pasta with egg and bacon sauce).

Da Lucia   Trattoria €

Map p176 (☎ 06 580 36 01; Vicolo del Mattonato 2; meals €30; ⊙Tue-Sun; ☒Piazza Trilussa) Eat beneath the fluttering knickers of the neighbourhood at this terrific trattoria, frequented by hungry locals and tourists, and packed with locals for Sunday lunch. On a cobbled backstreet that is classic Trastevere, it serves up a cavalcade of Roman specialities including *trippa all romana* (tripe with tomato sauce) and *pollo con peperoni* (chicken with peppers), as well as bountiful antipasti and possibly Rome's best tiramisu. Cash only.

Da Augusto   Trattoria €

Map p176 (☎ 06 580 37 98; Piazza de' Renzi 15; meals €25; ⊙lunch & dinner Fri-Wed; ☒Piazza Trilussa) For a true Trastevere feast, plonk yourself at one of Augusto's rickety tables and prepare to enjoy some mamma-style cooking. The hard-working waiters dish out hearty platefuls of *rigatoni all'amatriciana and stracciatella* (clear broth with egg and Parmesan) among a host of Roman classics.

Pizzeria Ivo   Pizzeria €

Map p176 (☎ 06 581 70 82; Via di San Francesco a Ripa 158; pizzas €6.5-8.80; ⊙dinner Wed-Mon; ☒ or ☒Viale di Trastevere) With the TV on in the corner and the tables full, and with a lively strip out on the street when the weather's good enough, Ivo's a noisy and vibrant place where the crispy, though not huge, pizzas are some of Rome's most delicious and traditional, and the waiters fit the gruff-and-fast stereotype.

Forno la Renella   Pizzeria €

Map p176 (☎ 06 581 72 65; Via del Moro 15-16; pizza slices from €2; ⊙9am-1am; ☒Piazza Trilussa) The wood-fired ovens at this historic Trastevere bakery have been firing for decades, producing a delicious daily batch of pizza, bread and biscuits. Piled-high toppings (and fillings) vary seasonally. Popular with everyone from skinheads with big dogs to elderly ladies with little dogs.

Le Mani in Pasta   Pasta €

Map p176 (☎ 06 581 60 17; Via dei Genovesi 37; meals €40; lunch daily, dinner Tue-Sun; ☒ or ☒ Viale di Trastevere; ✱ ♟) Lively and popular, this narrow and secret-feeling place has an open kitchen that serves up delicious fresh pasta topped with whatever's in season, which could be, if you're lucky, *calamari e carciofi* (squid and artichokes).

⊙ Drinking & Nightlife

Enchantingly pretty, Trastevere is one of the city's most popular areas to wander, drink and decide what to do afterwards. Foreign visitors love it, as do those who love foreign visitors, but it's also a local haunt.

Trastevere

Ma Che Siete Venuti a Fà   Bar

Map p176 (Via Benedetta 25; ⊙3pm-2am; ☒ or ☒Piazza Sonnino) Also known as the Football Pub, the name means 'What did you come here for?' (it's a football chant), but the answer, rather than anything to do with the beautiful game, could be atmosphere and beer. It's pint-sized place, but packs a huge number of artisanal beers into its interior, with delicious caramel-like tipples such as Italiano Bibock (by Bir-rificio Italiano), Old Man or London Honey. A small/large beer costs €4/6.

Bar San Calisto   Bar
Map p176 (Piazza San Calisto; ⏱5.30am-2am Mon-Sat; 🚊 or 🚌Piazza Sonnino) Those in the know head to the down-at-heel 'Sanca' for its basic, stuck-in-time atmosphere and dirt-cheap prices (a beer costs from €1.50). It's famous for its chocolate – drunk hot with cream in winter, eaten as ice cream in summer.

Freni e Frizioni   Bar
Map p176 (📞06 583 34 210; Via del Politeama 4; ⏱6.30pm-2am; 🚊Piazza Trilussa) Everyone's favourite hip Trastevere hang-out: in a former life, this bar and cafe was a garage, hence its name ('brakes and clutches'). The arty crowd flocks here to slurp well-priced drinks (especially mojitos) and pack the piazza in front. Feast on the good-value *aperitivo*.

Ombre Rosse   Bar
Map p176 (📞06 588 41 55; Piazza Sant'Egidio 12; ⏱8am-2am Mon-Sat, 11am-2am Sun; 🚊Piazza Trilussa) Another seminal Trastevere hang-

out; grab a table on the terrace and watch the world go by. The cosmopolitan clientele ranges from elderly Italian wide boys to chic city slickers. Tunes are slinky and there's live music (jazz, blues, world) on Thursday and Sunday evenings from September to April.

La Meschita   Wine Bar
Map p176 (📞06 583 33 920; Piazza Trilussa 41; 🚊Piazza Trilussa) This tiny bar inside the entrance to upmarket restaurant Enoteca Ferrara serves fantastic *aperitivo* and has a wide range of wines by the glass, from €7.

Gianicolo
Il Barretto   Bar
Map p176 (📞06 583 65 422; Via Garibaldi 27; ⏱6am-2am Mon-Sat, 5pm-2am Sun; 🚊 or 🚌Piazza Sonnino) Venture a little way up the Gianicolo, up a steep flight of steps from Trastevere. Go on, it's so worth it: you'll discover this cocktail bar, an architectural triumph. The bar is mostly huge plate-glass windows overlooking the district, and there's a garden terrace.

Cafe on Piazza Santa Maria in Trastevere (p174)

Entertainment

Big Mama
Live Music

Map p176 (06 581 25 51; www.bigmama.it, in Italian; Vicolo di San Francesco a Ripa 18; annual membership €14; ⏰9pm-1.30am, show 10.30pm Thu-Sat, closed Jun-Sep; 🚊 or 🚋Viale di Trastevere) To wallow in the Eternal City blues, there's only one place to go – this cramped Trastevere basement, hosting jazz, funk, soul and R&B. Weekly residencies from well-known Italian musicians and songwriters, and frequent concerts by international artists.

Lettere Caffè Gallery
Live Music

Map p176 (☎06 972 70 991; Vicolo San Francesco a Ripa 100/101; ⏰ 7pm-2am daily, closed mid-Aug–mid-Sep; 🚋Piazza Trilussa) Like books? Poetry? Blues and jazz? Then you'll love this place – a clutter of barstools and books, where there are regular live gigs, poetry slams, comedy and gay nights, followed by DJ sets playing indie and new wave.

🔒 Shopping

Trastevere

La Cravatta su Misura
Accessories

Map p176 (☎06 581 66 76; Via Santa Cecilia 12; ⏰10am-2pm & 3.30-7pm Mon-Fri, 10am-2pm Sat; 🚊 or 🚋Viale di Trastevere) With ties draped over the wooden furniture, this inviting shop resembles the study of an absent-minded professor. But don't be fooled: these guys know their ties. Only the finest Italian silks and English wools are used in neckwear

made to customers' specifications. At a push, a tie can be ready in a few hours.

Officina della Carta
Gifts

Map p176 (☎06 589 55 57; Via Benedetta 26b; 🚋Piazza Trilussa) A perfect present pitstop, this tiny workshop produces attractive hand-painted paper-bound boxes, photo albums, recipe books, notepads, photo frames, diaries and charming marionette theatres.

Scala Quattorodici
Clothing

Map p176 (☎Via della Scala 13-14; 🚋Piazza Trilussa) Make yourself over à la Audrey Hepburn with these classically tailored clothes in beautiful fabrics – either made-to-measure or off-the-peg. Pricey (a frock will set you back €600 or so) but oh so worth it.

Porta Portese
Market

Map p176 (⏰7am-1pm Sun; Via Portuense; 🚊 or 🚋Viale di Trastevere) To see another side of Rome head to this mammoth flea market. With thousands of stalls selling everything from rare books to spare bike parts, from Peruvian shawls to iPods, it's crazily busy and a lot of fun. Keep your valuables safe and wear your haggling hat.

Roma-Store
Perfume

Map p176 (☎06 581 87 89; Via della Lungaretta 63; ⏰10am-8pm; 🚊 or 🚋Viale di Trastevere) With no sign, Roma-Store is an enchanting perfume shop crammed full of deliciously enticing bottles of scent, including lots of unusual brands as well as English Floris, Italian Aqua di Parma and French Etat Libre d'Orange.

Vatican City, Borgo & Prati

The Vatican, the world's smallest sovereign state (a mere 0.44 sq km), sits atop the low-lying Vatican hill. Centred on the domed bulk of St Peter's Basilica and Piazza San Pietro, it contains an incredible wealth of masterpieces.

You'll need at least half a day to do justice to the Vatican Museums. The highlight is the Michelangelo-decorated Sistine Chapel, but there's enough art on display to keep you busy for years.

Between the Vatican and the river lies the cobbled, medieval district of the Borgo – before Mussolini bulldozed through Via dei Conciliazione, all the streets around St Peter's were like this. The main sight here is Castel Sant'Angelo, the big drum-shaped castle overlooking the river.

The Vatican, Borgo and Prati districts are all easy to reach by public transport: via Ottaviano–San Pietro metro station, or by bus from Stazione Termini or the Centro Storico.

View of Vatican Gardens (p196) from St Peter's Basilica (p192) **183**

Vatican City, Borgo & Prati Highlights

Sistine Chapel (p191)

Gazing heavenwards at Michelangelo's cinematic ceiling frescoes in the Sistine Chapel is an experience of unparalleled wonder. To visit is to be enveloped on all sides by an incredible saturation of colour and energy – an experience for which no reproduction can prepare you. Michelangelo's works are filled with movement, solidity and beauty; you could spend hours here examining the details of his painting.

RUSSELL MOUNTFORD/LONELY PLANET IMAGES ©

St Peter's Basilica (p192)

The super-sized opulence of the Catholic Church's foremost place of worship will blow you away. Whatever your faith, or lack of it, the majesty of the ensemble is undeniable. Highlights include Michelangelo's dome and his tenderly sculpted *Pietà*, Bernini's Baldacchino, the views from the top of the dome, and a visit to St Peter's Tomb.

WILL SALTER/LONELY PLANET IMAGES ©

Piazza San Pietro (p196)

Embraced on either side by long colonnades that represent the enfolding arms of the church, this is a glorious public space that forms a harmonious whole with the splendours of the towering Basilica of St Peter's. It's very much in use by the faithful, as the Pope addresses the gathered crowds from a central window every Sunday (save in summer, when he decamps to Castel Gandolfo).

Castel Sant'Angelo (p197)

There's something otherworldly about this huge, drum-like edifice on the banks of the Tiber; once the mighty mausoleum of Hadrian and later an essential papal fortress. It's appeared in works as diverse as Puccini's *Tosca* and Dan Brown's *Angels and Demons*. The castle has an extraordinary history and beautifully frescoed interior, and the views from the roof terrace are stupendous.

Stanze di Raffaello (p190)

A complete vision of the High Renaissance, these rooms contain works of virtuoso genius, which create perspective and solidity out of two dimensions. They also convey the tenets of Renaissance thinking, with paintings such as the *School of Athens* summing up the intellectual achievements of humanity. It's incredible to think that these were painted at the same time as the Sistine Chapel, a few rooms away.

Vatican City, Borgo & Prati Walk

Vatican City may be the world's smallest state, but it contains enough treasures for a huge country. Take a walk around to see some extraordinary masterpieces and amazing architecture.

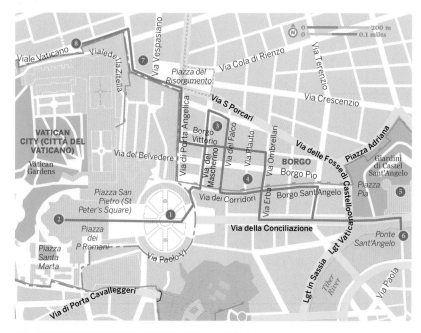

1 Piazza San Pietro

Start your walk in Bernini's elliptical **piazza** (p196). Bernini intended the piazza to appear as a surprise, after the tangle of the surrounding medieval streets, but Mussolini put paid to this subtle approach by bulldozing through the grand boulevard Via D Conciliazione.

2 St Peter's Basilica

Overwhelmingly grandiose in style and scale, **St Peter's** (p192) is a solid incarnation of the power and authority of the Catholic Church. From the piazza you can see the central window through which the Pope makes his Sunday address. Inside, the wealth of masterpieces includes Michelangelo's haunting *Pietà*.

3 Angeli a Borgo

From St Peter's, take Via delle Mascherino north to Borgo Angelico and turn right. There is a glut of substandard eateries around the Vatican, but unpretentious **Angeli a Borgo** (p197) in the Borgo – the medieval-seeming, picturesque district that edges St Peter's – is an exception. It's an ideal place to stop and recharge on homecooked pasta or pizza after a morning in the basilica.

4 Corridori Borgo Sant'Angelo

From Borgo Angelico, take Via del Falco south until you meet a thick, arched, fortified wall. Above it is the Corridori, an enclosed, **elevated walkway**, which was built in the 13th century to connect Vatican City with Castel Sant'Angelo. Popes used it as an escape route to the castle's fortified quarters during times of unrest.

5 Castel Sant'Angelo

Follow the wall of the Corridorio east to reach **Castel Sant'Angelo** (p197). Hadrian's mausoleum was built in the 2nd century, serving as the imperial tomb until being converted into a fortress in 403. In 1367 its church was consecrated by Pope Urbano V. The fortress is surmounted by a stone angel, hence its name.

6 Ponte Sant'Angelo

Leading across the river from the castle, this **bridge** (p197) also dates from the 2nd century. The 10 angels along its length, however, were designed by Bernini, chief architect and sculptor in baroque Rome. Executions used to take place on the bridge – Italian noblewoman Beatrice Cenci, accused of the murder of her father, was beheaded here in 1599.

7 Old Bridge

Once you've wandered back through the Borgo, it's a short walk towards the entrance of the Vatican Museums. On your way you'll pass a small hole-in-the-wall **ice cream shop** (p197), which serves mountains of delicious gelato. Just the ticket to help fuel a museum visit.

8 Vatican Museums

Carry on alongside the great wall and you'll shortly reach the entrance to the **Vatican Museums** (p188). There's always a queue, but if you've been smart and booked your ticket in advance, you can sail past.

 ## The Best...

PLACES TO EAT

Angeli a Borgo Charmingly no-nonsense restaurant serving crowd-pleasing pasta and pizza in the picturesque Borgo. (p197)

Pizzarium The Sistine Chapel of *pizza al taglio* (by the slice), created by pizza maestro Gabriele Bonci. (p201)

Osteria dell'Angelo Book ahead for this neighbourhood trattoria, owned by former rugby player Angelo. (p200)

PLACES TO DRINK

Alexanderplatz Rome's foremost jazz club. (p201)

Fonclea Lively pub with regular live music. (p201)

OVERGROUND & UNDERGROUND

Dome of St Peter's Basilica (p194) Climb 330 steps through narrow passages and up spiral staircases to be rewarded with sensational panoramas across the piazza and beyond.

Terrace of Castel Sant'Angelo Inspirational views across Rome, a cafe, and location for the climax of Puccini's *Tosca*. (p197)

Tomb of St Peter Feel the layers of Roman history as you descend to the saint's tomb. (p194)

Colonnade on Piazza San Pietro

Don't Miss
Vatican Museums

With some 7km of exhibitions and more masterpieces than many small countries, this vast museum complex, housed in the 5.5-hectare Palazzo Apostolico Vaticano, contains one of the world's greatest art collections.

Map p198

☎ 06 698 84 676

http://mv.vatican.va

Viale Vaticano

adult/reduced €15/8, last Sun of the month free, audioguide €7

🕐 9am-6pm Mon-Sat, last admission 4pm, 9am-2pm last Sun of month, last admission 12.30pm

Ⓜ Ottaviano–San Pietro

Pinacoteca

The papal picture gallery boasts some 460 paintings with works by Giotto, Fra Angelico, Filippo Lippi, Guido Reni, Guercino, Nicholas Poussin, Van Dyck and Pietro da Cortona. Look out for Raphael's *Madonna di Foligno* (Madonna of Folignano) and his last painting, *La Trasfigurazione* (Transfiguration), completed by his students after his death.

Museo Gregoriano Egizio

Founded by Pope Gregory XVI in 1839, this museum contains pieces taken from Egypt in Roman times. The collection is small but there are fascinating exhibits including the *Trono di Rameses II*, vividly painted sarcophagi dating from around 1000 BC, and some macabre mummies.

Museo Chiaramonti

This museum is effectively the long corridor that runs down the lower east side of the Belvedere Palace. Its walls are lined with thousands of statues representing everything from immortal gods to ugly Roman patricians. Near the end of the hall, off to the right, is the **Braccio Nuovo** (New Wing), which contains a famous sculpture of Augustus and a statue depicting the Nile as a reclining god covered by 16 babies.

Museo Pio-Clementino

This spectacular museum contains some of the Vatican Museums' finest classical statuary. To the left, as you enter the **Cortile Ottagono** (Octagonal Courtyard), is the *Apollo Belvedere* – a Roman 2nd-century copy of a 4th- century-BC Greek bronze. It's considered one of the great masterpieces of classical sculpture. Nearby, the 1st-century *Laocoön* depicts a muscular Trojan priest and his two sons in mortal struggle with two sea serpents.

Back inside the museum, the **Sala degli Animali** is filled with sculptures and some magnificent 4th-century mosaics. Continuing through the sala, you come to the **Galleria delle Statue**, which has several important classical pieces: the **Sala delle Buste**, which contains hundreds of Roman busts; and the **Gabinetto delle Maschere**, named after the floor mosaics

Don't Miss List

BY SILVIA PROSPERI,
TOUR GUIDE

1 **CORTILE OTTAGONO (OCTAGONAL COURTYARD)**
This used to be an orange tree garden for the guests of Pope Julius II. It is decorated with masterpieces of Greek–Roman classical art, such as the *Laocoon, Apollo, Venus* and *Hermes*. These spectacular statues inspired Renaissance artists such as Michelangelo and Raffaello.

2 **PAINTING GALLERY**
This shows the evolution of Italian art from Giotto to Caravaggio and beyond. The fragments of the fresco *Christ in Glory Between Angels and Apostles* by Melozzo da Forlì represent an incredible rescue – they were saved when the apse of the Church SS Apostoli was demolished, and are a true example of angelic beauty.

3 **STANZE DI RAFFAELLO**
In the Raphael Rooms, look carefully at the *Liberation of St Peter* in the Heliodorus Room. This was proof of the great talent of the young Raphael, who had just arrived in Rome, as night scenes with different sources of light are particularly hard to realise in fresco.

4 **SISTINE CHAPEL**
The entire chapel is overwhelming and captivating, and it is impossible to pick the best of thousands of characters, all defined in intricate detail. However, the Lybian Sybil is amazing evidence of Michelangelo's development over five years working on the chapel: the transparent veil over the sybil's legs, the brilliance of her orange dress, and the feminine twist of her body all show the touch of a genius.

5 **MUSEO GREGORIANO PROFANO**
The mosaic of the 'unswept floor' (which includes a little mouse nibbling leftovers!) is a good example of the level of perfection reached by the Greek–Roman artists in this art form. I suggest visiting the tranquil Museo Gregoriano Profano, where this and other neglected masterpieces can be enjoyed away from the usual crowds.

189

Jump the Queue

Here's how to jump the ticket queue. Book tickets at the museums' online ticket office (http://biglietteriamusei.vatican.va/musei/tickets). On payment, you'll receive email confirmation, which you should print and present, along with valid ID, at the museum entrance.

of theatrical masks. To the east, the **Sala delle Muse** (Room of the Muses) is centred on the *Torso Belvedere,* another of the museum's must-sees.

Galleria delle Carte Geografiche & Sala Sobieski

One of the unsung heroes of the Vatican Museums, the 120m-long Map Gallery is hung with 40 huge topographical maps. They were all created between 1580 and 1583 for Pope Gregory XIII, and based on drafts by Ignazio Danti, a leading cartographer of his day.

Stanze di Raffaello

Even in the shadow of the Sistine Chapel, the *Stanze di Raffaello* (Raphael Rooms) stand out. They were part of Pope Julius II's private apartment; in 1508 he commissioned the 25-year-old, relatively unknown Raphael to decorate them. The frescoes cemented Raphael's reputation, establishing him as a rising star.

But while they carry his name, not all were completed by Raphael: he painted the **Stanza della Segnatura** (Study) and **Stanza d'Eliodoro** (Waiting Room), while the **Stanza dell'Incendio di Borgo** (Dining Room) and **Sala di Costantino** (Reception Room) were decorated by students following his designs.

Sala di Costantino was finished by Giulio Romano in 1525, five years after Raphael's death. It is dominated by the huge *Battaglia di Costantino contro Maxentius* (Battle of the Milvian Bridge), celebrating the victory of Constantine, Rome's first Christian emperor, over Maxentius.

Leading off this are the **Sala dei Chiaroscuri**, featuring a Raphael-designed ceiling, and the **Cappella di Niccolo V**, Pope Nicholas V's private chapel. Often closed to the public, this tiny chapel features a superb cycle of frescoes by Fra Angelico.

The **Stanza d'Eliodoro**, which was used for private audiences, was painted between 1512 and 1514. It takes its name from the *Cacciata d'Eliodoro* (Expulsion of Heliodorus from the Temple). To the right of this is the *Messa di Bolsena* (Mass of Bolsena), showing Julius II paying homage to the relic of a 13th-century miracle at the lake town of Bolsena. Next is *Incontro di Leone Magno con Attila* (Encounter of Leo the Great with Attila) by Raphael and his school, and on the fourth wall the *Liberazione di San Pietro* (Liberation of St Peter), one of Raphael's most brilliant works.

The **Stanza della Segnatura**, Pope Julius' study and library, was the first room that Raphael painted, and it's here that you'll find his great masterpiece, *La Scuola d'Atene* (The School of Athens) featuring philosophers and scholars gathered around Plato and Aristotle. The seated figure in front of the steps is believed to be Michelangelo, while the figure of Plato is said to be a portrait of Leonardo da Vinci and Euclide (the bald man bending over) is Bramante. Raphael also included a self-portrait in the lower right corner (he's the second figure from the right in the black hat). Opposite is *La Disputa*

Myths Debunked

It is often said that Michelangelo worked alone. He didn't. He employed a steady stream of assistants to help with the plaster work (producing frescoes involves painting directly onto wet plaster). Another popular myth is that Michelangelo painted lying down. In fact, Michelangelo designed a curved scaffolding system that allowed him to work standing up, albeit in an awkward backward-leaning position.

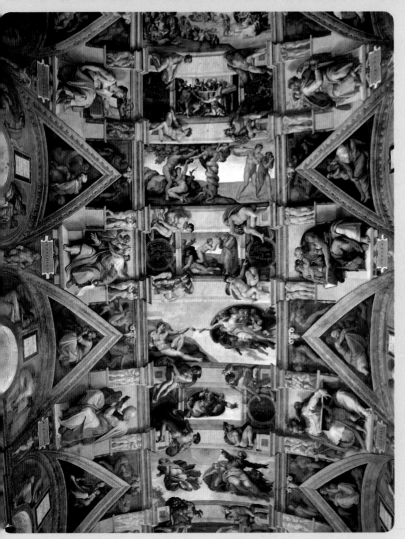

del Sacramento (Disputation on the Sacrament), also by Raphael.

Sistine Chapel

The jewel in the Vatican crown, the Sistine Chapel (Cappella Sistina) is home to two of the world's most famous works of art – Michelangelo's ceiling frescoes and his *Giudizio Universale* (Last Judgment). But the chapel is more than just an art gallery. It also serves as the pope's private chapel, and the place where the papal conclave meets to elect a new pope. The chapel was originally built for Pope Sixtus IV, after whom it is named, and consecrated on 15 August 1483. But it owes its modern fame to Michelangelo and his two unrivalled masterpieces. The ceiling was commissioned by Pope Julius II and painted between 1508 and 1512; the spectacular *Giudizio Universale*, was completed almost 30 years later in 1541. Together, they cover approximately 1000 sq m and represent one of the greatest feats of painting ever accomplished by a single man.

Don't Miss
St Peter's Basilica

In a city of outstanding churches, none can hold a candle to St Peter's Basilica (Basilica di San Pietro), Italy's biggest, richest and most spectacular church. The basilica is a huge place but it can still get very crowded and on busy days it attracts more than 20,000 visitors. If you want to be one of them, remember to dress appropriately – that means no shorts, miniskirts or bare shoulders.

Map p198

Piazza San Pietro

Admission free

Audioguide €5

⊙ 7am-7pm Apr-Sep, 7am-6pm Oct-Mar

Ⓜ Ottaviano–San Pietro

History

The first basilica was built by Constantine in the 4th century. Standing on the site of Nero's stadium, the Ager Vaticanus, where St Peter is said to have been buried, it was consecrated in AD 326. Like many early churches, it fell into disrepair and it wasn't until the mid-15th century that efforts were made to restore it. In 1506 Bramante came up with a design for a basilica based on a Greek-cross plan, with four equal arms and a huge central dome.

On Bramante's death in 1514, construction work ground to a halt as architects, including Raphael and Antonio da Sangallo, tried to modify his original plans. But little progress was made and it wasn't until Michelangelo took over in 1547 at the age of 72 that the situation changed. Michelangelo simplified Bramante's plans and drew up designs for what was to become his greatest architectural achievement, the dome. He never lived to see it built; Giacomo della Porta and Domenico Fontana to finish it in 1590.

With the dome in place, Carlo Maderno inherited the project in 1605. He designed the monumental facade and lengthened the nave towards the piazza.

Interior – Right Nave

At the beginning of the right aisle, Michelangelo's beautiful **Pietà** sits in its own chapel behind a panel of bullet-proof glass. Sculpted when he was a little-known 25-year-old (in 1499), it's the only work he ever signed – his signature is etched into the sash across the Madonna's breast.

Moving down the aisle you come to the **Cappella del Santissimo Sacramento,** a small chapel decorated in sumptuous baroque style. The iron grille was designed by Borromini; the gilt bronze ciborium above the altar is by Bernini; and the altarpiece, *The Trinity,* is by Pietro da Cortona.

Just beyond the chapel, the grandiose **Monument to Gregory XIII** sits near the **Cappella Gregoriana,** built by Gregory XIII from designs by Michelangelo. The outstanding work here is the 12th-century

1 SAN PIETRO PIAZZA

This project of architect Gian Lorenzo Bernini was completed in 1667, after 11 years of intense work. The oval of the piazza is enclosed by two porticos, formed of 284 columns of travertine marble (each 16m high). They are surmounted by 140 statues of the saints and martyrs of the church.

2 BERNINI'S BALDACCHINO

Underneath the dome, which forms a symbolic shelter to the great papal altar, you can gaze at the grand *baldacchino* commissioned by Pope Urbano VIII between 1624 and 1635. This monument, nearly 29m tall, features spiralling columns inspired by the marble columns around the tomb of St Peter in the ancient church.

3 CONFESSIO

The 'Confessio' – so-named as it was St Peter's confession of his faith that led to his martyrdom – is a place of veneration, a niche decorated by a mosaic of Christ. It was constructed over St Peter's original modest tomb, which had been enclosed by Constantine in a marble box. Three altars were later added – the most recent, which is generally used for papal celebrations, in 1594.

4 TOMB OF ST PETER & THE VATICAN NECROPOLIS

The best way discover the most profound roots of the basilica is by walking along the unpaved street that leads to the tomb of St Peter, which crosses a Roman necropolis. This was filled by Constantine in the 4th century to construct the first basilica, and rediscovered after 1600 years.

5 VATICAN GROTTOES

Under the central nave, the Grotte Vaticane are an integral part of the basilica's sacred space. There is a strong sense of devotion and faith, and the grottos still preserve some surviving parts of the revered and lost Constantine basilica.

fresco of the *Madonna del Soccorso* (Madonna of Succour), which was moved from the original basilica in 1578.

Much of the right-hand transept is roped off but from outside you can still see the **monument of Clement XIII**, one of Antonio Canova's most famous works.

Interior – Central Nave

Dominating the centre of the basilica is Bernini's 29m-high **baldachin**. Supported by four spiral columns and made with bronze taken from the Pantheon, it stands over the papal altar, also known as the Altar of the Confession, which itself sits on the site of St Peter's grave. In front, the elaborate **Confessione**, built by Carlo Maderno, is where St Peter was originally buried.

Above the baldachin, Michelangelo's **dome** rises to a height of 119m. This towering masterpiece is supported by four stone **piers** that rise around the papal altar. At the base of the **Pier of St Longinus,** to the right as you face the papal altar, is a much-loved bronze **statue of St Peter**, believed to be a 13th-century work by Arnolfo di Cambio, whose right foot has been worn down by centuries of caresses. On the Feast Day of St Peter and St Paul (29 June), the statue is dressed in papal robes.

Behind the altar in the tribune at the end of the basilica, the **throne of St Peter** (1665) is the centrepiece of Bernini's extraordinary **Cattedra di San Pietro**. In the middle of the elaborate gilded-bronze throne, supported by statues of Saints Augustine, Ambrose, Athanasius and John Chrysostom, is a wooden seat, which was once thought to have been St Peter's but in fact dates to the 9th century.

To the right of the throne, Bernini's **monument to Urban VIII** depicts the pope flanked by the figures of Charity and Justice.

Interior – Left Nave

In the roped-off left transept behind the **Pier of St Veronica**, the **Cappella della Madonna della Colonna** takes its name from the image of the Madonna that once adorned the old basilica but now stares out from Giacomo della Porta's marble altar. To its right, above the **tomb of St Leo the Great**, is a particularly fine relief by the baroque sculptor Alessandro Algardi. Opposite it, under the next arch, is Bernini's last work in the basilica, the **monument to Alexander VII**.

Continuing back towards the front of the basilica, you'll find the **Cappella della Presentazione**, which contains two of St Peter's most modern works: a black relief **monument to John XXIII** by Emilio Greco, and a **monument to Benedict XV** by Pietro Canonica.

Under the next arch are the so-called **Stuart monuments**. On the right is the monument to Clementina Sobieska, wife of James Stuart, by Filippo Barigioni, and on the left is Canova's vaguely erotic monument to the last three members of the Stuart clan, the pretenders to the English throne who died in exile in Rome.

Dome

To climb the **dome** (with/without lift €7/5; ⏰8am-5.45pm Apr-Sep, 8am-4.45pm Oct-Mar) look for the entrance to the right of the basilica. A small lift takes you halfway up but it's still a long climb (320 steps) to the top. It's worth the effort, but bear in mind it's steep, long and narrow.

Tomb of St Peter

Excavations beneath the basilica have uncovered part of the original church

and what archaeologists believe is the **Tomb of St Peter (admission €10, over 15s only)**. In 1942, the bones of an elderly, strongly built man were found in a box hidden behind a wall covered by pilgrims' graffiti. After more than 30 years of forensic examination, in 1976, Pope Paul VI declared the bones to be those of St Peter.

The excavations can be visited only on a 90-minute guided tour. To book a spot email the **Ufficio Scavi (**Excavations Office; ☎06 698 85 318; scavi@fsp.va)**, as far in advance as possible.

Vatican Grottoes

Extending beneath the basilica, the **Vatican Grottoes (admission free; ⊘9am-6pm Apr-Sep, 9am-5pm Oct-Mar)** contain the tombs of numerous popes, including John Paul II, whose simple sepulchre contrasts with many of the flamboyant monuments in the basilica above. You can also see several huge columns from the original 4th-century basilica.

Discover Vatican City, Borgo & Prati

Getting There & Away

○ Bus From Termini, No 40 is the quickest bus to the Vatican – it'll drop you off near Castel Sant'Angelo. You can also take No 64, which runs a similar route but stops more often. No 492 runs to Piazza del Risorgimento from Stazione Tiburtina, passing through Piazza Barberini and the *centro storico*.

○ Metro Take metro line A to Ottaviano–San Pietro. From the station signs direct you to St Peter's.

◎ Sights

Boasting priceless treasures at every turn, the Vatican is home to some of Rome's most popular sights.

Vatican City

St Peter's Basilica Church
See p192.

Piazza San Pietro Piazza
Map p198 (M Ottaviano–San Pietro) One of the world's great public spaces, the piazza was laid out by Gian Lorenzo Bernini between 1656 and 1667 for Pope Alexander VII. Seen from above, it resembles a giant keyhole with two semicircular colonnades, each consisting of four rows of Doric columns, encircling a giant ellipse that straightens out to funnel believers into the basilica. The effect was deliberate – Bernini described the colonnades as representing 'the motherly arms of the church'. The 25m obelisk in the centre was brought to Rome by Caligula from Heliopolis in Egypt and later used by Nero as a turning post for the chariot races in his circus.

Vatican Museums Museum
See p188.

Vatican Gardens Garden
Map p198 (http://biglietteriamusei.vatican .va; adult/reduced incl Vatican Museums €31/24) Up to half the Vatican is covered by the perfectly manicured Vatican Gardens, which contain fortifications, grottoes, monuments and fountains dating from the 9th century to the present day. Visits are by two-hour guided tour only, for which you'll need to book at least a week in advance.

Piazza San Pietro
IMAGES & STORIES/ALAMY ©

Papal Audiences

At 11am on Wednesday, the pope addresses his flock at the Vatican (in July and August in Castel Gandolfo near Rome). For free tickets, download the request form from the Vatican website (www.vatican.va) and fax it to the **Prefettura della Casa Pontificia** (fax 06 698 85 863). Pick up tickets at the office through the bronze doors under the colonnade to the right of St Peter's.

When he is in Rome, the Pope blesses the crowd in St Peter's Square on Sunday at noon. No tickets are required.

Borgo

Castel Sant'Angelo   Castle

Map p198 (☎06 681 91 11; Lungotevere Castello 50; adult/reduced €5/2.50; ◷9am-7.30pm, last admission 6.30pm Tue-Sun; 🚊Piazza Pia) Originally a mausoleum for the emperor Hadrian, this castle was converted into a papal fortress in the 6th century and named after an angelic vision that Pope Gregory had in 590. Thanks to a secret 13th-century passageway to the Vatican palaces, it provided sanctuary to many popes in times of danger, including Clemente VII who holed up here during the 1527 Sack of Rome.

Its upper floors boast lavishly decorated Renaissance interiors, including, on the 4th floor, the beautifully frescoed Sala Paolina. Two stories further up, the terrace, immortalised by Puccini in his opera *Tosca*, offers great views over Rome.

Ponte Sant'Angelo   Bridge

Map p198 (🚊Piazza Pia) Hadrian built the Ponte Sant'Angelo across the River Tiber in 136 to provide an approach to his mausoleum, but it was Bernini who brought it to life with his sculptures in the 17th century.

✖ Eating

Beware, hungry tourists: there are unholy numbers of overpriced, mediocre eateries around the Vatican and St Peter's. It's worth making the extra effort to find somewhere listed in this guide, as there are fabulous places amid the follies.

Vatican City

Old Bridge   Gelateria €

Map p198 (Via dei Bastioni di Michelangelo 5; cones/tubs from €1.50; 🚊Piazza del Risorgimento) Ideal for a pre- or post-Vatican pick-me-up, this tiny parlour has been cheerfully dishing up huge portions of delicious ice cream for over 20 years.

Borgo

Angeli a Borgo   Traditional Italian €€

Map p198 (☎06 686 96 74; www.angeliaborgo .com; Borgo Angelico 28; pizzas from €5.50, meals €25-30) It is possible to escape the crowds and eat well near St Peter's. Just a few blocks back from the basilica, this is a laid-back restaurant–pizzeria with a high brick ceiling, yellow walls and an ample menu.

La Veranda de l'Hotel
Columbus   Modern Italian €€€

Map p198 (☎06 687 29 73; www.laveranda.net; Borgo Santo Spirito; meals €70; 🚊Piazza del Risorgimento) Dine in romantic splendour under Pinturicchio frescoes in the loggia of the 15th-century Palazzo della Rovere. In line with the setting, dishes are based on superb Italian ingredients, such as Tuscan *chianina* beef, and accompanied by top-quality Italian and international wines. Prices are lower at lunch.

Prati

Gelarmony   Gelateria €

Map p198 (Via Marcantonio Colonna 34; ice cream from €1.50; ◷10am-late daily) This superb gelateria is the ideal place for a lunchtime

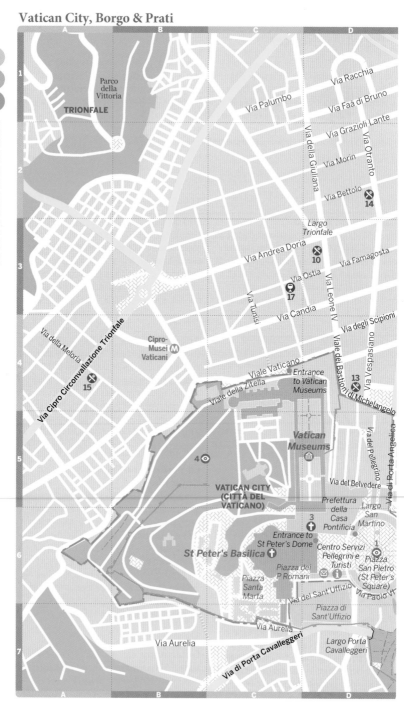

VATICAN CITY, BORGO & PRATI

Parco della Vittoria

TRIONFALE

Via Palumbo

Via Racchia

Via Faà di Bruno

Via Grazioli Lante

Via della Giuliana

Via Morin

Via Otranto

Via Bettolo

14

Largo Trionfale

Via Andrea Doria

10

Via Famagosta

Via Ostia

17

Via Leone IV

Via degli Scipioni

Via Tunisi

Via Candia

Via della Meloria

Via Cipro Circonvallazione Trionfale

Cipro-Musei Vaticani

Viale dei Bastioni di Michelangelo

Via Vespasiano

15

Viale Vaticano

Entrance to Vatican Museums

13

Viale della Zitella

Vatican Museums

Via del Pellegrino

Via di Porta Angelica

4

VATICAN CITY (CITTÀ DEL VATICANO)

Via del Belvedere

Prefettura della Casa Pontificia

Largo San Martino

3

Entrance to St Peter's Dome

St Peter's Basilica

Centro Servizi Pellegrini e Turisti

1

Piazza San Pietro (St Peter's Square)

Piazza dei P Romani

Piazza Santa Marta

Via del Sant'Uffizio

Via Paolo VI

Piazza di Sant'Uffizio

Via Aurelia

Via Aurelia

Via di Porta Cavalleggeri

Largo Porta Cavalleggeri

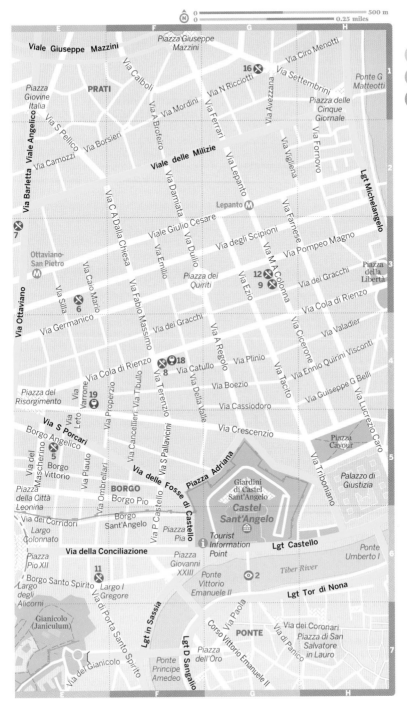

0 500 m
0 0.25 miles

Viale Giuseppe Mazzini

Piazza Giuseppe Mazzini

Via Ciro Menotti

16

Via Settembrini

Ponte G Matteotti

Piazza Giovine Italia

PRATI

Via Calboli

Via N Ricciotti

Via Avezzana

Piazza delle Cinque Giornale

Via S Pellico

Via A Broferio

Via Mordini

Via Ferrari

Via Fornovo

Viale Angelico

Via Borsieri

Via Camozzi

Viale delle Milizie

Via Damiata

Via Lepanto

Via Vigliena

Via Barletta

Via C A Dalla Chiesa

Lepanto M

Via Farnese

Lgt Michelangelo

7

Viale Giulio Cesare

Via degli Scipioni

Ottaviano-San Pietro M

Via Caio Mario

Via Duilio

Via Emilio

Via degli Scipioni

Via Pompeo Magno

Via M A Colonna

Via dei Gracchi

Piazza della Libertà

Via Ottaviano

Via Silla

Piazza dei Quiriti

12

9

Via Ezio

Via Cola di Rienzo

Via Germanico

6

Via Fabio Massimo

Via dei Gracchi

Via Cicerone

Via Valadier

Via Cola di Rienzo

Via Varrone

Via Properzio

Via Tibullo

Via A Regolo

Via Plinio

Via Tacito

Via Ennio Quirini Visconti

Via Catullo

8

18

Via Della Valle

Via Boezio

Via Guiseppe G Belli

Piazza del Risorgimento

Via Leto

Via Cancellieri

Via Terenzio

Via Cassiodoro

Via Lucrezio Caro

19

Via S Pallavicini

Via Crescenzio

Via S Porcari

Borgo Angelico

Via Plauto

Via delle Fosse di Castello

Piazza Adriana

Piazza Cavour

Via del Mascherino

5

Borgo Vittorio

Via Ombrellari

BORGO

Borgo Pio

Giardini di Castel Sant'Angelo

Via Triboniano

Piazza della Città Leonina

Via dei Corridori

Borgo Sant'Angelo

Via P Castello

Piazza Pia

Castel Sant'Angelo

Palazzo di Giustizia

Largo Colonnato

Tourist Information Point

Lgt Castello

Ponte Umberto I

Piazza Pio XII

Via della Conciliazione

Piazza Giovanni XXIII

2

Tiber River

Borgo Santo Spirito

11

Largo I Gregore

Ponte Vittorio Emanuele II

Lgt Tor di Nona

Largo degli Alicorni

Lgt in Sassia

Via di Porta Santo Spirito

Gianicolo (Janiculum)

Via Paola

PONTE

Via dei Coronari

Via di Panico

Piazza di San Salvatore in Lauro

Corso Vittorio Emanuele II

Lgt D Sangallo

Piazza dell'Oro

Via del Gianicolo

Ponte Principe Amedeo

Vatican City, Borgo & Prati

dessert, a mid-afternoon treat, an evening fancy – in fact, anything at any time. Alongside delicious ice cream, there's a devilish selection of creamy Sicilian sweets, including the best *cannoli* (pastry tubes filled with sweetened ricotta and candied fruit or chocolate pieces) this side of Palermo.

Mondo Arancina   Sicilian €

Map p198 (Via Marcantonio Colonna 38; arancine from €2) All sunny yellow ceramics, cheerful crowds and tantalising deep-fried snacks, this bustling takeaway brings a little corner of Sicily to Rome. Star of the show are the classic fist-sized *arancine*, fried rice balls stuffed with *ragù* and peas.

Osteria dell'Angelo   Trattoria €€

Map p198 (🕿 06 372 94 70; Via Bettolo 24; set menus €25 & €30; ⏱closed lunch Mon & Sat, Sun) Former rugby player Angelo presides over this hugely popular neighbourhood

trattoria (reservations are a must). The set menu features a mixed antipasti, a robust Roman-style pasta and a choice of hearty mains with a side dish. To finish off, you're offered lightly spiced biscuits to dunk in sweet dessert wine.

Hostaria Dino e Tony   Osteria €€

Map p198 (🕿 06 397 33 284; Via Leone IV; meals €30-35; ⏱Mon-Sat) Something of a rarity, Dino e Tony is an authentic osteria in the Vatican area. Kick off with the monumental antipasto, a minor meal in its own right, before plunging into its signature dish, *rigatoni all' amatriciana.* Finish up with a *granita di caffè,* a crushed ice coffee served with a full inch of whipped cream. No credit cards.

Settembrini Café   Modern Italian €

Map p198 (Via Settembrini 25; meals €15) A favourite lunchtime haunt of media execs from the nearby RAI TV offices, this trendy cafe does a roaring trade in tasty bar snacks and fresh pastas. Next door, the main **restaurant** (🕿 06 323 26 17; Via Settembrini 25; meals €60; ⏱closed Sat lunch & Sun) is highly regarded by Roman foodies for its modern cuisine and exemplary wine list.

Dolce Maniera   Bakery €

Map p198 (Via Barletta 27; ⏱24hr) This 24-hour basement bakery supplies much of the neighbourhood with breakfast. Head here for cheap-as-chips *cornetti,* slabs of pizza, *panini* and an indulgent array of cakes.

Del Frate   Wine Bar €€

Map p198 (🕿 06 323 64 37; www.enotecadelf rate.it; Via degli Scipioni 122; meals €40; ⏱Mon-Sat; Ⓜ Ottaviano–San Pietro) Locals love this upmarket wine bar with its simple wooden tables and high-ceilinged brick-arched rooms. There's a formidable wine list and a small, but refined, selection of beef and tuna tartares, appetising salads, cheeses and fresh pastas.

Franchi   Delicatessen €

Map p198 (🕿 06 687 46 51; Via Cola di Rienzo 198; snacks €2.50-4; ⏱9am-8.30pm;

MARTIN MOOS/LONELY PLANET IMAGES ©

Ⓜ Ottaviano–San Pietro) One of Rome's historic delicatessens, Franchi is great for a swift bite, or to stock up on stuff to take home. White-jacketed assistants work with practised dexterity slicing hams, cutting cheese, weighing olives and preparing *panini*, to take away or eat at stand-up tables.

Aurelio

Pizzarium   Pizza al Taglio €
Map p198 (Via della Meloria 43; pizza slice €2-3) It's worth searching for this unassuming takeaway near the Cipro–Musei Vaticani metro station for superb fried snacks and *pizza a taglio*. Pizza toppings are original and intensely flavoursome, and the pizza base manages to be both fluffy and crisp. Eat standing up, and wash it down with a chilled beer.

Ⓠ Drinking & Nightlife

The quiet area around the Vatican harbours a few charming wine bars and cafes. For nightlife there are a couple of live-music venues, including Italy's best jazz club.

Prati

Alexanderplatz   Live Music
Map p198 (📞 06 397 42 171; www.alexander platz.it; Via Ostia 9; admission €15; ⏰ 8pm-2am; Ⓜ Ottaviano–San Pietro) Rome's top jazz joint attracts top international performers and a passionate, knowledgeable crowd. You'll need to book a table if you want dinner, and the music starts around 10pm.

Fonclea   Live Music
Map p198 (📞 06 689 63 02; www.fonclea.it; Via Crescenzio 82a; ⏰ 7pm-2am Sep-May; 🚇 Piazza del Risorgimento) Fonclea is a great little pub venue for live music, with bands playing anything from jazz to soul, funk to rockabilly and African sounds (gigs start at around 9.30pm).

Castroni   Cafe
Map p198 (Via Cola di Rienzo 196; ⏰ 8am-8pm; Ⓜ Ottaviano–San Pietro) This landmark food shop has an in-store cafe that does a roaring trade in morning cappuccinos and *cornetti* (Italian croissants).

Villa Borghese & Northern Rome

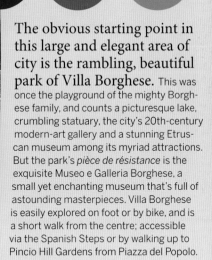

The obvious starting point in this large and elegant area of city is the rambling, beautiful park of Villa Borghese. This was once the playground of the mighty Borghese family, and counts a picturesque lake, crumbling statuary, the city's 20th-century modern-art gallery and a stunning Etruscan museum among its myriad attractions. But the park's *pièce de résistance* is the exquisite Museo e Galleria Borghese, a small yet enchanting museum that's full of astounding masterpieces. Villa Borghese is easily explored on foot or by bike, and is a short walk from the centre; accessible via the Spanish Steps or by walking up to Pincio Hill Gardens from Piazza del Popolo.

Northern Rome also harbours two of Rome's most important modern buildings: Renzo Piano's extraordinary cultural centre, Auditorium Parco della Musica, and Zaha Hadid's contemporary art gallery, MAXXI. To reach these, take a tram from Piazzale Flaminio up Via Flaminia.

Villa Borghese (p211)

Villa Borghese & Northern Rome Highlights

Museo e Galleria Borghese (p208)

This lavish rococo building, resembling an oversized jewellery box, is packed full of master-pieces. It's a survey of genius, from Gian Lorenzo Bernini's incredible marble sculptures on the lower floor, to a feast of works by Titian, Caravaggio and Raphael on the first. The size of the museum means you won't feel overwhelmed. It's essential to book ahead.

1

MOVEMENTWAY/IMAGEBROKER ©

Villa Borghese (p211)

2

Just north of Tridente and the Centro Storico, the bucolic park of Villa Borghese is a rambling expanse of rolling, umbrella pine-shaded space, with countless sun-dappled corners and some superb museums, including the Museo de Galleria Borghese and the Museo Nazionale Etrusco di Villa Giulia. It's ideal for a leisurely bicycle ride, a wander around the ornamental lake, or a restorative picnic.

YANNICK LUTHY/ALAMY ©

Auditorium Parco della Musica (p213) ③

The scarab-like pods of the Auditorium Parco della Musica contain three concert halls, whose interiors architect Renzo Piano fine-tuned by studying the construction of a lute – the resulting acoustics are heavenly. Rome's foremost cultural space also has a dazzling programme of music and dance, ranging from stars such as Patti Smith to myriad themed festivals and classical performances.

④ Museo Nazionale Etrusco di Villa Giulia (p210)

In any other city, this museum would be the centre of attention, with its wealth of ancient Etruscan artefacts housed in a magnificent villa in Villa Borghese park. But, this being Rome, it feels off the beaten track. Anyone intrigued by the rich culture that preceded the Roman Empire will be fascinated by this insight into Etruscan life.

⑤ MAXXI (p213)

MAXXI (Museo Nazionale delle Arti del XXI Secolo) is Rome's foremost contemporary art gallery. It opened in 2010 and was designed by Iraqi architect Zaha Hadid. To visit is a mesmerising experience. The walls, made of reinforced concrete, seem to wrap around you like undulating silk veils, and the meandering, intertwining tunnels, lit by natural light, invite you to get lost among the galleries.

Villa Borghese & Northern Rome Walk

This meander through the green, sun-dappled pathways of Villa Borghese park takes you to the major sights, including the Galleria e Museo Borghese and the boating lake, while allowing plenty of scope for rest and relaxation.

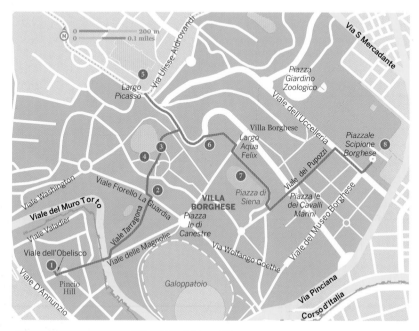

WALK FACTS

- **Start** Pincio
- **Finish** Galleria e Museo Borghese
- **Distance** 1.5km
- **Duration** Three hours

1 Pincio

Start your walk with a wonderful view across Rome's golden and russet rooftops and domes from the **Pincio Hill Gardens** (p104), which overlook Piazza del Popolo. Behind the viewpoint is a small square called Piazzale Napoleone I. Take Viale Adamo Mickievicz south out of the piazza and then turn left into Piazza Bucarest, from where you walk along Via Obelisco.

2 Museo Carlo Bilotti

Carry straight on along Via Obelisco, cross the footbridge, then take the left fork onto Viale Tarragona, which will eventually lead you to the Villa Borghese orangery. This houses the **Museo Carlo Bilotti**, the art collection of billionaire cosmetics magnate Carlo Bilotti, which includes works by Warhol and de Chirico.

3 Il Lago

Walk around to the back of the museum and take the path that leads out from the building (and joins Viale del Lago). Turn left and walk towards the small boating lake, **Il Lago**. This picturesque spot is very much of the Romantic age; the classical Temple of Aesculapius on the island dates to the 19th century.

④ Casina del Lago

If you fancy stopping for a drink or something to eat, the **Casina del Lago** (p216) is a graceful neoclassical pavilion, ideal for a coffee or a cocktail, in a serene setting close to the lake. The outside tables are a boon in summer.

⑤ Galleria Nazionale d'Arte Moderna

A short walk from the lake is **Galleria Nazionale Arte Moderna** (p211). Besides its 20th-century art collection, the gallery also includes works by Modigliani, de Chirico, Degas, Cezanne, Kandinsky and Mondrian, and has a particularly nice cafe. The park's other great museum, the **Museo Nazionale Etrusco** in the 16th-century Villa Giulia, is a short walk downhill from here.

⑥ Silvano Toti Globe Theatre

Take Viale di Valle Giulia back from the Galleria and en route you'll pass the **Silvano Toti Globe Theatre** (p217), a replica of an Elizabethan theatre that resembles the Globe Theatre in London. It hosts a busy programme of Shakespeare in Italian. Silvano Toti was a builder and patron of the arts.

⑦ Piazza di Siena

From the theatre, walk southeast to find this historic racetrack. Named for the Borghese family's city of origin, the beautifully set, 200m-long, oval **Piazza di Siena** (p211) saw its first equestrian event in 1922. It hosted Olympic events in 1960, and today is the venue for demonstrations and the CSIO Rome (the national showjumping event).

⑧ Museo e Galleria Borghese

From the Piazza di Siena, turn north up Viale dei Pupazzi, then right onto Viale dell'Uccelliera. Gloriously symmetrical, the **Casino Borghese** (p209) rises out of its manicured gardens like a rococo dream. The building itself is a pleasure to look at – its stone a pale pinkish-grey, surmounted by statuary that resembles cameo brooches. Inside, it's filled with a dazzling array of masterpieces, including works by Bernini, Titian and Caravaggio.

 The Best...

PLACES TO EAT

ReD The Auditorium's fashionable, loungey restaurant–bar, with creative cuisine and popular *aperitivo*. (p215)

Al Settimo Gelo Delicious artisanal ice cream that lives up to its name; a play on 'Seventh Heaven'. (p215)

PLACES TO DRINK

Casina del Lago Elegant neoclassical park cafe that is at its best in summer. (p216)

Brancaleone A former *centro sociale* (social centre), this is where to go for the funkiest house, electronica, hip hop and more, with big-name DJs. (p216)

MUSEUMS & GALLERIES

Museo e Galleria Borghese A perfect, masterful collection in a picturesque, bijou building. (p208)

Museo Nazionale Etrusco di Villa Giulia Fantastic array of ancient Etruscan artefacts, housed in a 16th-century papal palace. (p210)

Galleria Nazionale d'Arte Moderna Splendid and unsung 20th-century art collection housed in belle époque splendour. (p211)

MAXXI Zaha Hadid's spectacular building is worth a visit in itself, and harbours the latest in contemporary art. (p213)

Galleria Nazionale d'Arte Moderna
MARTIN MOOS/LONELY PLANET IMAGES ©

Don't Miss
Museo e Galleria Borghese

If you have time, or inclination, for only one art gallery in Rome, make it this one. Housing the 'queen of all private art collections', it provides the perfect introduction to Renaissance and baroque art without ever being overwhelming. To limit numbers, visitors are admitted at two-hourly intervals, so you'll need to call to prebook, and then enter at an allotted entry time, but trust us, it's worth it.

Map p212

📞 06 3 28 10

Piazzale del Museo Borghese 5

adult/reduced €8.50/5.25

audioguide €5

🕐 9am-7pm Tue-Sun, prebooking required

🚌 Via Pinciana

Villa

Known as the Casino Borghese, the villa was originally built by Cardinal Scipione to house his immense art collection. However, it owes its current neoclassical look to a comprehensive 18th-century facelift carried out by Prince Marcantonio Borghese, a direct descendant of the cardinal.

Ground Floor

The entrance hall features 4th-century floor mosaics of fighting gladiators and a 2nd-century *Satiro Combattente* (Fighting Satyr).

Sala I is centred on Antonio Canova's daring depiction of Napoleon's sister, Paolina Bonaparte Borghese, reclining topless as *Venere Vincitrice* (Venus Victrix; 1805–8).

But it's Gian Lorenzo Bernini's spectacular sculptures – flamboyant depictions of pagan myths – that really steal the show. Just look at Daphne's hands morphing into leaves in the swirling *Apollo e Dafne* (1622–5) in Sala III, or Pluto's hand pressing into the seemingly soft flesh of Persephone's thigh in the *Ratto di Proserpina* (Rape of Proserpina; 1621–2) in Sala IV.

Caravaggio, one of Cardinal Scipione's favourite artists, dominates Sala VIII.

Picture Gallery

With works representing the best of the Tuscan, Venetian, Umbrian and northern European schools, the upstairs picture gallery offers a wonderful snapshot of European Renaissance art.

In Sala IX don't miss Raphael's extraordinary *La Deposizione di Cristo* (The Deposition; 1507) and his charming *Dama con Liocorno* (Lady with a Unicorn; 1506).

Moving on, Sala XIV boasts two self-portraits of Bernini and Sala XVIII contains two significant works by Rubens: *Deposizione nel Sepolcro* (The Deposition; 1602) and *Susanna e I Vecchioni* (Susanna and the Elders; 1605–7). The highlight is Titian's early masterpiece, *Amor Sacro e Amor Profano* (Sacred and Profane Love; 1514) in Sala XX.

1 **VENERE VINCITRICE**
Antonio Canova's depiction of Napoleon's sister, Paolina Borghese, as Venere Vincitrice (Venus Victorious) is sublime. You could spend hours marvelling at how Canova managed to make the figure 'sink' into the cushions. The way the drapery flows so effortlessly over her body is equally impressive.

2 **RATTO DI PROSERPINA**
Gian Lorenzo Bernini's sculpture *The Rape of Proserpina* (1621–2) is incredible in that its twisting composition allows the simultaneous depiction of Pluto's abduction of Proserpina, their arrival in the underworld and her praying for release. To experience the narrative, start from the left, move to the front, and then view it from the right.

3 **RITRATTO DI GIOVANE DONNA CON UNICORNO**
Raphael's portrait *The Young Woman with a Unicorn* (c 1506) was inspired by da Vinci's *Lady with an Ermine* (1490). The painting originally depicted a woman holding a dog, a symbol of fidelity. But when the marriage did not take place, scholars believe, Raphael replaced the dog with a unicorn, a symbol of chastity or virginity.

4 **SATIRE SU DELFINO**
In Sala VII, the 'Egyptian Room', you'll find the *Satyr on a Dolphin*, dating from the 2nd century and probably intended for a fountain. The piece is believed to have inspired Raphael's design for the figure of *Jonah and the Whale* in the Chigi Chapel inside the Chiesa di Santa Maria del Popolo (p105).

5 **BACCHINO MALATO**
Of the many Caravaggio paintings, *Sick Bacchus* (1592–5) is particularly intriguing for its portrayal of the god of heady pleasures as a pale, tired-looking youth. Scholars believe the self-portrait was executed when Caravaggio was suffering from malaria. Cardinal Scipione Borghese, who formed the Borghese art collection, was a strong believer in the young artist's talent, buying pictures rejected by those who had commissioned them.

Discover Villa Borghese & Northern Rome

🔁 Getting There & Away

○ Bus Buses 116, 52 and 53 head up to Villa Borghese from Via Vittorio Veneto near Barberini metro station. There are regular buses along Via Nomentana and Via Salaria.

○ Metro To get to Villa Borghese by metro, follow the signs up from Spagna station (line A).

○ Tram Tram 2 trundles up Via Flaminia from Piazzale Flaminio above Flaminio metro station (line A).

Bioparco
GIORGIO COSULICH/GETTY IMAGES ©

 Sights

This large and attractive area boasts several fascinating sights including one of the city's best art galleries, a cutting-edge cultural centre and a couple of contemporary museums. Villa Borghese park provides a welcome escape from the bustle of the city centre.

Villa Borghese & Around

Museo e Galleria Borghese   Museum, Art Gallery
See p206.

Museo Nazionale Etrusco di Villa Giulia   Museum
Map p212 (☎ 06 322 65 71; Piazzale di Villa; adult/reduced €4/2; ⊘8.30am-7.30pm, last admission 6.30pm Tue-Sun; 🚍Viale delle Belle Arti) Italy's finest collection of Etruscan treasures is housed in Villa Giulia, Pope Julius III's Renaissance palace. There are thousands of exhibits, many of which came from burial tombs in the surrounding region, ranging from domestic utensils to extraordinary bronze figurines and dazzling jewellery. Perhaps the most famous piece is the 6th century BC *Sarcofago degli Sposi* (Sarcophagus of the Betrothed). Unearthed in 400 broken pieces in a tomb in Cerveteri, it depicts a husband and wife reclining on a stone banqueting couch.

Bioparco   Zoo
Map p212 (☎ 06 360 82 11; www.bioparco.it; Viale del Giardino Zoologico 1; adult/child over 1m & under 12yr/child under 1m €12.50/10.50/free; ⊘9.30am-6pm Apr-Oct, 9.30am-5pm Nov-Mar; 🚍Bioparco) A guaranteed kid-pleaser,

MOVEMENTWAY/IMAGEBROKER ©

 Don't Miss
Villa Borghese

Locals, lovers, tourists, joggers – no one can help heeding the call of this ravishing park just north of the historic centre. Originally the grounds of Cardinal Scipione Borghese's 17th-century residence, the park has various museums and galleries, as well as other attractions such as the 18th-century **Giardino del Lago** and **Piazza di Siena**, an amphitheatre used for Rome's top equestrian event in May.

Bike hire is available at various points, including Via delle Belle Arti, for about €5/15 per hour/day.

NEED TO KNOW

Map p212; entrances at Piazzale San Paolo del Brasile, Piazzale Flaminio, Via Pinciana, Via Raimondi; ☉dawn-dusk; ☐Porta Pinciana

Rome's zoo hosts a predictable collection of animals.

Galleria Nazionale d'Arte Moderna
Art Gallery

Map p212 (☏06 322 98 221; www.gnam.arti .beniculturali.it; Viale delle Belle Arti 131; adult/ reduced €8/4; ☉8.30am-7.30pm, last admission 6.45pm Tue-Sun; ☐Piazza Thorvaldsen) This oft-overlooked gallery of modern and contemporary art is definitely worth a visit. Set in a vast belle époque palace are works by some of the most impor- tant exponents of modern Italian art. There are canvases by the *macchiaioli* (the Italian Impressionists) and futurists, as well as several impressive sculp- tures by Canova and major works by Modigliani and De Chirico. International artists are also represented, with works by Degas, Cezanne, Kandinsky, Klimt, Mondrian and Pollock. The gallery's charming terrace cafe is the perfect place for a languorous breather. Entrance to the gallery for visitors with disabilities is at Via Antonio Gramsci 73.

Villa Borghese & Northern Rome

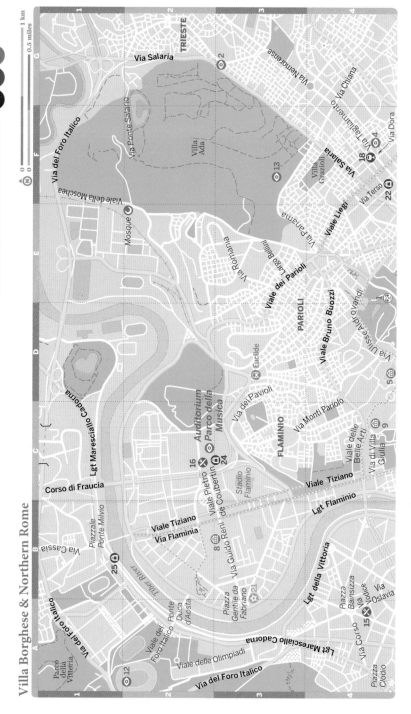

0.5 miles
1 km

TRIESTE

Via Salaria

Via Ponte Salario

Via del Foro Italico

Villa Ada

Viale della Moschea

Mosque

Via Nemorense

Via Chiana

Via Dora

Via Tagliamento

Villa Grazioli

Via Salaria

Via Terso

Viale Liegi

Via Panama

Via Romania

Largo Bellini

Viale dei Parioli

PARIOLI

Viale Bruno Buzzi

Via Ulisse Aldrovandi

Euclide

Via dei Pavioli

Via Monti Pariolo

FLAMINIO

Viale delle Belle Arti

Via di Villa Giulia

Lgt Marescialla Cadorna

Auditorium Parco della Musica

Corso di Fraucia

Viale Pietro de Coubertin

Stadio Flaminio

Viale Tiziano

Lgt Flaminio

Piazzale Ponte Milvio

Via Cassia

Viale Tiziano

Via Flaminia

Via Guido Reni

Tiber River

Piazza Gentile da Fabriano

Ponte Duca d'Aosta

Viale del Foro Italico

Viale delle Olimpiadi

Parco della Vittoria

Via del Foro Italico

Lgt Marescallo Cadorna

Via del Foro Italico

Lgt della Vittoria

Piazza Bainsizza

Via Vodice

Via Corso

Via Oslavia

Piazza Clodio

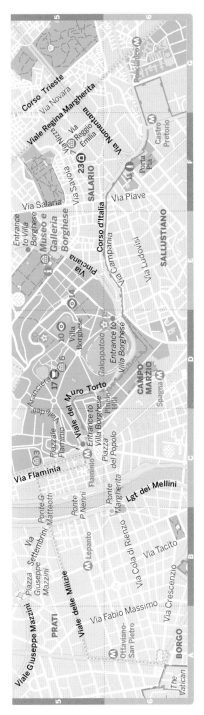

Flaminio

Auditorium Parco della Musica
Concert Hall

Map p212 (☎06 802 41 281; www.auditorium
.com; Viale Pietro de Coubertin 10; guided tours
adult/reduced €9/7; ⏱11am-8pm Mon-Fri,
10am-6pm Sat & Sun; 🚊🚌Viale Tiziano, or
shuttle bus from Stazione Termini) Rome's premier concert complex is not what you'd
expect. Designed by superstar architect
Renzo Piano and inaugurated in 2002, it
consists of three grey pod-like concert
halls set round a 3000-seat amphitheatre and the remains of a 300 BC Roman
villa, discovered shortly after construction work began. It's a truly audacious
work of architecture and is now one of
Europe's most popular arts centres – in
2010 more than a million people attended more than a thousand cultural
events. Guided tours cover the concert
halls, amphitheatre (known as the *cavea*)
and enormous foyer area, which is itself
home to a small archaeology museum
and stages temporary exhibitions. Tours
depart hourly 11.30am to 4.30pm on Saturday and Sunday, and by arrangement
from Monday to Friday.

Museo Nazionale delle Arti del XXI Secolo (MAXXI)
Art Gallery

Map p212 (☎06 321 01 81; www.fondazione
maxxi.it; Via Guido Reni 2f; adult/reduced €11/7;
⏱11am-7pm Tue, Wed, Fri & Sun, 11am-10pm Thu
& Sat; 🚊🚌Viale Tiziano) Rome's flagship
contemporary art gallery opened in May
2010 to grand fanfare and headlines
across the world. The star of the show
was, and still is, Zaha Hadid's stunning €150 million, 27,000 sq m gallery,
universally hailed as a triumph of modern
architecture. Housed in a former barracks,
the building is impressive inside and out.
The multi-layered geometric facade gives
on to a cavernous light-filled interior full of
snaking walkways, suspended staircases,
glass, cement and steel. The gallery has
a small permanent collection but more
interesting are the temporary exhibitions
and installations – check the website for
details.

Villa Borghese & Northern Rome

Explora – Museo dei Bambini di Roma   Museum

Map p212 (☎ 06 361 37 76; www.mdbr.it; Via Flaminia 82; adult/child over 3yr/child 1-3yr/child under 1yr €7/7/3/free; ☉ 9.30am-7.30pm Tue-Sun Sep-Jul, 11.30am-7pm Tue-Sun Aug; Ⓜ Flaminio) Rome's only dedicated kids' museum, Explora is aimed at the under-12s. It's set up as a miniature town where children can play at being grown-ups and with everything from a doctor's surgery to a TV studio, it's a hands-on, feet-on, full-on experience that your nippers will love. Outside there's also a free play park open to all.

Booking is advisable on weekdays, essential at weekends.

Salario & Beyond

Museo d'Arte Contemporanea di Roma (MACRO)   Art Gallery

Map p212 (☎ 06 06 08; www.macro.roma .museum; Via Nizza 138, cnr Via Cagliari; adult/ reduced €11/9; ☉ 11am-10pm Tue-Sun; ☒ Via Nizza) Along with MAXXI, this is Rome's most important contemporary art gallery. Exhibits, which include works by all of Italy's important post-WWII artists, are displayed in what was once a brewery.

The sexy black-and-red interior retains much of the building's original structure but sports a sophisticated steel-and-glass finish thanks to a revamp by French architect Odile Decq.

Catacombe di Priscilla   Catacombs

Map p212 (☎ 06 862 06 272; www.catacombe priscilla.com; Via Salaria 430; guided visit adult/ reduced €8/5; ☉ 8.30am-noon & 2.30-5pm Tue-Sun; ☒ Via Salaria) In the early Christian period, these creepy catacombs were something of a high-society burial ground, known as the Queen of Catacombs. Seven popes and various martyrs were buried in their 13km of tunnels between 309 and 555. They retain a lot of their original decoration, including the oldest ever image of the Madonna, a scratchy fresco dating to the beginning of the third century.

Villa Ada   Park

Map p212 (entrances at Via Salaria & Via Ponte Salario; ☒ Via Salaria) If you're in this neck of the woods and you need a breather, Villa Ada is the place. A big rambling park with wooded paths, lakes and lawns, it was once the private property of King Vittorio Emanuele III.

Nomentano

Porta Pia
Landmark

Map p212 (Piazzale Porta Pia; 🚇Via XX Settembre) This imposing crenellated structure, built near the ruins of the Porta Nomentana, one of the original gates in the ancient Aurelian walls, was Michelangelo's last architectural work.

Eating

Rome's wealthy northern suburbs are speckled with fine restaurants, and there's a cluster around the happening nightlife district of Ponte Milvio.

Flaminio

ReD
Modern Italian €€€

Map p212 (📞06 806 91 630; www.redrestaurant .roma.it; Viale Pietro de Coubertin 30; meals €50; ⊙noon-late; 🚋 or 🚇Viale Tiziano, or shuttle bus M from Stazione Termini) Mingle with the stars at the fashionable restaurant–bar of the Auditorium Parco della Musica. It's a glamorous, loungey place staffed by black-clad waiters and styled in designer red and apple greens. The food is duly creative, with a good selection of pastas and some delicious seafood mains. Also popular is the daily *aperitivo,* served between 6.30pm and 9pm, and the Sunday brunch.

Piazza Mazzini & Around

Al Settimo Gelo
Gelateria €

Map p212 (Via Vodice 21a; ⊙Tue-Sun; 🚇Piazza Giuseppe Mazzini) The name's a play on 'seventh heaven' and it's not a far-fetched title for one of Rome's finest gelaterie. Here at Al Settimo Gelo, there's a clear devotion to the best possible natural ingredients. Try the Greek ice cream or cardamom made to an Afghan recipe.

 Drinking & Nightlife

Many of the big galleries have excellent on-site cafes. Otherwise the drinking scene is centred on Piazzale Ponte Milvio, which is particularly popular with sashaying under-20s, dressed to the nines and driving tiny cars.

Museo d'Arte Contemporanea di Roma (MACRO)

Villa Borghese & Around

Casina del Lago
Cafe

Map p212 (Viale dell'Aranciera 2; 🚇Porta Pinciana) This elegant little cafe, housed in a neoclassical pavilion in Villa Borghese, is a lovely place for a coffee or cocktail, particularly in summer when the outdoor deck seating really comes into its own.

Salario & Beyond

Piper Club
Nightclub

Map p212 (www.piperclub.it; Via Tagliamento 9; 🚇Via Salaria) Keeping Rome in the groove since 1965, Piper has worked through its midlife crisis and is starting to rediscover its mojo as the life and soul of Rome's clubbing scene. As well as hosting funky party nights, it also stages some great gigs – previous performers have included White Lies, Babyshambles and Pete Yorn.

Nomentano

Brancaleone
Nightclub

(www.brancaleone.eu; Via Levanna 11; admission around €10; ⏱Oct-Jun; 🚇Via Nomentana) This former *centro sociale* is now one of Rome's top clubs. Blockbuster DJs ratch up the tempo, pumping up the young, alternative crowd with house, hip-hop, drum'n'bass, reggae and electronica. Everyone from serious musos to skate kids will be in their element. The club is some distance from the city centre, just off Via Nomentana in the outlying Montesacro district.

⭐ Entertainment

Auditorium Parco della Musica
Cultural Centre

Map p212 (📞06 802 41 281; www.auditorium .com; Viale Pietro de Coubertin 30; 🚇 or 🚇Viale Tiziano, or shuttle bus M from Stazione Termini) Rome's state-of-the-art concert complex combines architectural innovation with perfect acoustics: architect Renzo Piano apparently studied the interiors of lutes and violins as part of his design process. Its programme is eclectic, featuring everything from classical music concerts to tango exhibitions, book readings, art exhibitions and film screenings.

The Auditorium is also home to Rome's premier classical-music organisation, the Accademia di Santa Cecilia, and its world-class orchestra, the **Orchestra dell' Accademia Nazionale di Santa Cecilia** (www.santacecilia.it), directed by Antonio Pappano. The academy's programme includes a top-class symphonic season – featuring superstar guest conductors – and short festivals dedicated to single composers.

Teatro Olimpico
Theatre

Map p212 (📞06 326 59 91; www.teatroolimpico.it, in Italian; Piazza Gentile da Fabriano 17; 🚇🚇Piazza Mancini) This is home to the **Accademia Filarmonica Romana** (www.filarmonicaromana.org,

Auditorium Parco della Musica
VINCENZO LOMBARDO/GETTY IMAGES ©

in Italian), one of Rome's major classical music organisations. Past members have included Rossini, Donizetti and Verdi, and it still attracts star performers. Its varied programme concentrates on classical and chamber music but also features opera, ballet and contemporary multimedia events.

Casa del Cinema   Cinema
Map p212 (📞06 06 08; www.casadelcinema.it; Largo Marcello Mastroianni 1; 🚃Via Boncompagni) In Villa Borghese, the Casa del Cinema comprises an exhibition space, two projection halls and a popular cafe. It screens everything from documentaries to shorts, indie flicks and arthouse classics, sometimes in their original language, and hosts a regular programme of film-related events and book presentations.

Silvano Toti Globe Theatre Theatre
Map p212 (📞06 06 08; www.globetheatreroma .com; Largo Aqua Felix, Villa Borghese; 🚃Piazzale Brasile) Like London's Globe Theatre, but with better weather, this is an open-air Elizabethan theatre in the middle of Villa Borghese. The season – mainly Shakespeare – includes occasional productions in English. Tickets start at €10 for a place in the stalls, rising to €22.

🔒 Shopping

Libreria l'Argonauta   Bookstore
Map p212 (www.librerialargonauta.com; Via Reggio Emilia 89; 🚃Via Nizza) Off the main tourist trail, this travel bookshop is a lovely place to browse. The serene atmosphere and shelves of travel literature can easily spark daydreams of far-off places. Staff are friendly and happy to let you drift around the world in peace.

Notebook   Bookstore, Music
Map p212 (www.notebookauditorium.it, in Italian; Viale Pietro de Coubertin 30; ⏰10am-8pm, closed Aug; 🚃 or 🚃Viale Tiziano) Part of the Auditorium Parco della Musica complex, this attractive modern shop offers a sizeable collection of art, film, music, design

Olympic Stadium

Watching a football game at Rome's **Stadio Olimpico** (Map p212; Viale del Foro Italico; Ⓜ Ottaviano–San Pietro & 🚃32) is an unforgettable experience, although you'll have to keep your wits about you as crowd trouble is not unheard of. Throughout the season (September to May), there's a game most Sundays involving one of the city's two teams: AS Roma, known as the *giallorossi* (yellow and reds; www. asroma.it), or Lazio, the *biancazzuri* (white and blues; www.sslazio.it, in Italian). Ticket prices start at €10 and can be bought at Lottomatica (lottery centres), the stadium, ticket agencies, www.listicket.it or one of the many Roma or Lazio stores around the city – try the **AS Roma Store** (Piazza Colonna 360).

and travel books (mostly in Italian), as well as CDs, DVDs and Auditorium merchandise. Not surprisingly it's particularly good for classical music.

Borgo Parioli Market   Market
Map p212 (Via Tirso 14 & Via Metauro 21; ⏰10am-8pm Sat & Sun 1st three weekends of the month; 🚃Viale Regina Margherita) Parioli is Rome's most expensive residential area, and its weekend market is a hot date on the capital's monthly shopping calendar. Among the often-expensive bric-a-brac, you'll find original jewellery and accessories from the 1950s onwards, silverware, paintings, antique lamps and old gramophones.

Ponte Milvio   Market
Map p212 (Piazzale Ponte Milvio; ⏰9am-sunset 1st & 2nd Sun of the month, closed Aug; 🚃Ponte Milvio) The 2nd-century-BC Ponte Milvio is the scene of a great monthly antique market along the riverbank. On the first Sunday of every month stalls spring up between Ponte Milvio and Ponte Duca d'Aosta laden with antiques and collectable clobber.

25 km
15 miles

Tivoli

★ ROME

○ Ostia Antica

Tyrrhenian Sea

Day Trips

Ostia Antica (p220)

With preservation in places matching that of Pompeii, at the ancient Roman port of Ostia Antica you can wander through complete streets, gape at Roman toilets, and see an ancient Roman menu.

Tivoli (p221)

This hilltop town is home to two Unesco World Heritage sites: Villa Adriana, the mammoth country estate of Emperor Hadrian, and 16th-century Villa d'Este, with its fantastical gardens featuring musical fountains.

Carved marble at Piazzale delle Corporazioni (p221), Ostia Antica
MARTIN MOOS/LONELY PLANET IMAGES ©

Ostia Antica

Half a day or more would be ideal to explore the impressive remains of Ostia Antica. This ancient Roman city was a busy working port until 42 AD, and the ruins are substantial and well preserved. The main thoroughfare, the **Decumanus Maximus**, runs over 1km from the city's entrance (the Porta Romana) to the Porta Marina, which originally led to the sea, and it's still the main drag. The site gets busy at weekends, but is usually exhilaratingly empty during the week. Bring a picnic or time your visit so that you can eat at one of the restaurants in the town, as the site cafe feels rather like a canteen and can get busy. To get the most out of your visit, buy a handy site map from the ticket office (€2).

Getting There & Away

Car Take Via del Mare, parallel to Via Ostiense, and follow the signs for the *scavi* (ruins).

Train From Rome, take metro line B to Piramide, then the Ostia Lido train (half-hourly) from Stazione Porta San Paolo, getting off at Ostia Antica. The trip is covered by the standard BIT tickets (see boxed text p268).

Need to Know

- **Area Code** 00119
- **Location** 25km southwest of Rome
- **Information** Ostia Antica (www.ostiaantica.net)

⊙ Sights

Founded in the 4th century BC, Ostia (named for the mouth or *ostium* of the Tiber) became a great port and later a strategic centre for defence and trade, with a population of around 50,000, of whom 17,000 were slaves, mostly from Turkey, Egypt and the Middle East. In the 5th century AD barbarian invasions and the outbreak of malaria led to its abandonment followed by its slow burial – up to 2nd-floor level – in river silt, hence its survival. Pope Gregory IV re-established the town in the 9th century.

Ruins   Ruins

(Scavi Archeologici di Ostia Antica; ☎ 06 563 52 830; www.ostiantica.info, in Italian; Viale dei Romagnoli 717; adult/reduced/child €6.5/3.75/free, car park €2.50; ⊙8.30am-7.15pm Tue-Sun Apr-Oct, to 6pm Mar, to 5pm Nov-Feb, last admission 1hr before closing) Ostia was a busy working port until it began to decline in the 3rd century AD, and the town was made up of restaurants, laundries, shops, houses and public meeting places. These are clearly delineated in the ruins of the site, giving a good impression of what life must have been like when it was at its busiest.

Either side of the main thoroughfare, **Decumanus Maximus**, there are networks of narrow streets lined by buildings.

At one stage, Ostia had 20 baths complexes, including the **Terme di Foro** – these were equipped with a roomful of stone toilets (the *forica*) that remain largely intact. Pivot-holes show that the entrances had revolving doors, and there are 20 marble seats that remain intact. Water flowed along channels in front of the seats, into which the user would dip a sponge on a stick to clean themselves.

The most impressive mosaics on site are at the huge **Terme di Nettuno**, which occupied a whole block and date from Hadrian's renovation of the port. Make sure you climb the elevated platform and look at the three enormous mosaics here, including Neptune driving his seahorse chariot, surrounded by sea monsters, mermaids and mermen. In an adjacent room is a mosaic with Neptune's wife, Amphitrite, on a hippocampus, accompanied by Hymenaeus – the god of weddings – and tritons. In the centre of the baths complex are the remains of a large arcaded courtyard called the Palaestra, in which athletes used to train. There's an impressive mosaic depicting boxing and wrestling.

Next to the Nettuno baths is a good-sized **amphitheatre**, built by Agrippa and later enlarged to hold 4000 people. Stucco is still discernible in the entrance hall. In late antiquity, the orchestra could be flooded to present watery tableaus. By climbing to the top of the amphitheatre and looking over the site, you'll get a good idea of the original layout of the port and how it would have functioned.

Behind the amphitheatre is the **Piazzale delle Corporazioni** (Forum of the Corporations), the offices of Ostia's merchant guilds, which sport well-preserved mosaics depicting the different interests of each business. These include guilds, shippers and traders. The pictures represent dolphins, ships, the lighthouse at Portus (the older nearby settlement) and the grain trade. The symbols here indicate just how international the nature of business in Ostia was. Both Latin and Greek graffiti has been discovered on the walls of the city.

The **Forum**, the main square of Ostia, is dominated by the huge Capitolium, which was built by Hadrian, a temple dedicated to the main Roman deities, the Capitoline triad (Jupiter, Juno and Minerva).

Nearby is another of the highlights of the site: the **Thermopolium**, an ancient cafe. Check out the bar counter, surmounted by a frescoed menu, the kitchen and the small courtyard, where customers would have sat next to the fountain and relaxed with a drink.

The site has a complex comprising a cafeteria and bar (but a picnic is always a good idea) and museum, which houses statues and sarcophagi excavated on site.

Castello di Giulio II Castle
(☎ 06 563 58 013; Piazza della Rocca; ⌚ free 20-min guided tours 10am & noon Tue-Sun, plus 3pm Tue & Thu, max 30 people) Near the entrance to the excavations is this castle, an impressive example of 15th-century military architecture, which lost its purpose when a freak flood changed the course of the river, making the location less accessible.

 # Eating

Ristorante Cipriani Restaurant €€
(☎ 06 5635; 2956; meals €30; ⌚ lunch & dinner Thu-Sat, Mon & Tue, lunch Sun) If it's sunny enough to eat outside, this location can't be beat; dine on *cucina Romana*, with dishes such as *pasta alla' Gricia* (with lardons and onion) and *cacio e pepe* (cheese and pepper), while seated in a cobbled street in the old Borgo by the castle.

Ristorante Monumento Restaurant €€
(☎ 06 565 00 21; Piazza Umberto I 8; meals €30; ⌚ lunch & dinner Tue-Sun) This tucked-away restaurant near the ruins specialises in homemade pasta and fish and has a traditional interior decorated by blown-up old black-and-white photos.

Tivoli

For millennia, the hilltop town of Tivoli has been a summer escape for rich Romans, as amply demonstrated by its two Unesco World Heritage sites, both breathtaking hedonistic playgrounds. Villa Adriana was the mammoth country estate of Emperor Hadrian, and the 16th-century Villa d'Este is a wonder of the High Renaissance. You can visit both in a day, though you'll have to start early. Take a picnic, or organise your day to eat in Tivoli town before heading over to Villa Adriana (which is a short bus ride out of town).

Getting There & Away

Bus Tivoli is 30km east of Rome and is accessible by Cotral bus from outside the Ponte Mammolo station on metro line B (€1.60, every 15 minutes, 50 minutes). However, it's best to buy a Zone 3 BIRG ticket (€6), which will cover you for the whole day. The easiest way to visit both sites is to visit the Villa D'Este first, as it is close to Tivoli town centre. Then take the Cotral bus back towards Ponte Mammolo (€1) from Largo Garibaldi, asking the driver to stop close to Villa Adriana. After visiting the villa, you can then take the same bus (€2, 50 minutes) back to Ponte Mammolo.

Car Take either Via Tiburtina (SS5) or the faster Rome–L'Aquila autostrada (A24).

Train From Stazione Tiburtina (€2.30, 50 minutes to 1 hour 20 minutes, at least hourly).

Need to Know

- **Area Code** 00019
- **Location** 30km east of Rome
- **Tourist Office** Tourist information point (☎07 743 13 536; ⏱9am-5.30pm) On Piazza Garibaldi, where the bus arrives.

◉ Sights

Villa Adriana — Historical Site

(☎06 399 67 900; adult/reduced €8/4, car park €2; ⏱9am-7pm, last admission 5.30pm) Many powerful Romans had villas around Tivoli in ancient times, and this site is Emperor Hadrian's summer residence **Villa Adriana**, 5km outside Tivoli. It set new standards of luxury when it was built between AD 118 and 134, even given the excess of the Roman Empire – it covered around 300 acres, so it was more like a town than a summer house. A model near the entrance gives you an idea of the scale of the original complex, which you'll need several hours to explore. Consider hiring an audioguide (€5), which gives a helpful overview. There's a small cafeteria next to the ticket office, but a nicer option is to bring a picnic lunch or eat in Tivoli.

A great traveller and enthusiastic architect, Hadrian personally designed much of the complex, taking inspiration from buildings he'd seen around the world, in Greece and Egypt. The **pecile**, a large porticoed pool area where the emperor used to stroll after lunch, was a reproduction of a building in Athens. Similarly, the **canopo** is a copy of the sanctuary of Serapis near Alexandria, with a long canal of water, originally surrounded by Egyptian statues, representing the Nile.

To the east of the pecile is one of the highlights, Hadrian's private retreat, the **Teatro Marittimo**. Built on an island in an artificial pool, it was originally a minivilla accessible only by swing bridges, which the emperor would have raised when he felt like retreating into utter solitude. Nearby, the fish pond is encircled by an underground gallery where Hadrian liked to wander. There are also nymphaeums, temples and barracks, and a museum with the latest discoveries from ongoing excavations (often closed).

Villa d'Este — Palazzo

(☎199 766 166, 0445 230310; www.villadestetivoli.info; Piazza Trento; adult/reduced €8/4; ⏱8.30am-1hr before sunset Tue-Sun) In Tivoli's hill-top centre, the steeply terraced gardens of Villa d'Este are a superlative example of the High Renaissance garden, dotted by fantastical fountains that

Gargoyle in the Viale delle Cento Fontaine, Villa d'Este
RAIMUND KUTTER/IMAGEBROKER ©

are all powered by gravity alone, without pumps. The villa was once a Benedictine convent, converted by Lucrezia Borgia's son, Cardinal Ippolito d'Este, into a pleasure palace in 1550. It was extended by his various successors, but fell into romantic dilapidation in the 18th century.

However, renovations began under the tenure of Cardinal Alessandro d'Este, who also hosted Franz Liszt. The pianist, inspired by the gardens, wrote his compositions 'To the Cypresses of the Villa d'Este' and 'The Fountains of the Villa d'Este' during his stay.

The rich Mannerist frescoes of the villa interior merit a glance, but it's the garden that you're here for: the steep terraces harbour water-spouting gargoyles and elaborate avenues lined by deep-green, knotty cypresses. One fountain (designed by Gianlorenzo Bernini) used its water pressure to play an organ concealed in the top part of its structure, and this plays regularly throughout the day. Another highlight is the 130m-long 'Viale delle Cento Fontane' – this Path of 100 Fountains is lined by uniquely carved, gargoyle-like images, featuring grotesque faces, ships and eagles, among others, and joins the Fountain of Tivoli to the 'Rometta' (little Rome) fountain. The latter has a model of Tiberina island, with reproductions of the landmarks of Rome, the she-wolf and other symbols.

The villa is a two-minute walk north from Largo Garibaldi. Picnics are not permitted, but there's a stylish cafe.

Villa Gregoriana   Park
(06 399 67 701; Piazza Tempio di Vesta; adult/child €5/2.50; 10am-6.30pm Tue-Sun Apr–mid-Oct, 10am-2.30pm Mon-Sat, 10am-4pm Sun Mar & mid-Oct–Nov, by appointment Dec-Feb)
In 1826, there was a terrible flood when the waters of the Aniene river overflowed its banks, carrying away houses with the force of the water. As a result, Pope Gregory XVI ordered the river waters be diverted through a tunnel, creating a magnificent waterfall over a steep gorge, crashing down 120m to the bottom of the canyon, and known as the Cascata Grande (Great Waterfall). The architects of this used the old riverbed, the gorge, and the thickly wooded setting, full of caves, ravines and archaeological fragments, to create the park of Villa Gregoriana.

 # Eating

Sibilla   Restaurant €€
(0774 335281; Via della Sibilla 50; meals €50; May-Sep) Chef Adriano Baldassare, who studied under Antonello Colonna, serves up exciting creative cuisine that combines Roman traditions with innovation at this impressive restaurant, which has a glorious setting overlooked by two ruined temples and overlooking the slopes of Villa Gregoriana. The food lives up to the view, there's an extensive wine list, and it's less expensive than you would expect.

Trattoria del Falcone   Trattoria €€
(0774 312358; Via del Trevio 34; meals €30; Wed-Mon) In Tivoli town, this is a lively trattoria with exposed stone walls that's been serving up classic pasta dishes since 1918 and is popular with both tourists and locals.

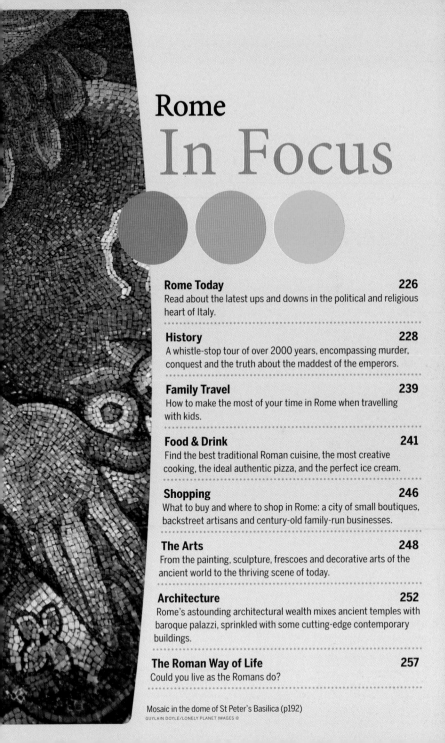

Rome
In Focus

Mosaic in the dome of St Peter's Basilica (p192)
GUYLAIN DOYLE/LONELY PLANET IMAGES ©

Rome Today

Vespa drivers passing in front of Castel Sant'Angelo (p197)

66
Despite its reputation as a chaotic city, Rome can put on a superb show when it wants to.
99

ethnicity (% of population)

90
Italian

10
Other

if Rome were 100 people

69 drive a car
18 ride a scooter
13 rely exclusive on public transport

population per sq km

Rome   Italy   ♦ ≈ 200 people

In the past decade, Rome has done much to pull itself into the 21st century. A major clean-up for the year 2000 Jubilee was followed by a frenzy of artistic and architectural activity in the mid-noughties. Since then, the pace of renovation has slowed and Rome today is a city of ups and downs; on the one hand striving to deal with economic uncertainty and political upheaval, on the other celebrating papal beatification and gay pride with festive abandon.

Rome Celebrates

Despite a reputation as a chaotic and traffic-clogged city – both merited – Rome can put on a superb show when it wants to. On 1 May 2011, Piazza San Pietro provided the lordly setting for the beatification of Pope John Paul II, a ceremony that drew hundreds of thousands of pilgrims from all over the world. A month later, more than 40 heads of state flew into town to join Rome's political leaders in celebrating 150 years

MIRKO MILOVANOVIC/IMAGEBROKER ©

the Roman air, and the next bout of major demonstrations saw a carnival atmosphere as thousands of people celebrated the ousting of Berlusconi in November 2011. After Berlusconi resigned, amid a mounting national debt crisis, economist Mario Monti took over as a non-party leader at the head of a government of technocrats, expecting to serve until the next election.

Cultural Ups & Downs

On the cultural front, the last couple of years have been fairly turbulent. There have been successes – a recent Caravaggio exhibition attracted up to 5000 visitors per day, and more than a million people attended events at the Auditorium in 2010 – but recent talk has been of spending cuts and the effect they will have on the city's high-maintenance monuments. Rome's mayor Gianni Alemanno has been actively pursuing private investment, and in spring 2011 he announced that Diego Della Valle, owner of Tod's (a luxury footwear and fashion company), had offered to finance restoration work at the Colosseum to the tune of €25 million. The news was hailed as a breakthrough in some quarters, but attacked by critics who condemned the idea of a private company holding a stake in a national treasure: under the terms of the deal, Della Valle gets exclusive rights to the Colosseum's image for 15 years.

of Italian unification. No less heartfelt were the festivities that accompanied the huge Gay Pride rally just a few days later.

Scandal & Political Protest

Politics have always been central to Roman life and the scandals surrounding former Italian prime minister Silvio Berlusconi have long been the talk of Rome (and most of the country). The seemingly irrepressible media mogul is facing trials for business-related corruption and fraud offences.

By the summer of 2011, Italy had one of the highest levels of public debt in the Eurozone, and political and economic gloom led to tensions running high in the capital. The riots that exploded in October 2011, off the back of the global anti-capitalism demonstrations, were the worst the city had seen for 30 years. Fortunately, despite the country's problems, there's little menace in

Tourism on the Up

Surprisingly, all this political turmoil has not adversely affected tourism, a mainstay of the Roman economy. According to figures released by the Bilateral Tourism Office of Lazio, there was a rise of around 10% in 2011, to almost 11 million visitors.

227

History

Lupa Capitolina (Capitoline Wolf), Capitoline Museums (p59)

Rome's history spans three millennia, from the classical myths of vengeful gods to the follies of Roman emperors, from Renaissance excess to swaggering 20th-century Fascism. Emperors, popes and dictators have come and gone. Martial ruins, Renaissance palazzi and flamboyant baroque basilicas all have tales to tell – of family feuding, historic upheavals, artistic rivalries, intrigues and dark passions.

Ancient Rome, the Myth

As much a mythical construct as a historical reality, Ancient Rome's image has been carefully nurtured throughout history. Intellectuals, artists and architects have sought inspiration from this skilfully constructed legend, while political and religious rulers have invoked it to legitimise their authority and serve their political ends.

Rome's original mythmakers were the first emperors. Eager to reinforce the city's

753 BC
According to legend, this is the year Romulus kills his twin brother Remus and founds Rome.

status as *Caput Mundi* (capital of the world), they turned to writers such as Virgil, Ovid and Livy to create an official Roman history. These authors, while adept at weaving epic narratives, were less interested in the rigours of historical research and frequently presented myth as reality. In the *Aeneid,* Virgil brazenly draws on Greek legends and stories to tell the tale of Aeneas, a Trojan prince who arrives in Italy and establishes Rome's founding dynasty.

Ancient Rome's rulers were sophisticated masters of spin; under their tutelage, art, architecture and elaborate public ceremony were employed to perpetuate the image of Rome as an invincible and divinely sanctioned power. Monuments such as the Ara Pacis, the Colonna di Traiano and the Arco di Costantino celebrated imperial glories, while gladiatorial games highlighted the Romans' physical superiority. The Colosseum, the Roman Forum and the Pantheon were not only supremely sophisticated feats of engineering, they were also impregnable symbols of Rome's might.

Legacy of an Empire

Rising out of the bloodstained remnants of the Roman Republic, the Roman Empire was the Western world's first great superpower. At its zenith under Emperor Trajan (r AD 98–117), it extended from Britannia in the north to North Africa in the south, from Hispania (Spain) in the west to Palestina (Palestine) and Syria in the east. Rome itself had more than 1.5 million inhabitants and the city sparkled with the trappings of imperial splendour: marble temples, public baths, theatres, circuses and libraries. Decline eventually set in during the 3rd century and by the latter half of the 5th century Rome was in barbarian hands.

In AD 285 the emperor Diocletian, prompted by widespread disquiet across the empire, split the Roman Empire into eastern and western halves – the west centred on Rome and the east on Byzantium (later called Constantinople) – in a move that was to have far-reaching consequences for centuries. In the west, the fall of the Western Roman Empire in AD 476 paved the way for the emergence of the Holy Roman Empire and the Papal States, while in the east Roman (later Byzantine) rule continued until 1453 when the empire was finally conquered by rampaging Ottoman armies.

Christianity & Papal Power

For much of its history Rome has been ruled by the pope, and today the Vatican still wields immense influence over the city.

146 BC

Carthage and Greece are defeated, and Rome becomes undisputed master of the Mediterranean.

73–71 BC

Spartacus leads a slave revolt against dictator Cornelius Sulla. Spartacus and 6000 followers are crucified along Via Appia Antica.

49 BC

'Alea iacta est' ('The die is cast'). Julius Caesar leads his army across the River Rubicon and marches on Rome.

The ancient Romans were remarkably tolerant of foreign religions. They themselves worshipped a cosmopolitan pantheon of gods, ranging from household spirits and former emperors to deities appropriated from Greek mythology (Jupiter, Juno, Neptune, Minerva etc). Religious cults were also popular – the Egyptian gods Isis and Serapis enjoyed a mass following, as did Mithras, a heroic saviour-god of vaguely Persian origin, who was worshipped by male-only devotees in underground temples.

Emergence of Christianity

Christianity entered this religious cocktail in the 1st century AD, sweeping in from Judaea, a Roman province in what is now Israel and the West Bank. Its early days were marred by persecution, most notably under Nero (r 54–68), but it slowly caught on, thanks to its popular message of heavenly reward and the evangelising efforts of Sts Peter and Paul. However, it was the conversion of Emperor Constantine (r 306–37) that really set Christianity on the path to European domination. In 313 Constantine issued the Edict of Milan, officially legalising Christianity, and later, in 378, Theodosius (r 379–95) made Christianity Rome's state religion. By this time, the Church had developed a sophisticated organisational structure based on five major sees: Rome, Constantinople, Alexandria, Antioch and Jerusalem. At the outset, each bishopric carried equal weight but in subsequent years Rome emerged as the senior party. The reasons for this were partly political – Rome was the wealthy capital of the Roman Empire – and partly religious – early Christian doctrine held that St Peter, founder of the Roman Church, had been sanctioned by Christ to lead the universal Church.

Papal Control

But while Rome had control of Christianity, the Church had yet to conquer Rome. This it did in the dark days that followed the fall of the Roman Empire by skilfully stepping into the power vacuum created by the demise of imperial power. And although no one person can take credit for this, Pope Gregory the Great (r 590–604) did more than most to lay the groundwork. A leader of considerable foresight, he won many friends by supplying free bread to Rome's starving citizens and restoring the city's water supply. He also stood up to the menacing Lombards, who presented a very real threat to the city.

It was this threat that pushed the papacy into an alliance with the Frankish kings, an alliance that resulted in the creation of the two great powers of medieval Europe: the Papal States and the Holy Roman Empire. In Rome, the battle between these two

The Best...
Historical Sites

1 Palatino (p54)

2 Roman Forum (p56)

3 The Vatican (p196)

4 Castel Sant'Angelo (p197)

5 Ostia Antica (p220)

44 BC
Julius Caesar is stabbed to death in the Teatro di Pompeo, on modern-day Largo di Torre Argentina (right).

AD 14
Augustus dies after 41 years as Rome's first emperor. His reign is successful, unlike those of his mad successors.

superpowers translated into endless feuding between the city's baronial families and frequent attempts by the French to claim the papacy for their own. This political and military fighting eventually culminated in the papacy transferring to the French city of Avignon between 1309 and 1377, and the Great Schism (1378–1417), a period in which the Catholic world was headed by two popes, one in Rome and one in Avignon.

As both religious and temporal leaders, Rome's popes wielded influence well beyond their military capacity. For much of the medieval period, the Church held a virtual monopoly on Europe's reading material (mostly religious scripts written in Latin) and was the authority on virtually every aspect of human knowledge. All innovations in science, philosophy and literature had to be cleared by the Church's hawkish scholars, who were constantly on the lookout for heresy.

Modern Influence

Almost a thousand years on and the Church is still a major influence on modern Italian life. In recent years, Vatican intervention in political and social debate has provoked fierce divisions within Italy.

This relationship between the Church and Italy's modern political establishment is a fact of life that dates to the establishment of the Italian Republic in 1946. For much of the First Republic (1946–94), the Vatican was closely associated with the Christian Democrat party (DC, *Democrazia Cristiana*), Italy's most powerful

Romulus & Remus, Rome's Legendary Twins

The most famous of Rome's many legends is the story of Romulus and Remus, the mythical twins who are said to have founded Rome on 21 April 753 BC.

Romulus and Remus were born to the vestal virgin Rhea Silva after she'd been seduced by Mars. At their birth they were immediately sentenced to death by their great-uncle Amulius, who had stolen the throne of Alba Longa from his brother, Rhea Silva's father, Numitor. But the sentence was never carried out, and the twins were abandoned in a basket on the banks of the Tiber. Following a flood, the basket ended up on the Palatino, where the babies were saved by a she-wolf and later brought up by a shepherd, Faustulus.

Years later, and after numerous heroic adventures, the twins decided to found a city on the site where they'd originally been saved. They didn't know where this was, so they consulted the omens. Remus, on the Aventino, saw six vultures; his brother over on the Palatino saw 12. The meaning was clear and Romulus began building, much to the outrage of his brother. The two subsequently argued and Romulus killed Remus, going on to found his city.

64

Rome is ravaged by a huge fire that burns for five and a half days. Some blame Nero, although he was in Anzio at the time.

67

St Peter and St Paul become martyrs as Nero massacres Rome's Christians.

285

To control anarchy within the Roman Empire, Diocletian splits the Roman Empire into two.

party and an ardent opponent of communism. At the same time, the Church, keen to weed communism out of the political landscape, played its part by threatening to excommunicate anyone who voted for Italy's Communist Party (PCI, *Partito Comunista Italiano*). Today, no one political party has a monopoly on Church favour, and politicians across the spectrum tread warily around Catholic sensibilities. But this reverence isn't limited to the purely political sphere; it also informs much press reporting and even law enforcement. In September 2008, Rome's public prosecutor threatened to prosecute a comedian for comments made against the pope, invoking the 1929 Lateran Treaty under which it is a criminal offence to 'offend the honour' of the pope and Italian president. The charge, which ignited a heated debate on censorship and the right to free speech, was eventually dropped by the Italian justice minister.

Renaissance, a New Beginning

Bridging the gap between the Middle Ages and the modern age, the Renaissance (*Rinascimento* in Italian) was a far-reaching intellectual, artistic and cultural movement. It emerged in 14th-century Florence but quickly spread to Rome, where it gave rise to one of the greatest makeovers the city had ever seen.

Humanism & Rebuilding

The movement's intellectual cornerstone was humanism, a philosophy that focused on the central role of humanity within the universe, a major break from the medieval world view, which had placed God at the centre of everything. It was not anti-religious, though. Many humanist scholars were priests and most of Rome's great works of Renaissance art were commissioned by the Church. In fact, it was one of the most celebrated humanist scholars of the 15th century, Pope Nicholas V (r 1447–84), who is generally considered the harbinger of the Roman Renaissance.

When Nicholas became pope in 1447 Rome was not in a good state. Centuries of medieval feuding had reduced the city to a semi-deserted battleground. In political terms, the papacy was recovering from the trauma of the Great Schism and attempting to face down Muslim encroachment in the east.

It was against this background that Nicholas decided to rebuild Rome as a showcase of Church power. To finance his plans, he declared 1450 a jubilee year, a tried and tested way of raising funds by attracting hundreds of thousands of pilgrims to the city (in a jubilee year anyone who comes to Rome and confesses receives a full papal pardon).

Over the course of the next 80 years or so, Rome underwent a complete overhaul. Pope Sixtus IV (r 1471–84) had the Sistine Chapel built and, in 1471, gave the people of Rome a selection of bronzes that became the first exhibits of the Capitoline Museums. Julius II (r 1503–13) laid Via del Corso and Via Giulia, and ordered Bramante to rebuild

313

Emperor Constantine issues the Edict of Milan, officially establishing religious tolerance.

476

The fall of Romulus Augustulus marks the end of the Western Empire.

754

Pope Stephen II and Pepin, king of the Franks, cut a deal resulting in the creation of the Papal States.

St Peter's Basilica. Michelangelo frescoed the Sistine Chapel and designed the dome of St Peter's, while Raphael inspired a whole generation of painters with his masterful grasp of perspective.

Sack of Rome & Protestant Protest

But outside Rome an ill wind was blowing. The main source of trouble was the longstanding conflict between the Holy Roman Empire, led by the Spanish Charles V, and the Italian city states. This simmering tension came to a head in 1527 when Rome was invaded by Charles' marauding army and ransacked as Pope Clement VII (r 1523–34) hid in Castel Sant'Angelo. The sack of Rome, regarded by most historians as the nail in the coffin of the Roman Renaissance, was a hugely traumatic event. It left the papacy reeling and gave rise to the view that the Church had been greatly weakened by its own moral shortcomings. That the Church was corrupt was well known, and it was with considerable public support that Martin Luther pinned his famous 95 Theses to a church door in Wittenberg in 1517, thus sparking off the Protestant Reformation.

Statue of Neptune, Capitoline Museums (p59)

800
Pope Leo III crowns Pepin's son, Charlemagne, Holy Roman Emperor during Christmas mass at St Peter's Basilica.

1084
Rome is sacked by a Norman army after Pope Gregory VII invites them in to help fight the Holy Roman Emperor Henry IV.

1300
Pope Boniface VIII proclaims Rome's first ever jubilee, offering a full pardon to any who make the pilgrimage to the city.

Counter-Reformation

The Catholic reaction to the Reformation was all-out. The Counter-Reformation was marked by a second wave of artistic and architectural activity, as the Church once again turned to bricks and mortar to restore its authority. But in contrast to the Renaissance, the Counter-Reformation was a period of persecution and official intolerance. With the full blessing of Pope Paul III, Ignatius Loyola founded the Jesuits in 1540, and two years later the Holy Office was set up as the Church's final appeals court for trials prosecuted by the Inquisition. In 1559 the Church published the *Index Librorum Prohibitorum* (Index of Prohibited Books) and began to persecute intellectuals and freethinkers. Galileo Galilei (1564–1642) was forced to renounce his assertion of the Copernican astronomical system, which held that the earth moved around the sun. He was summoned by the Inquisition to Rome in 1632 and exiled to Florence for the rest of his life. Giordano Bruno (1548–1600), a freethinking Dominican monk, fared worse. Arrested in Venice in 1592, he was burned at the stake eight years later in Campo de' Fiori. The spot is today marked by a sinister statue.

Despite, or perhaps because of, the Church's policy of zero tolerance, the Counter-Reformation was largely successful in re-establishing papal prestige. From being a

Carved relief of Giordano Bruno, Campo de' Fiori

1309
Fighting between French-backed pretenders to the papacy and Roman nobility ends in Pope Clement V transferring to Avignon.

1378–1417
Fighting between factions in the Catholic Church leads to the Great Schism. The pope rules in Rome; the antipope in Avignon.

1527
Pope Clement VII takes refuge in Castel Sant'Angelo as Rome is overrun by troops loyal to Charles V, king of Spain.

rural backwater with a population of around 20,000 in the mid-15th century, Rome had grown to become one of Europe's great 17th-century cities, home to Christendom's most spectacular churches and a population of some 100,000 people.

Power & Corruption

The exercise of power has long gone hand in hand with corruption. As the British historian Lord Acton famously put it in 1887, 'Power tends to corrupt; absolute power corrupts absolutely.'

Caligula

Of all Rome's cruel and insane leaders, few are as notorious as Caligula. A byword for depravity, Caligula was hailed as a saviour when he inherited the empire from his great-uncle Tiberius in AD 37. Tiberius, a virtual recluse by the end of his reign, had been widely hated, and it was with a great sense of relief that Rome's cheering population welcomed the 25-year-old Caligula to the capital.

Their optimism was to prove ill-founded. After a bout of serious illness, Caligula began showing disturbing signs of mental instability and by AD 40 had taken to appearing in public dressed as a god. He made his senators worship him as a deity and infamously tried to make his horse, Incitatus, a senator. He was accused of all sorts of perversions and progressively alienated himself from all those around him. By AD 41 his Praetorian Guard had had enough and on 24 January its leader, Cassius Chaerea, stabbed him to death.

Papal Foibles

Debauchery on such a scale was rare in the Renaissance papacy, but corruption was no stranger to the corridors of ecclesiastical power. It was not uncommon for popes to father illegitimate children, and nepotism was rife. The Borgia pope Alexander VI (r 1492–1503) fathered two illegitimate children with the first of his two high-profile mistresses. The second, Giulia Farnese, was the sister of the cardinal who was later to become Pope Paul III (r 1534–59), himself no stranger to earthly pleasures. When not persecuting heretics during the Counter- Reformation, the Farnese pontiff managed to sire four children.

Tangentopoli

Corruption has also featured in modern Italian politics, most famously during the 1990s *Tangentopoli* (Kickback City) scandal. Against a backdrop of steady economic growth, the controversy broke in Milan in 1992 when a routine corruption case – accepting bribes in exchange for public works contracts – blew up into a nationwide crusade against corruption.

1555

As fear pervades Counter-Reformation Rome, Pope Paul IV confines the city's Jews to the area known as the Jewish Ghetto.

1798

Napoleon marches into Rome, forcing Pope Pius VI to flee.

Led by the 'reluctant hero', magistrate Antonio di Pietro, the *Mani Pulite* (Clean Hands) investigations exposed a political and business system riddled with corruption. For once, no one was spared, not even the powerful Bettino Craxi (prime minister between 1983 and 1989), who, rather than face a trial in Italy, fled to Tunisia in 1993. He was subsequently convicted in absentia on corruption charges and died in self-imposed exile in January 2000.

Tangentopoli left Italy's entire establishment in shock, and as the economy faltered – high unemployment and inflation combined with a huge national debt and an extremely unstable lira – the stage was set for the next act in Italy's turbulent political history.

Chief among the actors were Francesco Rutelli, a suave media-savvy operator who oversaw a successful citywide cleanup as mayor of Rome (1993–2001), and the larger-than-life media magnate Silvio Berlusconi, whose three terms as prime minister (1994–5, 2001–06 and 2008–11) were dogged by controversy and scandal.

Ghosts of Fascism

Rome's fascist history is a deeply sensitive and highly charged subject. In recent years historians on both sides of the political spectrum have accused each other of recasting the past to suit their views: left-wing historians have accused their right-wing counterparts of glossing over the more unpleasant aspects of Mussolini's regime, while right-wingers have attacked their left-wing colleagues for whitewashing the facts to perpetuate an over-simplified myth of antifascism.

Mussolini

Benito Mussolini was born in 1883 in Forlì, a small town in Emilia-Romagna. As a young man he was an active member of the Italian Socialist Party, rising through the ranks to become editor of the party's official newspaper, *Avanti!* However, service in WWI and Italy's subsequent descent into chaos led to a change of heart and in 1919 he founded the Italian Fascist Party. Calling for rights for war veterans, law and order, and a strong nation, the party won support from disillusioned soldiers, many of whom joined the squads of Blackshirts that Mussolini used to intimidate his political enemies.

In 1921 Mussolini was elected to the Chamber of Deputies. His parliamentary support was limited but on 28 October 1922 he marched on Rome with 40,000 black-shirted followers. The march was largely symbolic but it had the desired effect. Fearful of civil war between the fascists and socialists, King Vittorio Emanuele III invited Mussolini to form a government. His first government was a coalition of fascists, nationalists and liberals, but victory in the 1924 elections left him much better placed to consolidate his personal power, and by the end of 1925 he had seized complete control of Italy. In order to silence the Church he signed the Lateran Treaty in 1929,

1870

Rome's city walls are breached at Porta Pia and Pope Pius IX is forced to cede the city to Italy. Rome becomes the Italian capital.

1883

In the small town of Forlì in Emilia-Romagna, Italy's future dictator Benito Mussolini is born.

1922

Some 40,000 fascists march on Rome. King Vittorio Emanuele III invites the 39-year-old Mussolini to form a government.

Berlusconi: Italy's Media King

After 1994 Silvio Berlsconi dominated Italian political and public life like a modern-day colossus. A colourful, charismatic and highly divisive character, he was Italy's longest-serving post-war PM and is one of the country's richest men, with a fortune that the US business magazine *Forbes* puts at US$7.8 billion. His business empire spans the media, advertising, insurance, food, construction and sport – he owns Italy's most successful football team, AC Milan.

For much of his controversial political career, he was criticised for his hold over Italy's media and, in particular, for his control of the nation's TV output. Italian TV is dominated by two networks – RAI, the Rome-based state broadcaster, and Mediaset, Italy's largest private media company – and Berlusconi has major interests in both camps. He's the controlling shareholder of Mediaset and as PM wielded enormous influence over RAI. This 'conflict of interest' long aroused debate, both inside and outside Italy, and was one of the reasons Freedom House, the US-based press watchdog, gives Italy only a 'partly free' freedom of press rating.

which made Catholicism the state religion and recognised the sovereignty of the Vatican State.

Abroad, Mussolini invaded Abyssinia (now Ethiopia) in 1935 and sided with Hitler in 1936. In 1940, from the balcony of Palazzo Venezia, he announced Italy's entry into WWII to a vast, cheering crowd. The good humour didn't last, as Rome suffered, first at the hands of its own fascist regime, then, after Mussolini was ousted in 1943, at the hands of the Nazis. Rome was liberated from German occupation on 4 June 1944.

Post-War Period

But defeat in WWII didn't kill off Italian fascism, and in 1946 hardline Mussolini supporters founded the *Movimento Sociale Italiano* (MSI; Italian Social Movement). For close on 50 years this overtly fascist party participated in mainstream Italian politics, while on the other side of the spectrum the *Partito Comunista Italiano* (PCI; Italian Communist Party) grew into Western Europe's largest communist party. The MSI was finally dissolved in 1994, when Gianfranco Fini rebranded it as the post-fascist *Alleanza Nazionale* (AN; National Alliance). AN remained an important political player until it was incorporated into Silvio Berlusconi's *Popolo delle Libertà* coalition in 2009.

Outside the political mainstream, fascism (along with communism) was a driving force of the domestic terrorism that rocked Italy during the *anni di piombo* (years of lead), between the late 1960s and early 1980s. In these years, terrorist groups

1946

The republic is born after Italians vote to abolish the monarchy. Two years later, the Italian constitution becomes law.

2000

Pilgrims pour into Rome from all over the world to celebrate the Catholic Church's Jubilee year.

2001

Charismatic media tycoon Silvio Berlusconi becomes prime minister for the second time.

emerged on both sides of the ideological spectrum, giving rise to a spate of politically inspired violence. Most famously, the communist Brigate Rosse (Red Brigades) kidnapped and killed former PM Aldo Moro in 1978, and the neo-fascist Armed Revolutionary Nuclei bombed Bologna train station in 1980, killing 85 people and leaving up to 200 injured.

In more recent years, extreme right-wing groups have been connected with organised football hooliganism. According to figures released by Italy's Home Ministry in 2009, up to 234 fan groups have been identified as having political ties, of which 61 are said to be closely associated with extreme right-wing movements.

Fascism once again hit the headlines in April 2008 when Gianni Alemanno, an ex-MSI activist and member of AN, was elected mayor of Rome. In his first year in office, Alemanno had to walk an ideological tightrope as he tried to sell himself as a mayor for everyone. Inevitably, though, his fascist past aroused discomfort. The sight of supporters hailing his election victory with the fascist salute – something he was quick to distance himself from – did not go down well in many quarters and in September 2008 he infuriated Rome's Jewish community by refusing to condemn fascism as 'absolute evil'. Ironically, two months later he won praise from the community's leader for leading a group of 250 schoolchildren to Auschwitz and urging them never to forget the tragedy of the Holocaust.

2005

Pope John Paul II dies. He is replaced by Josef Ratzinger (right), who takes the name Benedict XVI.

2008–11

Berlusconi bounces back for a third term as prime minister, but is ousted three years later during the Euro crisis.

Family Travel

JUPITERIMAGES/GETTY IMAGES ©

Despite Rome's lack of child-specific sights, there's plenty to keep the little 'uns occupied and Mum and Dad happy. The Italians love children (especially babies) too, which makes eating out with kids a pleasure.

Things to Do

Children love the Colosseum (p52) and you can fire their imaginations with tales of bloodthirsty gladiators and hungry lions. For maximum effect prep your kids beforehand with some Rome-based films – perhaps the *Lizzie McGuire Movie* or the Olsen Twins *When in Rome;* for older teenagers *Gladiator* is a good bet. Your children might want a photo with one of the costumed Roman legionnaires outside but note that these guys will expect payment of up to €5.

Rome's big art museums are not ideal for toddlers, but not far from Piazza del Popolo, Explora – Museo del Bambini di Roma (p214) is an interactive museum for kids under 12, and has a free play park outside.

For a run around, head to Villa Borghese (p211), Rome's largest central park, which has bicycles for hire. The park is also home to Bioparco (p210), Rome's zoo.

But you don't have to go to the zoo to see animals. There are hundreds of animal sculptures around the city. Kids should look out for an elephant (outside Chiesa di Santa Maria Sopra Minerva), lions (at the foot of the Cordonata staircase up to Piazza del Campidoglio), bees (in Bernini's fountain just off Piazza Barberini), horses, eagles and, of course, Rome's trademark wolf.

The catacombs (p160) on Via Appia Antica are fascinating, creepy underground tunnels, but not suitable for kids under about eight, especially as visits are in guided groups.

A sure-fire kid pleaser (over fives only) is the Time Elevator (p108) just off Via del Corso. Claiming to be Rome's first ever 5D cinema, it screens a virtual romp through Roman history that will have you rolling in your seat (literally).

Out of town, at Ostia Antica (p220) your kids can run along the ancient town's streets, among shops, and up the tiers of its impressive amphitheatre.

Eating & Drinking

All but the most upmarket restaurants are very welcoming to children, even if they don't have specific facilities for them. If there's no children's menu (which is likely), ask for a *mezza porzione* (child's portion). A *seggiolone* is a highchair. Pasta and pizza are ideal eats for children, and are available everywhere you look. While on the move, pizza *al taglio* (by the slice) is a godsend for parents of flagging children. Ice cream is also manna from heaven, served in *coppette* (tubs) or *coni* (cones).

Not For Parents

For an insight into Rome aimed directly at kids, pick up a copy of Lonely Planet's *Not for Parents: Rome*. Perfect for children aged eight and up, it opens up a world of intriguing stories and fascinating facts about Rome's people, places, history and culture.

Need To Know

- Buy baby formula and sterilising solutions at pharmacies. Disposable nappies (diapers; *pannolini*) are available from supermarkets and pharmacies.
- A small, manoeuvrable pram is the best choice if one is necessary – Rome's streets are cobbled and parked cars often block the narrow pavements.
- Under 10s travel free on all public transport.
- Check http://piccolituristi.turismoroma.it.

Food & Drink

Spaghetti alle vongole.

JEAN-BERNARD CARILLET/LONELY PLANET IMAGES ©

This is a city that lives to eat, rather than eats to live. There is an obsession with the best seasonal ingredients, and some of the city's corners of gastronomic heaven are deceptively simple: home-cooked trattoria food or heaven-sent slices of pizza. However, nowadays there are also many chances to sample cucina creativa (creative cooking), where masterful chefs concoct awe-inspiring takes on Roman cuisine.

Roman Cooking

The basics of Roman cuisine have remained the same throughout history, resting on the availability of local ingredients: olives, olive oil, lamb, offal, vegetables, wild greens, pecorino cheese, ricotta, wood-baked bread, pasta and fish.

Classic dishes

Roman favourites are all comfort foods that are seemingly simple (yet notoriously difficult to prepare well) and remarkably tasty. In the classic Roman comedy *I Soliti Ignoti* (Big Deal on Madonna Street; 1958) inept thieves break through a wall to burgle a safe, but find themselves in a kitchen by mistake, and console themselves by cooking *pasta e ceci* (pasta with chickpeas). Other iconic Roman dishes include *carbonara* (pasta with lardons and egg), *amatriciana* (with tomato and lardons) and *cacio e pepe* (with cheese and pepper), appear on almost every menu in Rome.

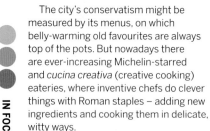

The city's conservatism might be measured by its menus, on which belly-warming old favourites are always top of the pots. But nowadays there are ever-increasing Michelin-starred and *cucina creativa* (creative cooking) eateries, where inventive chefs do clever things with Roman staples – adding new ingredients and cooking them in delicate, witty ways.

Roman-Jewish Cuisine

Most entrenched in culinary tradition is the Jewish Ghetto area, with its hearty Roman-Jewish cuisine, including deep-fried delights and particularly spectacular takes on the artichoke. Deep-frying is a staple of *cucina ebraico-romanesca* (Roman-Jewish cooking), and dates to the period between the 16th and 19th centuries when the Jews were confined to the city's ghetto. To add flavour to their limited ingredients – those spurned by the rich, such as courgette (zucchini) flowers – they began to fry everything from mozzarella to *baccalà* (salted cod).

Culinary Calendar

According to the culinary calendar, which was initiated by the Catholic Church to vary the nutrition of its flock, fish is eaten on Friday, and *baccalà* (salted cod) is often eaten with *ceci* (chickpeas), usually on Wednesday.

Thursday is the day for gnocchi (dumplings). The traditional, heavy Roman recipe uses semolina flour, but you can also find the typical gnocchi with potatoes.

Need to Know

PRICES

The pricing in this chapter refers to the average cost of a meal that includes *primo* (first course), *secondo* (second course) and *dolce* (dessert), plus a glass of wine. Don't be surprised to see *pane e coperto* (bread and cover charge; €1 to €5 per person) added to your bill.

€	under €25
€€	€25 to €50
€€€	over €50

ETIQUETTE

○ Brush up when eating out; Italians dress smartly at most meals.

○ Bite through hanging spaghetti rather than slurping it up.

○ Pasta is eaten with a fork (not fork and spoon).

○ It's OK to eat pizza with your hands.

○ In an Italian home you may *fare la scarpetta* (make a little shoe) with your bread and wipe plates clean of sauces.

○ If invited to someone's home, traditional gifts are a tray of *dolci* (sweets) from a *pasticceria* (pastry shop), a bottle of wine or flowers.

TIPPING

Although service is included, leave a tip: anything from 5% in a pizzeria to 10% in a more upmarket place. At least round up the bill.

Roman Staples
Pizza

Remarkably, pizza was only introduced to Rome post-WWII, by southern immigrants. But it's like it's been here forever, and every Roman's favourite casual meal remains the gloriously simple pizza, with Rome's signature wafer-thin, bubbling-topped pizzas slapped down on tables by waiters on a mission. A pizzeria will, of course, serve pizza, but many also offer a full menu including antipasti, pasta, meat and vegetable dishes. They're often open only in the evening. Most Romans will precede their pizza with a starter of *bruschetta* or *fritti* (mixed fried things, such as zucchini flowers, potato, olives etc) and wash it all down with beer.

For a snack on the run, Rome's *pizza al taglio* (pizza by the slice) places are hard to beat, with some combinations loaded atop thin, crispy, light-as-air, slow-risen bread that verge on the divine.

Seafood

It's by no means all about cheap cuts of meat. Seafood can be excellent in Rome; it's fished locally in Lazio. There are lots of dedicated seafood restaurants, usually upper-range places with delicate takes on fish such as sea bass, skate and tuna.

Offal

For the heart (and liver and brains) of the *cucina Romana,* head to Testaccio, a traditional working-class district, clustered around the city's former slaughter-house. This proximity led to the area specialising in offal – a major feature of Roman cooking. In the past, butchers who worked in the city abattoir were often paid in meat as well as money. But they got the cuts that the moneyed classes didn't want, the offal, and so they developed ways to cook them – usually extremely slowly, to develop the flavour and disguise their origins. The Roman staple *coda alla vaccinara* translates as 'oxtail cooked butcher's style'.

The Best...
Traditional Roman

1 Checchino dal 1887 (p152)

2 Giggetto al Portico D'Ottavia (p91)

3 Campana (p89)

4 Sora Margharita (p92)

Ice Cream

Eating gelato is as much part of Roman life as the morning coffee – try it and you'll understand why. The city has some of the world's finest ice-cream shops, which use only the finest seasonal ingredients. In these artisanal gelaterie you won't find strawberry ice cream in winter, for example, and ingredients are sourced from where they are reputedly the best, so, pistachios from Bronte, almonds from Avola. It's all come a long way since Nero snacked on snow mixed with fruit pulp and honey.

The following are all shining stars of the ice-cream scene, but a rule of thumb for elsewhere is to check the colour of the pistachio: ochre-green = good, bright-green = bad. Most places open from around 8am to 1am, though hours are shorter in winter. Prices range from around €1.50 to €3.50 for a *cona* (cone) or *coppetta* (tub).

Eat as the Romans Do
Breakfast

For *colazione* (breakfast), most Romans head to a bar for a cappuccino and *cornetto* – a croissant filled with *cioccolata* (chocolate), *marmellata* (marmalade) or *crema* (custard cream).

Lunch & Dinner

The main meal of the day is *pranzo* (lunch), eaten at about 1.30pm. Many shops and businesses close for three to four hours every afternoon to accommodate the meal and siesta that follows. On Sundays *pranzo* is sacred.

Cena (dinner), eaten any time from about 8.30pm, is usually a simple affair, although this is changing as fewer people make it home for the big lunchtime feast.

A full Italian meal consists of an antipasto (starter), a *primo piatto* (first course), a *secondo piatto* (second course) with an *insalata* (salad) or *contorno* (vegetable side dish), *dolci* (sweet), fruit, coffee and *digestivo* (liqueur). When eating out, however, you can do as most Romans do, and mix and match: order, say, a *primo* followed by an *insalata* or *contorno*.

Dessert

Dolci (desserts) tend to be the same at every trattoria: tiramisù, *pannacotta* ('cooked cream', with added sugar and cooled to set) and so on, but for a traditional Roman *dolce* you should look out for ricotta cakes – with chocolate chips or cherries or both – at a local bakery. Many Romans eat at a restaurant and then go elsewhere for a gelato and a coffee to finish off the meal.

Aperitivo

Aperitivo is a trend from Milan that's been taken up with gusto in Rome – a buffet of snacks to accompany evening drinks in bars and some restaurants, usually from around 6pm till 9pm, and costing around €8-10 for a drink and unlimited platefuls.

Vegetarians & Vegans

Panic not, vegetarians – you can eat well in Rome, with the choice of bountiful antipasti, pasta dishes, *insalati* (salad), *contorni* (side dishes) and pizzas. There are a couple of extremely good vegetarian restaurants, and some of the more creative restaurants have a greater choice of vegetarian dishes.

Be mindful of hidden ingredients not mentioned on the menu – for example, steer clear of anything that's been stuffed (like courgette flowers, often spiced up with anchovies) or check that it's *senza carne o pesce* (without meat or fish).

Vegans are in for a tougher time. Cheese is used universally, so you must specify that you want something 'senza formaggio' (without cheese). Also remember that pasta fresca, which may also turn up in soups, is made with eggs. The safest bet is to self-cater or try a dedicated vegetarian restaurant, which will always have some vegan options.

Where to Eat

Eateries are divided into several categories.

Fast Food

A tavola calda (hot table) offers cheap, pre-prepared pasta, meat and vegetable dishes. Quality is usually reasonable while atmosphere takes a back seat.

A rosticceria sells cooked meats but often has a larger selection of takeaway food. There are also takeaway pizza joints serving ready pizza al taglio (by the slice). When it's good, it's very good.

Enoteche (Wine Bars)

You can eat well at many enoteche, ie wine bars that usually serve snacks (such as cheeses or cold meats, bruschette and crostini) and some hot dishes. Where these are so good they are worth dining out at, they're listed under 'Eating' in the neighbourhood chapters.

Trattoria, Osteria or Restaurant?

Usually for a full meal you'll want a trattoria, an osteria (neighbourhood inn), a ristorante (restaurant) or a pizzeria. The difference between the different types of eatery is now fairly blurred. Traditionally, trattorias were family-run places that offered a basic, affordable local menu, and there are still lots of these around. There are also new incarnations of these, which use the faithful formula (gingham tablecloths, old friends on the menu) but offer innovative cuisine and scholarly wine lists. Ristoranti, however, offer more choice and smarter service, and are more expensive.

Ethnic restaurants are more prevalent these days, though in Rome Italian food remains king, and the old stalwart trattoria is still where every Roman returns, and some of the city's most memorable culinary experiences are to be had enjoying home-cooked food served by a shuffling matriarch.

Food & Wine Courses

Check out the **Città di Gusto** (City of Taste; ☎ 06 551 12 21; Via Enrico Fermi 161), a six-storey shrine to food created by Italian foodie organisation **Gambero Rosso** (www.gambero rosso.it, in Italian). It has cooking courses starring Rome's top chefs, a wine bar, pizza workshop, cookbook shop and the **Teatro del Vino** for demonstrations, tastings and lessons. For taste-sensation culinary events featuring the best in local produce, there's Rome's **Slow Food movement** (www.slowfoodroma.com, in Italian).

Cookery writer Diane Seed (The Top One Hundred Pasta Sauces) runs her **Roman Kitchen** (☎ 06 678 57 59; http://italiangourmet.com/) several times a year from her kitchen in the Palazzo Doria Pamphilj. There are one-day courses (which include a market visit) costing €200 per day and week-long courses for €1000.

The Best...
Value

1 Da Enzo (p178)

2 Enoteca Corsi (p87)

3 Open Colonna (lunch; p135)

4 Sora Margherita (p92)

IN FOCUS FOOD & DRINK

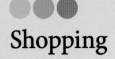

Shopping

Cartier store on Via dei Condotti

RAIMUND KUTTER/IMAGEBROKER ©

Rome's shops, studios and boutiques make retail therapy diverting enough to distract you from the incredible cityscape. Wander the capital's backstreets and you'll find yourself glancing into dusty workshops. Narrow lanes are dotted by beautiful boutiques and department stores have an old-style glamour. This is a city still dominated by the individual shop.

What to Buy

Italy's reputation for quality is deserved, and Rome is a splendid place to shop for designer clothes, shoes and leather goods.

There is also a wonderful array of small designers selling one-off, hand-made outfits, places to buy bespoke shoes, and work-of-art jewellery and leather goods.

Foodstuffs are, of course, the tops, and designer homewares are another Italian speciality.

High Fashion

Big-name designer boutiques glitter and gleam in the Tridente area. The immaculately clad high-fashion spine is Via dei Condotti, but there's also lots of high fashion in Via Borgognona, Via Frattina, Via della Vite and Via del Babuino.

One-Off Boutiques & Vintage

Best for cutting-edge designer boutiques and vintage clothes is bohemian Via del Governo Vecchio, running from a small square just off Piazza Navona, the area around Campo de' Fiori, and the Monti district, which is dotted with artisanal jewellers and small designer clothing boutiques.

Antiques

For antiques shopping, Via dei Coronari, Via Margutta, Via Giulia and Via dei Banchi Vecchi are the best places to look – quality is high, as are the prices.

Artisans

Rome's shopping scene has a surprising number of artists and artisans who create goods on the spot, with several places in Tridente and the Centro Storico where you can commission a bespoke bag, wallet or belt.

Foodstuffs

You're in the Italian capital, so of course it's deli heaven. Prepare to enter some of the world's great temples to food, breathe in sweet and savoury scents, and get lost among all the tantalising jars and bottles. Prime among Rome's foodstuff stores are Vineri Roscioli Salumeria (p90) and Teichner (p118).

The Best...
Shops

1 Confetteria Moriondo & Gariglio (p97)

2 Vertecchi (p116)

3 Lucia Odescalchi (p119)

4 Armando Rioda (p116)

5 Bottega di Marmoraro (p117)

Need to Know

PRICES & SALES

While prices here are not as steep as they are in, say, London or Paris, they're still not cheap. To grab a bargain, you should try to time your visit to coincide with the *saldi* (sales). Winter sales run from early January to mid-February and summer sales from July to early September.

PAYMENT & RECEIPTS

Most shops accept credit cards and many accept travellers cheques. Note that you're required by Italian law to have a *ricevuta* (receipt) for your purchases.

TAXES & REFUNDS

Non-EU residents who spend more than €155 at shops with a 'Tax Free for Tourists' sticker are entitled to a tax rebate. You'll need to fill in a form in the shop and get it stamped by customs as you leave Italy.

The Arts

Rome's turbulent history and magical cityscape have inspired countless painters, sculptors, filmmakers, writers and musicians. Roman antiquity fired the imagination of Renaissance artists; the Counter-Reformation fuelled baroque art; and the experience of Mussolini and WWII found expression in gritty neorealist cinema.

Painting & Sculpture

Rome's churches contain more masterpieces than many midsize countries and the city's galleries are packed with famous works of art.

Etruscan Groundwork

The Etruscans placed great importance on their funerary rites and they developed sepulchral decoration into a highly sophisticated artform, an example is the *Sarcofago degli Sposi* (Sarcophagus of the Betrothed) in the Museo Nazionale Etrusco di Villa Giulia. To see bright Etruscan frescoes, architecture and treasures in situ head out of town to Cerveteri and Tarquinia.

Roman Developments

In art, as in architecture, the ancient Romans borrowed heavily from the Etruscans and Greeks. By the 1st century BC, floor mosaics were a popular form of home decor. Wall mosaics, however, were the preserve of only the wealthiest citizens. In the Museo Nazionale Romano: Palazzo Massimo alle Terme, you'll find some spectacular wall mosaics from Nero's villa in Anzio, as well as some superb 1st-century-BC frescoes from Villa Livia, one of the homes of Livia Drusilla, Augustus' wife.

Sculpture was an important element of Roman art, and was largely influenced by Greek styles. Early Roman sculptures were often made by Greek artists or were copies of Greek works. They were largely concerned with visions of male beauty in mythical settings – the *Apollo Belvedere* and the *Laocoön* in the Vatican Museums' Museo Pio-Clementino are classic examples.

However, over time, Roman sculpture lost its obsession with form and began to focus on accurate representation, mainly in the form of sculptural portraits.

From the time of Augustus (r 27 BC–AD 14), art was increasingly used to serve the state, and artists came to be regarded as little more than state functionaries. This new narrative art often took the form of relief decoration recounting the story of great military victories – the Colonna di Traiano and Ara Pacis are two examples.

Early Christian Art

Rome's earliest preserved Christian artworks are the faint biblical frescoes in the Catacombe di Priscilla on Via Salaria and the Catacombe di San Sebastiano on Via Appia Antica.

With the legalisation of Christianity in the 4th century, these images began to move into the public arena, appearing in mosaics across the city; beautiful examples may be seen in the Basilica di Santa Maria Maggiore.

Eastern influences became much more pronounced between the 7th and 9th centuries, when Byzantine styles swept in from the east – you can see such brighter, golden works in the Basilica di Santa Maria in Trastevere.

Renaissance

Originating in Florence, the Renaissance arrived in Rome in the latter half of the 15th century, and was to have a profound impact on the city as the top artists of the day, including Michelangelo Buanarroti and Raphael (Raffaello Sanzio), were summoned to decorate the many new buildings going up around town.

Counter-Reformation & Baroque

The baroque burst onto Rome's art scene in the early 17th century. Combining a dramatic sense of dynamism with highly charged emotion, it was enthusiastically appropriated by the Catholic Church. At the time the Church was viciously persecuting Counter-Reformation heresy and the powerful popes of the day saw baroque art as an ideal propaganda tool. A key, if not typical, painter of the period was the Milan-born Caravaggio (1573–1610), whose realistic interpretations of religious subjects caused consternation in Rome's art world. But while Caravaggio shocked his patrons, Gian Lorenzo Bernini (1598–1680) delighted his by combining emotion, sensuality and dramatic action, and helped to shape modern Rome with his many architectural and sculptural works.

20th Century

In artistic terms, the early 20th century was marked by the development of two movements: futurism and metaphysical painting (*pittura metafisica*), an early form of surrealism.

In contrast to the brash vitality of futurism, metaphysical paintings were peopled by mysterious images conjured up from the subconscious world. Key works from both movements may be seen at the Galleria Nazionale d'Arte Moderna.

Contemporary Scene

Rome's contemporary arts scene now has two flagship arts centres: the Museo Nazionale delle Arti del XXI Secolo (MAXXI), and the Museo d'Arte Contemporanea di Roma (MACRO), with small permanent collections and regular changing exhibitions.

Literature

Rome has a rich literary tradition, encompassing everything from ancient satires to contemporary thrillers.

Classics

Famous for his blistering oratory, Marcus Tullius Cicero (106–43 BC) was the Roman Republic's pre-eminent author. A brilliant barrister, he became consul in 63 BC and subsequently published many philosophical works and speeches. His contemporary, Catullus (c 84–54 BC) cut a very different figure. A passionate and influential poet, he is best known for his epigrams and erotic verse.

On becoming emperor, Augustus (aka Octavian) encouraged the arts, and Virgil (70–19 BC), Ovid, Horace and Tibullus all enjoyed freedom to write. Of the works produced in this period, it's Virgil's rollicking *Aeneid* that stands out.

Rome as Inspiration

With its magical cityscape and historic atmosphere, Rome has provided inspiration for legions of foreign authors.

In the 18th century, historians and Grand Tourists poured into Rome from northern Europe. The German author Johann Wolfgang von Goethe captures the elation of discovering ancient Rome in his travelogue *Italian Journey* (1817). The city was also favoured by the Romantic poets: John Keats (who died here, of TB), Lord Byron, Percy Bysshe Shelley, Mary Shelley and other writers all spent time here. In the 19th century, American author Nathaniel Hawthorne wrote *The Marble Faun* (1860) after two years in Italy. Henry James' *Italian Hours, Daisy Miller* and *Portrait of a Lady* all feature the city, and Dickens visited in 1844, writing *Pictures from Italy*.

In more recent fiction, Rome has provided a setting for many a blockbuster: Dan Brown's thriller *Angels and Demons* (2001) is set in Rome, as is Kathleen A Quinn's warm-hearted love story *Leaving Winter* (2003). Jeanne Kalogridis evokes the 15th century in her sumptuous historical novel *The Borgia Bride* (2006).

Robert Harris's accomplished fictional biography of Cicero, *Imperium* (2006), evokes 1st-century Rome. Steven Saylor's *Triumph of Caesar* (2009) skilfully describes the passion, fear and violence that hung in the air during Julius Caesar's last days. Similarly stirring is *Antony and Cleopatra* (2008), the last in Colleen McCullough's Masters of Rome series.

Current Crop

Born in Rome in 1966, Niccolò Ammaniti is the king of Rome's literary young guns. In 2007 he won the Premio Strega, Italy's top literary prize for his novel, *Come Dio Comanda* (As God Commands), but he's best known for *Io Non Ho Paura* (I'm Not Scared; 2001), about a young boy's discovery that his father is involved in a child kidnapping.

The Best...
Frescoes

1 Sistine Chapel (p191)

2 Stanze di Raffaello (p190)

3 Museo Nazionale Romano – Palazzo Massimo alle Terme (p135)

4 Villa Farnesina (p173)

Cinema

Despite financial setbacks, the Italian film industry continues to thrive. Most films are aimed at the Italian market but some make international waves, like Nanni Moretti's *Habemus Papam*, which debuted to critical praise at the 2011 Cannes Film Festival.

Italian filmmakers have long had a good relationship with Cannes, and 2008 was a recent highpoint. Matteo Garrone, a young Roman director, took the Grand Prix for *Gomorra* (Gomorrah), an exposé of Neapolitan organised crime, and Paolo Sorrentino scooped the Special Jury Prize for *Il Divo,* a portrayal of Giulio Andreotti, Italy's most famous postwar politician.

The 1940s was Roman cinema's Golden Age, when Roberto Rossellini (1906–77) produced a trio of neorealist masterpieces. The first and most famous was the brutal *Roma Città Aperta* (Rome Open City; 1945). Vittorio de Sica (1901–74) kept the neorealist ball rolling in 1948 with *Ladri di Biciclette* (Bicycle Thieves); both were filmed in Rome's sprawling suburbs.

Federico Fellini (1920–94) took the creative baton from the neorealists, producing his era-defining hit *La Dolce Vita* (1960), starring Marcello Mastroianni and Anita Ekberg. The films of Pier Paolo Pasolini (1922–75) similarly expose the city's gritty underbelly during the post-war period.

Music

Despite cutbacks in public funding, Rome's music scene is in good health. International orchestras perform to sell-out audiences, jazz greats jam in steamy clubs and rappers delight in the underground.

Opera

Rome is often snubbed by serious opera buffs who prefer their Puccini in Milan, Venice or Naples. However, in recent years the city's main opera company, the Teatro dell'Opera di Roma, has upped its standards and performances are passionately followed.

Giacomo Puccini's *Tosca* (1900) not only premiered in Rome but is also set in the city. The first act takes place in the Chiesa di Sant'Andrea della Valle, the second in Palazzo Farnese and the final act in Castel Sant'Angelo, the castle from which Tosca jumps to her death.

Jazz & Hip Hop

Introduced by US troops during WWII, jazz grew in popularity during the post-war period and took off in the 1960s. Today Rome still loves jazz, and has some superb clubs and an excellent summer festival. Hip hop and rap are also favoured sounds in the city, usually found at underground clubs or social centres.

Nanni Moretti

The Roman director Moretti falls into no mainstream tradition. A politically active writer, actor and director, his films are often whimsical and self-indulgent. Arguably his best work, *Caro Diario* (Dear Diary; 1994) earned him the best director prize at Cannes in 1994 – an award that he topped in 2001 when he won the Palme d'Or for *La Stanza del Figlio* (The Son's Room). His 2011 film, *Habemus Papam* (We have a Pope), also won multiple awards.

Architecture

Fountain in Piazza della Rotunda with Pantheon (p74)

MARTIN MOOS/LONELY PLANET IMAGES ©

From ancient ruins and Renaissance basilicas, to baroque churches and hulking fascist palazzi, Rome's architectural legacy is unparalleled. Michelangelo, Bramante, Borromini and Bernini are among the architects who have stamped their genius on Rome's remarkable cityscape. But it's not all about history. In recent years a number of high-profile building projects have drawn the world's top architects to Rome.

The Ancients

Architecture was central to the success of the ancient Romans. In building their great capital, they were the first people to use architecture to tackle problems of infrastructure, urban management and communication. To do this the Romans advanced methods devised by the Etruscans and Greeks, developing construction techniques and building materials that allowed them to build on a hitherto unseen scale.

Etruscan Roots

By the 7th century BC the Etruscans were the dominant force on the Italian peninsula; they built with wood and brick, which didn't last, and much of what we now know about the Etruscans derives from findings unearthed in their impressive cemeteries. These were constructed outside the city walls and harboured richly decorated stone vaults covered by mounds of earth. The best examples of Etruscan tombs are to be found in Cerveteri and Tarquinia, north of Rome.

Roman Developments

When Rome was founded in 753 BC (if legend is to be believed), the Etruscans were at the height of their power and Greeks colonists were establishing control over southern Italy. Against this background, Roman architects borrowed heavily from their rivals' traditions, gradually developing their own styles and techniques.

Temples

Early Republican-era temples were based on Etruscan designs, but over time the Romans turned to the Greeks for their inspiration. But whereas Greek temples had steps and colonnades on all sides, the classic Roman temple had a high podium with steps leading up to a deep porch. Greek temples were designed to stand apart and be viewed from all sides, but Roman ones were built into the city's urban fabric, and meant to be approached from the front.

The Roman use of columns was also Greek in origin, even if the Romans favoured the more slender Ionic and Corinthian columns over the plain Doric pillars – to see how these differ study the exterior of the Colosseum, which incorporates all three styles.

Aqueducts & Sewers

One of the Romans crowning architectural achievements was the development of a water supply infrastructure. To meet demand, the Romans constructed a complex system of aqueducts to bring water in from the hills of central Italy and distribute it around the city.

The first aqueduct to serve Rome was the 16.5km Aqua Appia, which became fully operational in 312 BC. Over the next 700 years or so, up to 800km of aqueducts were laid out in the city. The system depended entirely on gravity, without the use of pumps. All aqueducts, whether underground pipes, as most were, or vast overland viaducts, were built at a gradient to allow the water to flow.

Residential Housing

While Rome's emperors and aristocrats lived in luxury in vast palaces up on the Palatino (Palatine hill), the city's poor huddled together in large residential blocks called *insulae.* These poorly built structures were sometimes up to six or seven storeys high,

Rococo Frills

In the early days of the 18th century, the rococo burst into theatrical life. Drawing on the excesses of the baroque, it was a short-lived fad but one that left a memorable mark.

The **Spanish Steps**, built between 1723 and 1726 by Francesco de Sanctis, provided a focal point for the many Grand Tourists who were busy discovering Rome's classical past. A short walk to the southwest, Piazza Sant'Ignazio was designed by Filippo Raguzzini (1680–1771) in 1728 to provide a suitably melodramatic setting for the **Chiesa di Sant'Ignazio di Loyola**, Rome's second Jesuit church. Most spectacular of all, however, was the **Trevi Fountain**, designed in 1732 by Nicola Salvi (1697–1751) and completed three decades later.

accommodating hundreds of people in dark, unhealthy conditions. Little remains of these early *palazzi* but near the foot of the Aracoeli staircase – the steps that lead up to the Chiesa di Santa Maria in Aracoeli – you can still see a section of what was once a typical city-centre *insula*.

Concrete & Monumental Architecture

Grandiose constructions such as Colosseum, the Pantheon, the Terme di Caracalla and the Forums, still standing some 2000 years after they were built, are not only reminders of the sophistication and intimidatory scale of ancient Rome, but also monuments to the vision and bravura of the city's ancient architects.

One of the key breakthroughs the Romans made, and one that allowed them to build on an ever-increasing scale, was the invention of concrete in the 1st century BC. Made by mixing volcanic ash with lime and an aggregate, often tufa rock or brick rubble, concrete was quick to make, easy to use and cheap. Furthermore, it freed architects from their dependence on skilled stonemasons

Early Christian

The most startling reminders of early Christian activity are the catacombs, a series of underground burial grounds built under Rome's ancient roads. Christian belief in the resurrection meant that the Christians could not cremate their dead, as was the custom in Roman times, and with burial forbidden inside the city walls they were forced to go outside the city.

The Christians began to abandon the catacombs in the 4th century and increasingly opted to be buried in the churches the emperor Constantine was building in the city. The most notable of the many churches that Constantine commissioned is the Basilica di San Giovanni in Laterano. Built between 315 and 324 and re-formed into its present shape in the 5th century, it was the model on which many subsequent basilicas were based. Other showstoppers of the period include the Basilica di Santa Maria in Trastevere and the Basilica di Santa Maria Maggiore.

A second wave of church-building hit Rome in the period between the 8th and 12th centuries. As the early papacy battled for survival against the threatening Lombards, its leaders took to construction to leave some sort of historical imprint, resulting in the Basilica di Santa Sabina, the Chiesa di Santa Prassede and the 8th-century Chiesa di Santa Maria in Cosmedin, better known as home to the Bocca della Verità (Mouth of Truth).

The 13th and 14th centuries were dark days for Rome as internecine fighting raged between the city's noble families, and little of lasting value was being built in Rome. The one great exception is the city's only Gothic church, the Chiesa di Santa Maria Sopra Minerva.

Renaissance

Many claim it was the election of Pope Nicholas V in 1447 that sparked the Renaissance in Rome, and ensuing artistic and architectural explosion. Nicholas believed that as head of the Christian world Rome had a duty to impress, a theory that was endorsed by his successors, and it was at the behest of the great papal dynasties – the Barberini, Farnese and Pamphilj – that the leading artists of the day were summoned to Rome.

It was under Julius II (1503–13) that the Roman Renaissance reached its peak, thanks largely to a classically minded architect from Milan, Donato Bramante (1444–1514).

Considered the high priest of Renaissance architecture, Bramante arrived in Rome in 1499. Here, inspired by the ancient ruins, he developed a refined classical style that was to prove hugely influential. His 1502 Tempietto is a masterpiece of elegance.

In 1506 Julius commissioned him to start work on the job that would finally finish him off – the rebuilding of St Peter's Basilica (Basilica di San Pietro).

St Peter's Basilica occupied most of the other notable architects of the High Renaissance, most notably Michelangelo, who took over in 1547, creating the basilica's crowning dome.

The Best...
Baroque

1 St Peter's Basilica (p192)

2 Piazza Navona (p79)

3 Chiesa di Santa Maria della Vittoria (p107)

4 Museo e Galleria Borghese (p208)

Baroque

The Catholic Church became increasingly powerful in the 16th century. But with power came corruption and calls for reform. These culminated in Martin Luther's 95 Theses and the far-reaching Protestant Reformation, which prompted the Counter-Reformation (1560–1648), a vicious and sustained campaign to get people back into the Catholic fold. In the midst of this great offensive, art and architecture emerged as an effective form of propaganda. Baroque architecture aims for a dramatic sense of dynamism, an effect that it often achieves by combining spatial complexity with clever lighting and a flamboyant use of decorative painting and sculpture.

One of the first great Counter-Reformation churches was the Jesuit Chiesa del Gesù, designed by the leading architect of the day, Giacomo della Porta (1533–1602).

The end of the 16th century and the papacy of Sixtus V (1585–90) marked the beginning of major urban-planning schemes. Domenico Fontana (1543–1607) and other architects created a network of major thoroughfares to connect parts of the sprawling medieval city, and decorative obelisks were erected at vantage points throughout Rome. Fontana also designed the main facade of Palazzo del Quirinale, the immense palace that served as the pope's summer residence for almost three centuries.

Bernini vs Borromini

No two people did more to fashion the face of Rome than Gian Lorenzo Bernini and Francesco Borromini. Naples-born Bernini, confident and suave, is best known for his work in the Vatican. He designed St Peter's Square (Piazza San Pietro), famously styling the colonnade as 'the motherly arms of the Church', and was chief architect at St Peter's Basilica from 1629. While working on the basilica, he created the baldachin (altar canopy) above the main altar, using bronze stripped from the Pantheon.

Under the patronage of the Barberini pope Urban VIII, Bernini was given free rein to transform the city, and his churches, *palazzi,* piazzas and fountains remain landmarks to this day. However, his fortunes nose-dived when the pope died in 1644. Urban's successor, Innocent X, wanted as little contact as possible with the favourites of his hated predecessor and instead turned to Borromini, from Lombardy.

Borromini, the son of an architect and well versed in stonemasonry and construction techniques, created buildings involving complex shapes and exotic geometry. Throughout their careers, the two geniuses were often at each other's throats. Borromini was deeply envious of Bernini's early success and Bernini, in turn, was scathing of Borromini's complex geometrical style.

Fascism, Futurism & the 20th Century

Rome entered the 20th century in good shape. During the last 30 years of the 19th century it had been treated to one of its periodic makeovers – this time after being made capital of the Kingdom of Italy in 1870. Piazzas were built – Piazza Vittorio Emanuele II, at the centre of a new upmarket residential district, and neoclassical Piazza della Repubblica, over Diocletian's bath complex – and roads were laid. To celebrate unification and pander to the ego of the ruling Savoy family, the Vittoriano monument was built between 1885 and 1911.

Influenced by the German Bauhaus movement, architectural rationalism was all the rage in 1920s Europe. Gruppo Sette, its main Italian proponents, incorporated classical elements into their modernistic designs. Aesthetically and politically, this tied in perfectly with Mussolini's vision of Fascism as the modern bearer of ancient Rome's imperialist ambitions.

Mussolini's most famous architectural legacy is the EUR district in the extreme south of the city, built for the Esposizione Universale di Roma in 1942.

Modern Rome

Rome's recent past has witnessed a flurry of architectural activity. Renzo Piano worked on the acclaimed auditorium, American Richard Meier built the new pavilion for the 1st-century AD Ara Pacis, Anglo-Iraqi Zaha Hadid designed MAXXI, and Odile Decq from France created the new MACRO.

The Roman Way of Life

Outdoor cafe, Piazza della Rotonda (p73), Centro Storico

MARTIN MOOS/LONELY PLANET IMAGES ©

As a visitor, it's often difficult to see beyond Rome's spectacular veneer to the large, modern city that lies beneath, a living, breathing capital, home to nearly three million people. So how do the Romans live in their city? Where do they work?

A Day in the Life

Rome's Mr Average, Signor Rossi, lives with his wife in a small, two-bedroom apartment in the suburbs and works in a government ministry.

His morning routine is a quick breakfast (usually nothing more than a sweet, black espresso) followed by a short bus ride to the nearest metro station. On the way he'll stop at an *edicola* (kiosk) to pick up his daily newspaper (*Il Messaggero*) and share a joke with the kiosk owner, a manic Roma supporter. Rome's metro is not a pleasant place to be in *l'ora di punta* (the rush hour), but the regulars are resigned to the discomfort. On arriving at work Signor Rossi has time for another coffee and a cornetto at the bar underneath his office.

His work, like many in the swollen state bureaucracy, is not the most interesting, nor the best paid, but it's secure as he has

Religion in Roman Life

With the Vatican as a neighbour, the Church is a constant presence in Roman life.

Yet the role of religion in modern Italian society is ambiguous. Approximately 90% of Italians consider themselves Catholic, but only about a third attend church regularly. The Church's line on ethical and social issues is always given an airing in the largely sympathetic national press, yet public support tends to be patchy.

Recent increases in the city's immigrant population have led to a noticeable Muslim presence. This has largely been a pain-free process but in 2007 Rome's right-wing administration blocked plans to open a mosque in the multi-ethnic Piazza Vittorio Emanuele II area.

a *contratto a tempo indeterminato* (permanent contract), in contrast to his younger colleagues, who are in constant fear that their temporary contracts will not be renewed.

Lunch, which is taken around 1.30pm, is usually a slice of *pizza al taglio* (pizza by the slice) from a nearby takeaway, followed by another espresso. Clocking-off time in most ministries is typically from 5pm onwards, when the rush-hour traffic begins to swell until about 7pm. Once home, Signor Rossi dines on pasta at around 8.30pm.

Work

Employment in the capital is largely based on Italy's bloated state bureaucracy. Other important employers include the tourist sector, banking, finance and culture – Italy's historic film industry is based in Rome and there are hundreds of museums and galleries across town.

Staying at Home

Italy's single most successful institution is the family. It's still the rule rather the exception for young Romans to stay at home until they marry, which they typically do at around 30. Local house prices are high and young Romans are reluctant to downgrade and move away from their home patch.

But while faith in the family remains, the family is shrinking. Italy's birth rate is one of the lowest in Europe and almost half of all Italian children (46.5%) have no brothers or sisters.

Survival
Guide

Outdoor bar, Trastevere
KRZYSZTOF DYDYNSKI/LONELY PLANET IMAGES ©

Sleeping

Rome has accommodation to please everyone, from the fussiest prince to the most impecunious nun. But while there's plenty of choice, rates are high and you'll need to book early to be assured of a room and to get the best deal.

Accommodation Types

Pensioni & Hotels

The bulk of accommodation in Rome is made up of *pensioni* and *albergi* (hotels).

A *pensione* is a small hotel or guesthouse. In Rome, they are generally housed in converted apartments. Rooms are simple, and although most come with a private bathroom, those that don't will usually have a basin and bidet.

Hotels are bigger and pricier than *pensioni*, although at the cheaper end of the market there's often little difference between the two.

A common complaint in Rome is that hotel rooms are small. This is especially true in the Centro Storico and Trastevere, where many hotels are housed in converted *palazzi* (mansions).

Breakfast in cheaper hotels is rarely worth setting the alarm for, so if you have the option save a few bob and pop into a bar for a coffee and *cornetto* (croissant).

B&Bs & Guesthouses

Alongside the hundreds of traditional B&Bs (private homes offering rooms to paying guests), Rome has numerous boutique-style guesthouses that offer chic, upmarket accommodation at mid- to top-end prices. Note also that breakfast in a Roman B&B is usually continental – a croissant and tea or coffee.

Hostels

Rome's hostels have smartened up their act in recent years and now cater to everyone from backpackers to budget-minded families. Many of these newer style hostels offer traditional dorms as well as smart hotel-style rooms with private bathrooms.

Rental Accommodation

For longer stays, renting an apartment might well work out cheaper than an extended hotel sojourn. Bank on spending about €900 per month for a studio apartment or a small one-bedroom place. For longer-term stays, you will probably have to pay bills on top, plus a condo-minium charge for building maintenance. A room in a shared apartment will cost from €600 per month, plus bills. You'll usually be asked to pay a deposit equal to one or two months' rent and the first month in advance.

Costs

The majority of hotels offer discounts from November to March (excluding the Christ-

Need to Know

PRICE RANGES

In this chapter prices quoted are the minimum-maximum for rooms with a private bathroom, and unless otherwise stated include breakfast.

- €   under €120
- €€   €120 to €250
- €€€   over €250

RESERVATIONS

- Always try to book ahead, especially if coming in high season or for a major religious festival.

- If you want a double bed, ask for a *camera matrimoniale*. A *camera doppia* (double room) is a room with twin beds.

- There's a **hotel reservation service** (☎06 699 10 00; booking fee €3; ☽7am-10pm) next to the tourist office at Stazione Termini.

CHECKING IN & OUT

- Check out is usually between 10am and noon. In hostels, it's around 9am.

- Some guesthouses require you to arrange a time to check in.

- If you're going to arrive late, mention this when you book your room.

mas and New Year period) and from mid-July through August. Throughout this chapter we've given prices for the low-season minimum and high-season maximum, unless there's a single year-round price. Most mid- and top-range hotels accept credit cards.

As of January 2011, all non-residents overnighting in Rome have to pay a nightly room occupancy tax. This amounts to: €2 per person per night for a maximum of 10 days in *agriturismi* (farm stay accommodation), B&Bs, guesthouses and 1-, 2- and 3-star hotels; and €3 per person per night for a maximum of 10 days in 4- and 5-star hotels. Prices quoted in this chapter do not include the tax.

Useful Websites

Comune di Roma (www.060608.it) Publishes an extensive list of B&Bs, rentals and hotels (with prices).

Bed & Breakfast Italia (www.bbitalia.com) Rome's longest-established B&B network.

Italian Youth Hostel Association (www.aighostels .com) For information on Rome, and Italy's, official HI hostels.

Lonely Planet (hotels. lonelyplanet.com) Author-reviewed accommodation options; book directly online.

Accommodations Rome (www.accomodationsrome.com) Useful rental resources.

Bed & Breakfast Association of Rome (www.b-b.rm.it) Lists B&Bs and short-term apartment rentals.

Flat in Rome (www .flatinrome.it) Owner-managed apartment rentals.

Sleeping Rome (www .sleepingrome.com) Offers B&Bs and has good short-term flat rentals.

Italy Accom (www.italy -accom.com) Holiday rentals.

Where to Stay

NEIGHBOURHOOD	FOR	AGAINST
ANCIENT ROME	Close to sights like Colosseum and Roman Forum; quiet at night.	Not cheap; restaurants tend to be touristy.
CENTRO STORICO	Most atmospheric part of Rome with everything on your doorstep.	Priciest part of town; can be noisy.
TRIDENTE, TREVI & THE QUIRINALE	Good for Spanish Steps, Trevi Fountain and designer shopping; excellent mid- to top-end options; good transport links.	Upmarket area with prices to match; subdued after dark.
MONTI, ESQUILINO & SAN LORENZO	Lots of budget accommodation; top eating options in Monti and San Lorenzo; good transport links.	Some dodgy streets in Termini area, which is not Rome's most characterful.
TRASTEVERE & GIANICOLO	Gorgeous, atmospheric area; party atmosphere; some interesting sights.	Noisy, particularly in summer; expensive; hotel rooms often small.
VATICAN CITY, BORGO & PRATI	Near St Peter's Basilica and the Vatican Museums; decent range of accommodation; on the metro.	Not much nightlife; packed during religious holidays.

Best Places to Stay

NAME		REVIEW
HOTEL FORUM €€€	Ancient Rome	Survey all of Ancient Rome from the rooftop; the interior features antiques and dangling chandeliers.
FORTY SEVEN €€€	Ancient Rome	Lovely retreat at the back of the Roman Forum, with a bright modern interior and wonderful rooftop lounge bar.
CAESAR HOUSE €€	Ancient Rome	Quiet, friendly, on busy Via Cavour, a refined apartment hotel. Rooms have warm, peachy decor, four-poster beds and small bathrooms.
HOTEL CAMPO DE' FIORI €€€	Centro Storico	Rakish four-star with the lot – sexy decor, an enviable location, attentive staff and a panoramic roof terrace.
TEATROPACE 33 €€	Centro Storico	Just off Piazza Navona, classy choice with 23 beautifully appointed rooms decorated with parquet flooring, damask curtains and wood beams.
HOTEL DUE TORRI €€	Centro Storico	Lovely, refined, classic hotel, with huge gilt-framed mirrors, antiques, parquet floors and plump pot plants.
BABUINO 181 €€€	Tridente, Trevi & the Quirinale	A beautifully renovated old palazzo in the heart of the shopping district, Babuino offers discreet luxury, with chic rooms and excellent breakfasts.
GREGORIANA €€€	Tridente, Trevi & the Quirinale	Low-key, polished art deco hotel, set behind the Spanish Steps. Rooms have beautiful circular maple-wood headboards.
HOTEL LOCARNO €€€	Tridente, Trevi & the Quirinale	With an ivy-clad exterior and rattling cage-lift, the art deco Locarno is the kind of place Hercule Poirot might stay when in town.
PENSIONE PANDA €	Tridente, Trevi & the Quirinale	Only 50m from the Spanish Steps, the friendly, efficient Panda is an anomaly in this district, a budget pension, and a splendid one.
OKAPI ROOMS €€	Tridente, Trevi & the Quirinale	Same ownership as Pensione Panda and close to Piazza del Popolo. Rooms are simple, small, airy affairs with cream walls, terracotta floors and double glazing.
HOTEL DE RUSSIE €€€	Tridente, Trevi & the Quirinale	A favourite of Hollywood celebs, the historic de Russie is almost on Piazza del Popolo, and has exquisite terraced gardens.
HASSLER VILLA MEDICI €€€	Tridente, Trevi & the Quirinale	Sumptuously surmounting the Spanish Steps, the Hassler is a byword for old-school luxury. A long line of VIPs have stayed here, enjoying the ravishing views.
HOTEL MOZART €€	Tridente, Trevi & the Quirinale	A credit-card's flourish from Via del Corso, the Mozart has classic, immaculate rooms, decorated in dove greys, eggshell blues and rosy pinks.

✆ 06 679 24 46; www.hotelforumrome.com; Via Tor de' Conti 25; s €160-220, d €240-360; M Cavour; P ❄ 🛜	Ancient City views.
✆ 06 678 78 16; www.fortysevenhotel.com; Via Petroselli 47; s €190-285, d €190-300; 🚌 Via Petroselli; ❄ @ 🛜	A tranquil stay.
✆ 06 679 26 74; www.caesarhouse.com; Via Cavour 310; s €150-230, d €170-270; M Cavour; ❄ 🛜	Good value.
✆ 06 687 48 86; www.hotelcampodefiori.com; Via del Biscione 6; r & apt €99-599; 🚌 Corso Vittorio Emanuele II; ❄ @ 🛜	Glamour and in-the-thick-of-it location.
✆ 06 687 90 75; www.hotelteatropace.com; Via del Teatro Pace 33; s €69-150, d €110-240; 🚌 Corso Vittorio Emanuele II; ❄	Great location and value.
✆ 06 6880 6956; www.hotelduetorriroma.com; Vicolo del Leonetto 23; s €125-150, d €170-230; 🚌 Via di Monte Brianzo; ❄ 🛜	Tranquility and tradition.
✆ 06 3229 5295; www.romeluxurysuites.com/babuino; Via del Babuino 181; r €180-250; ⊖ ❄ 🛜	Glamour for those in the know.
✆ 06 679 42 69; www.hotelgrego riana.it; Via Gregoriana 18; s €148-198, d €228-288; M Spagna; ⊖ ❄	Art deco loveliness.
✆ 06 361 08 41; www.hotellocarno.com; Via della Penna 22; s €150-180, d €150-250; M Flaminio; ⊖ ❄ @ 🛜	Art deco character.
✆ 06 678 01 79; www.hotelpanda.it; Via della Croce 35; s with/without bathroom €80/68, d with/without bathroom €108/78; M Spagna; ❄ 🛜	A well-kept bargain.
✆ 06 3260 9815; www.okapirooms.it; Via della Penna 57; s €65-80, d €85-120; M Flaminio; ❄ 🛜	A great deal.
✆ 06 32 88 81; www.hotelderussie.it; Via del Babuino 9; d €450-690; M Flaminio; P ❄ @	Celeb-spotting and terraced gardens.
✆ 06 69 93 40; www.hotelhassler.com; Piazza della Trinità dei Monti 6; d €450-500; M Spagna; ❄ @ 🛜	Feeling like a movie star.
✆ 06 3600 1915; www.hotelmozart.com; Via dei Greci 23b; s €110-165, d €140-245; M Spagna; P ❄ @ 🛜	Shopping, comfort and value.

HOTEL BAROCCO €€	Tridente, Trevi & the Quirinale	This well-run, welcoming 41-room hotel overlooking Piazza Barberini (the pricier rooms have views) has rooms featuring oil paintings, gleaming linen and gentle colour schemes.
LA PICCOLA MAISON €	Tridente, Trevi & the Quirinale	The excellent Piccola Maison is housed in a 19th-century building in a great location close to Piazza Barberini, and has pleasingly plain, neutrally decorated rooms and thoughtful staff.
VILLA SPALLETTI TRIVELLI €€€	Monti, Esquilino & San Lorenzo	With 12 rooms in a glorious mansion in central Rome, this has upped the ante for luxurious stays in the capital.
HOTEL DUCA D'ALBA €	Monti, Esquilino & San Lorenzo	Appealing four-star hotel in Monti; rooms have fabric-covered or handpainted walls, wood-beamed ceilings, big flat-screen TVs and sleek button-studded headboards.
HOTEL ARTORIUS €€	Monti, Esquilino & San Lorenzo	An art deco–flavoured lobby looks promising, and the rest delivers too in this small Monti hotel, with simple, plain rooms – not large, but perfectly comfortable.
BEEHIVE €	Monti, Esquilino & San Lorenzo	Rome's best hostel, with artworks and funky modular furniture. Beds are in a spotless, eight-person mixed dorm or six private double rooms, all with fans.
RESIDENZA CELLINI €€	Monti, Esquilino & San Lorenzo	With grown-up furnishings featuring potted palms, polished wood, pale yellow walls, oil paintings and a hint of chintz, this is a charming, family-run hotel.
DONNA CAMILLA SAVELLI €€€	Trastevere & Gianicolo	A converted convent designed by baroque genius Borromini; muted colours complement the serene concave and convex architectural curves, and service is excellent.
RESIDENZA ARCO DE' TOLOMEI €€	Trastevere & Gianicolo	Next to Arco del Lauro, this is decorated with polished antiques and rich contrasting chintzes that make the interiors feel like a country cottage.
ARCO DEL LAURO €€	Trastevere & Gianicolo	Six-roomed fab B&B in an ancient *palazzo*. A find, with gleaming white rooms that combine rustic charm with minimalist simplicity.
HOTEL SANTA MARIA €€	Trastevere & Gianicolo	Surrounding a tranquil modern cloister (a former convent site), shaded by orange trees, the spacious rooms are cool and comfortable, with slightly fussy décor.
VILLA LAETITIA €€€	Vatican, Borgo & Prati	A graceful riverside villa owned and styled by members of the famous Fendi fashion family, with 14 gorgeous rooms; each comes with its own kitchen facilities.
HOTEL BRAMANTE €€	Vatican, Borgo & Prati	In the atmospheric Borgo, Hotel Bramante exudes country-house charm, with 16 quietly elegant rooms – think oriental rugs, wood-beamed ceilings and antiques.
BIBI E ROMEO'S HOME €	Vatican, Borgo & Prati	Up from a broad cafe-lined avenue, this peaceful, personable B&B has rooms decorated in stylish mixes of white, brown and grey.

☎ 06 487 20 01; www.hotelbarocco.com; Piazza Barberini 9; d €160-330; Ⓜ Barberini; ⊖ ❋ @ 📶 — Service, style and location.

☎ 06 4201 6331; www.lapiccolamaison.com; Via dei Cappuccini 30; s €50-140, d €70-200; Ⓜ Vittorio Emanuele; ⊖ ❋ 📶 — Location and price.

☎ 06 4890 7934; www.villaspal letti.it; Via Piacenza 4; r €330-345; Ⓜ Spagna; ⊖ Ⓟ ❋ @ 📶 — Spectacular indulgence and a country estate feel.

☎ 06 48 44 71; www.hotelducadalba.com; Via Leonina 14; s €90-190, d €100-240; Ⓜ Vittorio Emanuele; ⊖ ❋ @ 📶 — Snugness, charm and the neighbourhood.

☎ 06 482 11 96; www.antica-locanda.com; Via del Boschetto 13; d €160-185; Ⓜ Cavour; ❋ @ 📶 — Value in vibrant Monti.

☎ 06 4470 4553; www.the-beehive.com; Via Marghera 8; dm €20-25, d without bathroom €70-80; Ⓜ Termini; ⊖ @ 📶 — Style on a budget.

☎ 06 4782 5204; www.residenzacel lini.it; Via Modena 5; d €145-240; Ⓜ Repubblica; ⊖ ❋ @ 📶 — Elegance at a reasonable price.

☎ 06 58 88 61; www.hotelsavelli.com; Via Garibaldi 27; d €200-260; � or 🚋 Viale di Trastevere; ⊖ Ⓟ ❋ @ 📶 — Architecture and service.

☎ 06 5832 0819; www.bbarcodeitolomei.com; Via Arco de' Tolomei 27; d €145-220; 🚋 or 🚋 Viale di Trastevere; ⊖ ❋ 📶 — Cosy cottage feel in characterful Trastevere.

☎ 06 9784 0350; www.arcodellauro.it; Via Arco de' Tolomei 27; s €75-125, d €95-145; 🚋 Viale di Trastevere; ⊖ ❋ 📶 — Inexpensive charm.

☎ 06 589 46 26; www.hotelsanta maria.info; Vicolo del Piede 2; s €90-190, d €130-260; 🚋 or 🚋 Piazza Sonnino; Ⓟ ⊖ ❋ @ 📶] — Larger rooms; suits families.

☎ 06 322 67 76; www.villalaetitia.com; Lungotevere delle Armi 22; d €190-350; Ⓜ Lepanto; ❋ 📶 — Stay in a work of haute couture.

☎ 06 6880 6426; www.hotelbramante.com; Vicolo delle Palline 24-25; s €100-160, d €150-220; Ⓜ Ottaviano–San Pietro; ❋ 📶 — Country-house feel in the city.

☎ 346 965 69 37; www.bbromeo.com; Via Andrea Doria 36; s €50-80, d €60-130, tr €90-130, q €100-150; Ⓜ Ottaviano–San Pietro; ❋ 📶 — Value, location and style.

Transcript

Getting To Rome

Most people arrive in Rome by plane, landing at one of its two airports: Leonardo da Vinci, better known as Fiumicino, or Ciampino, the hub for European low-cost airlines. For details of budget airlines flying to Rome check out www.fly cheapo.com. Domestic flights connect Rome with airports across Italy.

As an alternative to short-haul flights, trains serve Rome's main station, Stazione Termini, from a number of European destinations as well as cities across Italy.

Long-distance domestic and international buses arrive at the Autostazione Tiburtina.

You can also get to Rome by boat. Ferries serve Civitavecchia, some 80km north of the city, from a number of Mediterranean ports.

Flights, tours and rail tickets can be booked online at lonelyplanet.com/bookings.

 Air

Leonardo da Vinci Airport

Rome's main international airport, **Leonardo da Vinci** (FCO; ☑ 06 6 59 51; www.adr .it), aka Fiumicino, is situated on the coast 30km west of the city. It is divided into four terminals: Terminal 1 for domestic flights; Terminal 2 for charter flights; Terminal 3 for international flights; Terminal 5 for flights to the USA and Israel. Terminals 1, 2 and 3 are within easy walking distance of each other in the main airport building; Terminal 5 is accessible by shuttle bus from Terminal 3.

The easiest way to get to/from the airport is by train but there are also bus services and private shuttle services.

Leonardo Express train
(adult/child €14/free) Runs to/from platforms 27 and 28 at Stazione Termini. Departures from Termini every 30 minutes between 5.52am and 10.52pm, from the airport between 6.36am and 11.36pm. Journey time is 30 minutes.

FR1 train (one way €8)
Connects the airport to Trastevere, Ostiense and Tiburtina stations, but not Termini. Departures from the airport every 15 minutes (hourly on Sunday and public holidays) between 5.57am and 11.27pm, from Tiburtina between 5.05am and 10.33pm.

Cotral bus (www.cotralspa.it; one way €4.50 or €7 if bought on bus) Runs to/from Stazione

Tiburtina via Stazione Termini. Eight daily departures including night services from Tiburtina at 12.30am, 1.15am, 2.30am and 3.45am and from the airport at 1.15am, 2.15am, 3.30am and 5am. Journey time is one hour.

SIT bus (☑ 06 591 68 26; www.sitbusshuttle.it; one way €8) Regular departures from Via Marsala outside Stazione Termini between 5am and 8.30pm, from the airport between 8.30am and 12.30am. Tickets available on the bus. Journey time is one hour.

Airport Connection Services (☑ 06 338 32 21; www.airportconnection.it) Transfers to/from the city centre start at €37 per person.

Airport Shuttle (☑ 06 420 13 469; www.airportshuttle.it) Transfers to/from your hotel for €25 for one person, then €6 for each additional passenger up to a maximum of eight.

Taxi The set fare to/from the city centre is €40, which is valid for up to four passengers including luggage. Note that taxis registered in Fiumicino charge a set fare of €60, so make sure you catch a Comune di Roma taxi.

Car Follow signs for Roma out of the airport complex and onto the autostrada. Exit at EUR, following signs for the *centro*, to link up with Via Cristoforo Colombo, which will take you directly into the centre. All major car-hire

companies are present at Fiumicino.

Ciampino Airport

Ciampino (CIA; ☎ 06 6 59 51; www.adr.it), 15km southeast of the city centre, is used by European low-cost airlines and charter operators.

The best option to get here is to take one of the regular bus services into the city centre. You can also take a bus to Ciampino station and then pick up a train to Stazione Termini.

Terravision bus (www .terravision.eu; one way/return €4/8) Twice hourly departures to/from Via Marsala outside Stazione Termini. From the airport services are between 8.15am and 12.15am, from Via Marsala between 4.30am and 9.20pm. Buy tickets at Terracafé in front of the Via Marsala bus stop. Journey time is 40 minutes.

SIT bus (www.sitbusshuttle .com; one way/return €6/8) Regular departures from Via Marsala outside Stazione Termini between 4.30am and 9.30pm, from the airport between 7.45am and 11.15pm. Tickets available on the bus. Journey time is 45 minutes.

Cotral bus (www.cotralspa.it; one way/return €3.90/6.90) Runs 15 daily services to/from Via Giolitti near Stazione Termini.
Terravision bus (www. terravision.eu; one way/return €4/8) Twice hourly departures to/from Via Marsala outside Stazione Termini. Also buses to/from Anagnina metro station (€1.20) and Ciampino train

station (€1.20) where you can connect with trains to Stazione Termini (€1.30).

Airport Connection Services (☎ 06 338 32 21; www.airportconnection.it) Transfers to/from the city centre start at €37 per person.

Airport Shuttle (☎ 06 420 13 469; www.airport shuttle.it) Transfers to/ from your hotel for €25 for one person, then €5 for each additional passenger up to a maximum of eight.

Taxi The set rate to/from the airport is €30.

Car If you want to hire a car, you'll find all the major rental companies in the arrivals hall. Exit the station and follow Via Appia Nuova straight into the city centre.

🚆 Train

Almost all trains arrive at and depart from **Stazione Termini**, Rome's main train station and principal transport hub. There are regular connections to other European countries, all major Italian cities and many smaller towns. Train information is available from the **train information office** (🕑 6am– midnight) next to platform 1, online at www .ferroviedellostato.it or, if you speak Italian, by calling ☎ 89 20 21.

From Termini, you can connect with both metro lines (line A, which is colour-coded orange; and line B, which is marked with blue signs) or take a bus from the

Climate Change & Travel

Every form of transport that relies on carbon-based fuel generates CO_2, the main cause of human-induced climate change. Modern travel is dependent on aeroplanes, which might use less fuel per kilometre per person than most cars but travel much greater distances. The altitude at which aircraft emit gases (including CO_2) and particles also contributes to their climate change impact. Many websites offer 'carbon calculators' that allow people to estimate the carbon emissions generated by their journey and, for those who wish to do so, to offset the impact of the greenhouse gases emitted with contributions to portfolios of climate-friendly initiatives throughout the world. Lonely Planet offsets the carbon footprint of all staff and author travel.

bus station on Piazza dei Cinquecento out front. Taxis are outside the main exit.

🚌 Bus

Long-distance national and international buses use the **Autostazione Tiburtina** (Piazzale Tiburtina). From the bus station cross under the overpass for the Tiburtina train station where you can pick up the metro (line B) and connect with Termini for onward buses, trains or metro line A.

Tickets, Please

Public-transport tickets are valid on all Rome's bus, tram and metro lines, except for routes to Fiumicino airport. They come in various forms:

BIT (*biglietto integrato a tempo,* a single ticket valid for 75 minutes and one metro ride) €1

BIG (*biglietto integrato giornaliero,* a daily ticket) €4

BTI (*biglietto turistico integrato,* a three-day ticket) €11

CIS (*carta integrata settimanale,* a weekly ticket) €16

Abbonamento mensile (a monthly pass) €30

You can buy tickets at *tabacchi* (tobacconist's shop) and newsstands and from vending machines at metro, bus and train stations. They must be purchased before you get on the bus or train, then validated in the yellow machine once on board, or at the entrance gates for the metro. You risk a €50 fine if you're caught without a validated ticket. Children under 10 travel free.

The **Roma Pass** (www.romapass.it) comes with a three-day travel pass valid within the city boundaries. The **Vatican and Rome card** (1/3 days €20/25) provides unlimited travel on all public transport within the city and on the Open buses operated by Roma Christiana (see p270).

Boat

Rome's port is at Civitavecchia, about 80km north of Rome. Ferries sail here from destinations across the Mediterranean including Barcelona, Malta and Tunis, as well as Sicily and Sardinia. Check out www.traghettiweb.it for route details, prices and bookings.

From Civitavecchia there are half-hourly trains to Stazione Termini (€4.50 to €12.50, one hour). Civitavecchia's station is about 700m from the entrance to the port.

● ● ●

Getting Around Rome

Rome is a sprawling city, but the historic centre is relatively compact and it's quite pos-

sible to explore much of it on foot. The city's public transport system includes buses, trams, metro and a suburban train system.

Bicycle

The centre of Rome doesn't lend itself to cycling: there are steep hills and treacherous cobbled roads, and the traffic is terrible. However, if you want to pedal around town, pick up *Andiamo in Bici a Roma* (€7), a useful map published by L'Ortensia Rossa, which details Rome's main cycle paths.

○ On Saturdays, Sundays and weekdays after 8pm, you can take your bike on the metro and the Lido di Ostia train. You have to use the front carriage and buy a separate ticket for the bike.

○ On Sundays and holidays you can carry bikes on bus 791.

○ On regional trains marked with a bike icon on the timetable, you can carry a bike on payment of a €3.50 supplement.

○ Rome has a bike-sharing scheme. You can sign up at the ATAC ticket offices at Termini, Spagna and Lepanto metro stations. There's a €5 signing on fee and a €5 minimum charge. On signing up you're provided with a rechargeable smartcard that allows you to pick up a bike from one of the 27 stations across the city, and use it for up to 24 hours within a single day. On the road, you pay €0.50 for every 30 minutes. For further information see www.bikesharing.roma.it or call ☏06 5 70 03.

Hire

Appia Antica Regional Park Information Point (📞 06 513 53 16; www.parcoappiaantica.org; Via Appia Antica 58-60; per hr/day €3/10)

Bici e Baci (📞 06 482 84 43; www.bicibaci.com; Via del Viminale 5; per hr/day €4/11)

Eco Move Rent (📞 06 447 04 518; www.ecomoverent.com; Via Varese 48-50; per hr/day €4/10)

Treno e Scooter (📞 06 489 05 823; www.trenoescooter .com; Piazza dei Cinquecento; per hr/day €4/10)

Villa Borghese (Via delle Belle Arti; per hr/day €4/15)

🚌 Bus & Tram

○ Rome's buses and trams are run by **ATAC** (📞 06 5 70 03; www.atac.roma.it).

○ The main bus station is in front of Stazione Termini on Piazza dei Cinquecento, where there's an **information booth** (🕐7.30am-8pm). Other important bus stops are at Largo di Torre Argentina, Piazza Venezia and Piazza San Silvestro.

○ Buses generally run from about 5.30am until midnight, with limited services throughout the night.

🚇 Metro

○ Rome has two metro lines, A (orange) and B (blue), which cross at Termini, the only point at which you can change from one line to the other.

○ Trains run approximately every five to 10 minutes between 5.30am and 11.30pm (to 1.30am on Friday and Saturday).

○ All the metro stations on line B have wheelchair access except for Circo Massimo, Colosseo and Cavour (direction Laurentina), while on line A Cipro–Musei Vaticani station is one of the few stations equipped with lifts.

○ Take line A for the Trevi Fountain (Barberini), Spanish Steps (Spagna) and St Peter's (Ottaviano–San Pietro).

○ Take line B for the Colosseum (Colosseo).

Taxi

○ Official licensed taxis are white with the symbol of Rome and an identifying number on the doors. Always go with the metered fare, never an arranged price (the set fares to and from the airports are exceptions).

○ In town (within the ring road) flag fall is €2.80 between 7am and 10pm on weekdays, €4 on Sundays and holidays, and €5.80 between 10pm and 7am. Then it's €0.92 per km. Official rates are posted in taxis and on www .viviromaintaxi.eu.

○ You can hail a taxi, but it's often easier to wait at a rank or phone for one. There are major taxi ranks at the airports, Stazione Termini, Largo di Torre Argentina, Piazza San Silvestro, Piazza della Repubblica, Piazza del Colosseo, Piazza Belli in Trastevere and in the Vatican at Piazza del Pio XII and Piazza Risorgimento.

○ You can book a taxi by phoning the Comune di Roma's automated **taxi line** (📞060609) or calling a taxi company direct.

La Capitale (📞 06 49 94)

Pronto Taxi (📞 06 66 45)

Radio Taxi (📞 06 35 70) The website www.060608 has a list of taxi companies – click on the transport tab, then getting around & by taxi.

Note that when you call for a cab, the meter is switched on straight away and you pay for the cost of the journey from wherever the driver receives the call.

● ● ●

Tours
🚶 Walking

A Friend in Rome (📞 06 661 40 987; www .afriendinrome.it) Silvia Prosperi organises private tailor-made tours (on foot, by bike or scooter) to suit your interests. She covers the Vatican and main historic centre as well as neighbourhoods such as the Aventino, Trastevere, Celio and the Monti. Rates are €50 per hour, with a minimum of three hours for most tours. Silvia can also arrange mosaic lessons, cooking classes and coastal cruises.

Dark Rome (📞 06 833 60 561; www.darkrome.com) Runs a range of themed tours, costing from €22 to €91. Popular choices include the Crypts and Catacombs tour, which takes in Rome's buried treasures, and the Semi-Private Vatican Museums Tour, which takes you into the museums before they're opened to the public.

Enjoy Rome (📞 06 445 18 43; www.enjoyrome.com; Via Marghera 8a) Offers three-hour walking tours of the Vatican (under/over 26 yr €25/30) and Ancient & Old Rome (under/over 26 yr €25/30) as well as various other tours – see the website for further details. Note that tour prices do not cover admission charges to the Vatican Museums and Colosseum.

Through Eternity Cultural Association (📞 06 700 93 36; www.througheternity.com) Another reliable operator offering a range of private and group tours led by English-speaking experts. Walks include a group twilight tour of Rome's piazzas and fountains (€29, 2½ hours), the Vatican Museums and St Peter's Basilica (€41, five hours), and an Angels and Demons tour (€31, 3½ hours) based on Dan Brown's bestselling book.

Roma Cristiana (📞 06 698 96 380; www.operaromanapellegrinaggi.org) Runs various walking tours, including visits to the Vatican Museums (adult/reduced €26/17) and St Peter's Basilica (€12). Tickets are available online or at the meeting point just off Piazza San Pietro.

Bicycle & Scooter

Bici & Baci (📞 06 482 84 43; www.bicibaci.com; Via del Viminale 5; €35; ⊙ 10am, 3pm & 7pm Mar-Oct, on request Nov-Feb) Bici & Baci runs daily bike tours of central Rome, taking in the historic centre, Campidoglio and the Colosseum, as well as tours on vintage Vespas and in classic Fiat 500 cars. For the Vespa and Fiat 500 tours you'll need to book 24 hours ahead. Routes and prices vary according to your requests.

Boat

Battelli di Roma (📞 06 977 45 498; www.battellidiroma.it; adult/reduced €16/12) Runs hour-long hop-on hop-off cruises along the Tiber between Ponte Sant'Angelo and Ponte Nenni. Trips depart at 10am from Ponte Sant'Angelo, 10.10pm from Isola Tiberina, and then hourly until 6.30pm.There are also dinner cruises (€58, 2¼ hours), wine-bar cruises (€39, 2¼ hours) and a bus–boat combination tour (adult/reduced €32/19). Tickets are available online or at the embarkation points on Molo Sant'Angelo and Isola Tiberina.

Bus

Trambus 110open (📞 800 281 281; www.trambusopen.com; family/adult/reduced €50/20/18; ⊙ every 15min

8.30am-8.30pm) This open-top, double-decker bus departs from Piazza dei Cinquecento in front of Termini station, and stops at the Colosseum, Bocca della Verità, Piazza Venezia, St Peter's, Ara Pacis and Trevi Fountain. The entire tour lasts two hours, but the tickets, which are available on board, from the info boxes on Piazza dei Cinquecento and at the Colosseum, or from authorised Trambus Open dealers, are valid for 48 hours and allow you to hop off and on as you please.

Trambus Archeobus (📞 800 281 281; www.trambusopen.com; family/adult €40/12; ⊙ every half-hr 9am-4.30pm) A stop-and-go bus that takes sightseers down Via Appia Antica, stopping at points of archaeological interest along the way. It departs from Piazza dei Cinquecento and tickets, valid for 48 hours, can be bought online, on board, at the Piazza dei Cinquecento or Colosseum info boxes and at Trambus Open authorised dealers.

Open Bus Cristiana (📞 06 698 96 380; www.operaromanapellegrinaggi.org; 24hr/one circuit €18/13; ⊙ every 20 min 8.40am-7pm) The Vatican-sponsored Opera Romana Pellegrinaggi runs a hop-on, hop-off bus departing from Via della Conciliazione and Termini. Tickets are available on board the bus, online or at the meeting point just off Piazza San Pietro.

A-Z

Directory

Business Hours

Banks	8.30am-1.30pm & 2.45pm-4.30pm Mon-Fri
Bars & cafes	7.30am-8pm, sometimes until 1am or 2am
Shops	9am-7.30pm or 10am-8pm Mon-Sat, some 11am-7pm Sun; smaller shops 9am-1pm & 3.30-7.30pm (or 4-8pm) Mon-Sat.
Clubs	10pm-4am
Restaurants	noon-3pm & 7.30pm-11pm (later in summer)

Customs Regulations

Within the European Union you are entitled to tax-free prices on fragrances, cosmetics and skincare; photographic and electrical goods; fashion and accessories; gifts, jewellery and souvenirs where they are available, and there there are no longer any allowance restrictions on these tax-free items.

If you're arriving from a non-EU country you can import, duty free, 200 cigarettes, 1L of spirits (or 2L fortified wine), 4L wine, 60ml perfume, 16L beer and goods, including electronic devices, up to a value of €300; anything over this value must be declared on arrival and the duty paid. On leaving the EU, non-EU residents can reclaim value-added tax (VAT) on expensive purchases (see p247).

Emergency

Ambulance (📞 118)

Fire (📞 115)

Police (📞 113)

Gay & Lesbian Travellers

Hardly San Fran on the Med, Rome nevertheless has a thriving, if low-key gay scene.

The main gay cultural and political organisation is the **Circolo Mario Mieli di Cultura Omosessuale** (📞 06 541 39 85; www.mariomieli.it, in Italian; Via Efeso 2a), which organises debates, cultural events and social functions, including **Muccassassina** (www.muccassassina.com) clubnights and the city's annual Gay Pride march. The national organisation for lesbians is the **Coordinamento Lesbiche Italiano** (CLI; 📞 06 686 42 01; www.clrbp.it, in Italian; Via San Francesco di Sales 1b), who hold regular conferences and literary evenings.

Electricity

120V/60Hz

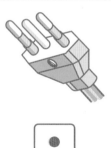

120V/60Hz

Legal Matters

The most likely reason for a brush with the law is to report a theft. If you do have something stolen and you want to claim it on insurance, you

Practicalities

○ Vatican Radio (www.radiovaticana.org; 93.3 FM & 105 FM in Rome, in Italian, English and other languages).

○ RAI-1, RAI-2 and RAI-3 (www.rai.it) National broadcaster.

○ Radio Città Futura (www.radiocittafutura.it) Good for contemporary music.

○ State-run TV channels: RAI-1, RAI-2 and RAI-3 (www.rai.it)

○ Main commercial stations (mostly run by Silvio Berlusconi's Mediaset company): Canale 5 (www.canale5.mediaset.it), Italia 1 (www.italia1.mediaset.it), Rete 4 (www.rete4.mediaset.it) and La 7 (www.la7.it).

○ Weights and measures use the metric system.

○ Smoking is banned in public spaces, such as bars, cafes and restaurants.

○ Italy's currency is the euro. The seven euro notes come in denominations of €500, €200, €100, €50, €20, €10 and €5. The eight euro coins are in denominations of €2 and €1, and 50, 20, 10, five, two and one cents.

must make a statement to the police as insurance companies won't pay up without official proof of a crime.

Rome's **Questura (police headquarters; ☎ 06 4 68 61; Via San Vitale 15; ⊘ 9am-midday Mon, Wed & Fri)** is just off Via Nazionale.

Medical Services

For emergency treatment, you can go to the *pronto soccorso* (casualty) section of an *ospedale* (public hospital), where it's also possible to receive emergency dental treatment, but be prepared for a long wait. For less serious ailments call the **Guardia Medica (☎ 06 57 06 00).**

A more convenient course, if you have insurance and can afford to pay up front, would be to call a private doctor to come

to your hotel or apartment. The callout/treatment fee will probably be around €130. Try **Roma Medica (☎ 338 622 48 32; ⊘24hr).** Pharmacists will serve prescriptions and can provide basic medical advice.

If you need an ambulance, call ☎118.

Emergency Rooms

Ospedale Fatebenefratelli (☎ 06 6 83 71; Piazza Fatebenefratelli, Isola Tiberina)

Ospedale San Camillo Forlanini (☎ 06 5 87 01; Circonvallazione Gianicolense 87)

Ospedale San Giacomo (☎ 06 3 62 61; Via A Canova 29)

Pharmacies

Marked by a green cross, *farmacie* (pharmacies) open

from 8.30am to 1pm and 4pm to 7.30pm Monday to Friday and on Saturday mornings. Outside these hours they open on a rotational basis, and all are legally required to post a list of places open in the vicinity. Night pharmacies are listed in daily newspapers and in pharmacy windows.

Money

Exchange rates are given inside the front cover of this book. For the latest rates, check out www.xe.com. For a guide to costs, see p44.

ATMs

ATMs (known in Italy as *bancomat*) are widely available in Rome and most will accept cards tied into the Visa, MasterCard, Cirrus and Maestro systems. The daily limit for cash withdrawal is €250.

Remember that every time you withdraw cash, you'll be charged a transaction fee (usually around 3% with a minimum of €3 or more) as well as a 1% to 3% conversion charge. Check with your bank to see how much this is.

Changing Money

You can change your money in banks, at post offices or at a *cambio* (exchange office). There are exchange booths at Stazione Termini and at Fiumicino and Ciampino airports. In the centre, there are numerous bureaux de change, including **American Express** (☎ 06 6 76 41; Piazza di Spagna 38; ⊘ 9am-5.30pm Mon-Fri, 9am-12.30pm Sat). Post offices and banks tend to offer the best rates. A few banks also provide automatic exchange machines that accept notes from most major currencies.

Always make sure you have your passport, or some form of photo ID, at hand when exchanging money.

Credit Cards

Credit cards are widely accepted but it's still a good idea to carry a cash back-up. Virtually all midrange and top-end hotels accept credit cards, as do most restaurants and large shops. You can also use them to obtain cash advances at some banks. Some of the cheaper *pensioni* (guesthouses), trattorias and pizzerias accept nothing but cash.

Major cards such as Visa, MasterCard, Eurocard, Cirrus and Eurocheques are widely accepted. Amex is also recognised, although it's less common than Visa or MasterCard.

Note that using your credit card in ATMs can be costly. On every transaction there's a fee, which with some credit-card issuers can reach US$10, as well as interest per withdrawal. Check with your issuer before leaving home.

If your card is lost, stolen or swallowed by an ATM, telephone to have an immediate stop put on its use.

Amex (☎ 06 7290 0347)

Diners Club (☎ 800 39 39 39)

MasterCard (☎ 800 87 08 66)

Visa (☎ 800 81 90 14)
The Amex office (American

Express (☎ 06 6 76 41; Piazza di Spagna 38; ☉ 9am-5.30pm Mon-Fri, 9am-12.30pm Sat) can issue customers with new cards, usually within 24 hours and sometimes immediately, if they have been lost or stolen.

●●● Public Holidays

Most Romans take their annual holiday in August. This means that many businesses and shops close for at least part of the month, particularly around Ferragosto (Feast of the Assumption) on 15 August. August is not considered high season by Rome's hoteliers (as Italians tend to vacate the city), many of whom offer discounts to avoid empty rooms.

Public holidays:

Capodanno (New Year's Day) 1 January

Epifania (Epiphany) 6 January

Pasquetta (Easter Monday) March/April

Giorno della Liberazione (Liberation Day) 25 April

Festa del Lavoro (Labour Day) 1 May

Festa della Repubblica (Republic Day) 2 June

Festa dei Santi Pietro e Paolo (Feast of St Peter & St Paul) 29 June

Ferragosto (Feast of the Assumption) 15 August

Festa di Ognisanti (All Saints' Day) 1 November

Festa dell'Immacolata Concezione (Feast of the Immaculate Conception) 8 December

Natale (Christmas Day) 25 December

Festa di Santo Stefano (Boxing Day) 26 December

For further details of Rome's holiday calendar, see p40.

●●● Telephone
Domestic Calls

Rome's area code is 06. Area codes are an integral part of all Italian phone numbers and must be dialled even when calling locally. Mobile phone numbers are nine or 10 digits long and begin with a three-digit prefix starting with a 3. Toll-free numbers are known as *numeri verdi* and usually start with ☎ 800. Some six-digit national-rate numbers are also in use (such as those for Alitalia and Trenitalia).

For directory inquiries, dial ☎ 1240.

International Calls

To call abroad from Italy dial ☎ 00, then the relevant country and area codes, followed by the telephone number.

Try to avoid making international calls from a hotel, as you'll be stung by high rates. It's cheaper to call from a private call centre or from a public payphone with an international calling card. These are available at newsstands and tobacconists, and are often good value. Another alternative is to use a direct-dialling service such as AT&T's USA Direct (access

Discount Cards

CARD	PRICE (ADULT/ REDUCED)	VALIDITY	ADMISSION TO
Appia Antica Card	€6/3	7 days	Terme di Caracalla, Mausoleo di Cecilia Metella and Villa dei Quintili.
Archaeologia Card	€23/12	7 days	Entrance to the Colosseum, Palatino, Terme di Caracalla, Museo Nazionale Romano (Palazzo Altemps, Palazzo Massimo alle Terme, Terme di Diocleziano, Crypta Balbi), Mausoleo di Cecilia Metella and Villa dei Quintili.
Roma Pass (www. romapass.it)	€27	3 days	Includes free admission to two museums or sites (you choose from a list of 38) as well as reduced entry to extra sites, unlimited public transport within Rome, access to the bike-sharing scheme, and reduced-price entry to other exhibitions and events. Roma & Più pass includes some of the surrounding province.

number ☎ 800 172 444) or Telstra's Australia Direct (access number ☎ 800 172 610), which allows you to make a reverse-charge call at home-country rates. Skype is also available at many internet cafes.

To make a reverse-charge (collect) international call from a public telephone, dial ☎ 170. All phone operators speak English.

Mobile Phones

Italian mobile phones operate on the GSM 900/1800 network, which is compatible with the rest of Europe and Australia but not with the North American GSM 1900 or Japanese systems (although some GSM 1900/900 phones do work here).

If you have a GSM dual- or tri-band phone that you can unlock (check with your service provider), it can cost as little as €10 to activate a prepaid *(prepagato)* SIM card in Italy. **TIM** (Telecom Italia Mobile; www.tim.it, in Italian),

Wind (www.wind.it, in Italian) and **Vodafone** (www.vodafone .it, in Italian) all offer SIM cards and have retail outlets across town. Note that by Italian law all SIM cards must be registered in Italy, so make sure you have a passport or ID card with you when you buy one. Also, if you're buying a SIM card abroad, check that the provider offers a registration service.

Public Phones

Despite the fact that Italy is one of the most mobile-saturated countries in the world, you can still find public payphones around Rome. Most work and most take telephone cards *(schede telefoniche)*, although you'll still find some that accept coins or credit cards. You can buy phonecards (€5, €10 or €20) at post offices, tobacconists and newsstands.

Time

Italy is in a single time zone, one hour ahead of GMT. Daylight-saving time, when clocks move forward one hour, starts on the last Sunday in March. Clocks are put back an hour on the last Sunday in October.

Italy operates on a 24-hour clock, so 6pm is written as 18:00.

Tourist Information

Telephone & Internet Resources

Comune Call Centre (☎ 06 06 06; ⏰ 24hr) Very useful for practical questions such as: where's the nearest hospital? Where can I park? When are the underground trains running? The centre is staffed 24 hours and there are staff who speak English, French, Arabic, German, Spanish, Italian and Chinese available from 4pm to 7pm.

Tourist Information Line
(📱 06 06 08; www.060608 .com; 🕙 9am-9pm) A free multilingual tourist information line and website providing information on culture, shows, hotels, transport, etc; you can also book theatre, concert, exhibition and museum tickets on this number.

Turismo Roma
(www .turismoroma.it) The official website of Rome Tourist Board with accommodation and restaurant lists, as well as details of upcoming events, museums and much more.

Tourist Offices

Centro Servizi Pellegrini e Turisti
(📱 06 6988 1662; Piazza San Pietro; 🕙 8.30am-6.15pm Mon-Sat) The Vatican's official tourist office.

Enjoy Rome
(📱 06 445 18 43; www.enjoyrome.com; Via Marghera 8a; 🕙 9am-5.30 Mon-Fri, 8.30am-2pm Sat) This is a private tourist office that arranges guided tours and books accommodation.

Meridiana Information Point
(📱 06 8530 4242; www.villaborghese.it; Viale dell'Uccelliera 35; 🕙 9am-5pm daily year-round, to 7pm Fri-Sun Apr-Sep) For information on Villa Borghese; closed for renovation at the time of research.

Rome Tourist Board
(APT; 📱 06 06 08; www .turismoroma.it; Terminal B, International Arrivals; 🕙 9am-6pm) At Fiumicino airport. The Comune di Roma also runs tourist information points throughout the city:

Castel Sant'Angelo
(Piazza Pia; 🕙 9.30am-7pm)

Ciampino airport
(International Arrivals, baggage reclaim area; 🕙 9am-6.30pm)

Fiumicino airport
(Terminal C, International Arrivals; 🕙 9am-6.30pm)

Piazza Navona
(🕙 9.30am-7pm) Near Piazza delle Cinque Lune.

Piazza Santa Maria Maggiore
(Via dell'Olmata; 🕙 9.30am-7pm)

Piazza Sonnino
(🕙 9.30am-7pm)

Stazione Termini
(🕙 8am-8.30pm) Next to platform 24.

Trevi Fountain
(Via Marco Minghetti; 🕙 9.30am-7pm) Nearer to Via del Corso than the fountain.

Via Nazionale
(🕙 9.30am-7pm)

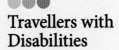

Travellers with Disabilities

Rome isn't an easy city for travellers with disabilities. Cobbled streets, blocked pavements and tiny lifts are difficult for the wheelchair-bound, while the relentless traffic can be disorienting for partially sighted travellers or those with hearing difficulties.

Getting around on public transport is difficult, although efforts are being made to improve accessibility. On metro Line B all stations have wheelchair access except for Termini, Circo Massimo, Colosseo, Cavour and EUR Magliana, while on Line A few of the central stations have facilities except for Cipro-Musei Vaticani. Note that bus 590 covers the same route as metro Line A and is wheelchair accessible. Rome's newer buses and trams can generally accommodate wheelchairs.

If you are travelling by train, ring the national helpline 📱199 30 30 60 to arrange assistance. At Stazione Termini, the **Sala Blu Assistenza Disabili** (📱 06 488 17 26; 🕙 7am-9pm) next to platform 1 can provide information on wheelchair-accessible trains and help with transport in the station. Contact the office 24 hours ahead if you know you're going to need assistance.

Airline companies should be able to arrange assistance at airports if you notify them of your needs in advance. Alternatively, contact **ADR Assistance** (www.adrassistance.it) for assistance at Fiumicino or Ciampino airports.

Some taxis are equipped to carry passengers in wheelchairs; ask for a taxi for a *sedia a rotelle* (wheelchair). For taxi company contact numbers, see p269.

Visas

EU citizens do not need a visa to enter Italy. Nationals of some other countries, including Australia, Canada, Israel, Japan, New Zealand, Switzerland and the USA do not need a visa for stays of up to 90 days.

Italy is one of the 15 signatories of the Schengen Convention, an agreement whereby participating countries abolished customs checks at common borders. The standard tourist visa for a Schengen country is valid for 90 days. You must apply for it in your country of residence and you cannot apply for more than two in any 12-month period. They are not renewable inside Italy.

Technically, all foreign visitors to Italy are supposed to register with the local police within eight days of arrival. However, if you're staying in a hotel you don't need to bother as the hotel does this for you.

Up-to-date visa information is available on www.lonelyplanet.com – follow links through to the Italy destination guide.

Language

Italian pronunciation isn't difficult as most sounds are also found in English. The pronunciation of some consonants depends on which vowel follows, but if you read our pronunciation guides below as if they were English, you'll be understood just fine. Just remember to pronounce double consonants as a longer, more forceful sound than single ones. The stressed syllables in words are in italics in our pronunciation guides.

To enhance your trip with a phrasebook, visit **lonelyplanet.com**. Lonely Planet iPhone phrasebooks are available through the Apple App store.

BASICS

Hello.
Buongiorno./Ciao. (pol/inf)   bwon·*jor*·no/chow
How are you?
Come sta?   *ko*·me sta
I'm fine, thanks.
Bene, grazie.   *be*·ne *gra*·tsye
Excuse me.
Mi scusi.   mee *skoo*·zee
Yes./No.
Sì./No.   see/no
Please. (when asking)
Per favore.   per fa·*vo*·re
Thank you.
Grazie.   *gra*·tsye
Goodbye.
Arrivederci./Ciao. (pol/inf)   a·ree·ve·*der*·chee/chow
Do you speak English?
Parla inglese?   *par*·la een·*gle*·ze
I don't understand.
Non capisco.   non ka·*pee*·sko
How much is this?
Quanto costa?   *kwan*·to *ko*·sta

ACCOMMODATION

I'd like to book a room.
Vorrei prenotare   vo·*ray* pre·no·*ta*·re
una camera.   oo·na *ka*·me·ra
How much is it per night?
Quanto costa per   *kwan*·to *kos*·ta per
una notte?   oo·na *no*·te

EATING & DRINKING

I'd like ..., please.
Vorrei ..., per favore.   vo·*ray* ... per fa·*vo*·re
What would you recommend?
Cosa mi consiglia?   *ko*·za mee kon·*see*·lya
That was delicious!
Era squisito!   *e*·ra skwee·*zee*·to
Bring the bill/check, please.
Mi porta il conto,   mee *por*·ta eel *kon*·to
per favore.   per fa·*vo*·re

I'm allergic (to peanuts).
Sono allergico/a   so·no a·*ler*·jee·ko/a
(alle arachidi). (m/f)   (a·le a·*ra*·kee·dee)
I don't eat ...
Non mangio ...   non *man*·jo ...
  fish   pesce   *pe*·she
  meat   carne   *kar*·ne
  poultry   pollame   po·*la*·me

EMERGENCIES

I'm ill.
Mi sento male.   mee *sen*·to *ma*·le
Help!
Aiuto!   a·*yoo*·to
Call a doctor!
Chiami un medico!   *kya*·mee oon *me*·dee·ko
Call the police!
Chiami la polizia!   *kya*·mee la po·lee·*tsee*·a

DIRECTIONS

I'm looking for (a/the) ...
Cerco ...   *cher*·ko ...
  bank
  la banca   la *ban*·ka
  ... embassy
  la ambasciata de ...   la am·ba·*sha*·ta de ...
  market
  il mercato   eel mer·*ka*·to
  museum
  il museo   eel moo·*ze*·o
  restaurant
  un ristorante   oon rees·to·*ran*·te
  toilet
  un gabinetto   oon ga·bee·*ne*·to
  tourist office
  l'ufficio del turismo   loo·*fee*·cho del too·*reez*·mo

Behind the Scenes

This Book

This 1st edition of Lonely Planet's *Discover Rome* guidebook was researched and written by Abigail Blasi and Duncan Garwood. This guidebook was commissioned in Lonely Planet's London office, and produced by the following:

Commissioning Editor Joe Bindloss
Coordinating Editor Bella Li
Coordinating Cartographer Csanad Csutoros
Coordinating Layout Designer Adrian Blackburn
Managing Editors Bruce Evans, Angela Tinson
Managing Cartographer Amanda Sierp
Managing Layout Designer Jane Hart
Assisting Editor Cathryn Game
Cover Research Naomi Parker
Internal Image Research Nicholas Colicchia
Language Content Annelies Mertens

Thanks to Laura Crawford, Janine Eberle, Ryan Evans, Liz Heynes, Carol Jackson, Laura Jane, Yvonne Kirk, Wayne Murphy, Trent Paton, Mik Ruff, Laura Stansfeld, Gerard Walker, Clifton Wilkinson, Juan Winata

Author Thanks

ABIGAIL BLASI

Huge thanks to Duncan Garwood, the excellent contributing author on this book, and to Joe Bindloss for commissioning me to work on my favourite city. *Molto grazie* to Luca, Gabriel and Jack, to Anna and Marcello, to Carlotta and Alessandro, and to Mum and Dad. A huge thank you to the unparalleled Barbara Lessona for all her kind assistance, to Silvia Prosperi for her interview and all her generous help and insider knowledge on the Vatican, to Roberto Egidi and La Fabbrica di San Pietro for their interviews, and to Paola Zagnarelli, Stéphanie Santini, Alessandro Sauda and Francesca Mazzà for their help with research.

Acknowledgments

Illustrations p64, p65 by Javier Martinex Zarracina.

Cover photographs Front: Colosseum, Rome, Atlantide Phototravel/Corbis. Back: Outdoor dining at Piazza della Rotonda, Rome, Russell Mountford/Lonely Planet Images.

Many of the images in this guide are available for licensing from Lonely Planet Images: www.lonelyplanetimages.com.

Index

See also separate subindexes for:

 Eating p283

 Drinking & Nightlife p284

 Entertainment p285

 Shopping p285

Sights 000
Map pages 000

279

Sights 000
Map pages 000

Sights 000
Map pages 000

Sights 000
Map pages 000

Sights 000
Map pages 000

How to Use This Book

These symbols will help you find the listings you want:

⊙ Sights
✴ Eating
🟢 Drinking & Nightlife

✦ Entertainment
🅰 Shopping
🟢 Sports & Activities

These symbols give you the vital information for each listing:

🎵 Telephone Numbers
⊙ Opening Hours
🅿 Parking
🚭 Nonsmoking
❄ Air-Conditioning
@ Internet Access

📶 Wi-Fi Access
🏊 Swimming Pool
🥗 Vegetarian Selection
🄴 English-Language Menu
👪 Family-Friendly
🐾 Pet-Friendly

🚌 Bus
⛴ Ferry
Ⓜ Metro
Ⓢ Subway
🚇 London Tube
🚊 Tram
🚆 Train

Reviews are organised by author preference.

Look out for these icons:

FREE No payment required

 A green or sustainable option

Our authors have nominated these places as demonstrating a strong commitment to sustainability – for example by supporting local communities and producers, operating in an environmentally friendly way, or supporting conservation projects.

Map Legend

Sights
⊙ Beach
⊕ Buddhist
⊙ Castle
✛ Christian
⊛ Hindu
☪ Islamic
✡ Jewish
❶ Monument
🏛 Museum/Gallery
⊙ Ruin
⊛ Winery/Vineyard
🐾 Zoo
⊙ Other Sight

Activities, Courses & Tours
⊜ Diving/Snorkelling
🜨 Canoeing/Kayaking
🜨 Skiing
🜨 Surfing
⊜ Swimming/Pool
🜨 Walking
🜨 Windsurfing
⊙ Other Activity/ Course/Tour

Sleeping
🛏 Sleeping
⛺ Camping

Eating
✴ Eating

Drinking
🟢 Drinking
🟢 Cafe

Entertainment
✦ Entertainment

Shopping
🅰 Shopping

Information
✉ Post Office
ℹ Tourist Information

Transport
✈ Airport
⊗ Border Crossing
🚌 Bus
🚠 Cable Car/ Funicular
🚲 Cycling
⛴ Ferry
Ⓜ Metro
🚝 Monorail
🅿 Parking
Ⓢ S-Bahn
🚕 Taxi
🚆 Train/Railway
🚊 Tram
🚇 Tube Station
Ⓤ U-Bahn
● Other Transport

Routes
Tollway
Freeway
Primary
Secondary
Tertiary
Lane
Unsealed Road
Plaza/Mall
Steps
Tunnel
Pedestrian Overpass
Walking Tour
Walking Tour Detour
Path

Boundaries
International
State/Province
Disputed
Regional/Suburb
Marine Park
Cliff
Wall

Population
❸ Capital (National)
◉ Capital (State/Province)
● City/Large Town
● Town/Village

Geographic
🏠 Hut/Shelter
🏮 Lighthouse
👁 Lookout
▲ Mountain/Volcano
🌴 Oasis
❸ Park
)(Pass
🏞 Picnic Area
🏞 Waterfall

Hydrography
River/Creek
Intermittent River
Swamp/Mangrove
Reef
Canal
Water
Dry/Salt/ Intermittent Lake
Glacier

Areas
Beach/Desert
Cemetery (Christian)
Cemetery (Other)
Park/Forest
Sportsground
Sight (Building)
Top Sight (Building)

Our Story

A beat-up old car, a few dollars in the pocket and a sense of adventure. In 1972 that's all Tony and Maureen Wheeler needed for the trip of a lifetime – across Europe and Asia overland to Australia. It took several months, and at the end – broke but inspired – they sat at their kitchen table writing and stapling together their first travel guide, *Across Asia on the Cheap*. Within a week they'd sold 1500 copies. Lonely Planet was born.

Today, Lonely Planet has offices in Melbourne, London and Oakland, with more than 600 staff and writers. We share Tony's belief that 'a great guidebook should do three things: inform, educate and amuse'.

Our Writers

ABIGAIL BLASI

Coordinating Author Abigail moved to Rome in 2003, her first son was born in Rome and she was married on the banks of nearby Lago Bracciano. Nowadays she divides her time between Rome, Puglia and London. She has worked on numerous editions of Lonely Planet's *Italy* and *Rome* guides, wrote the *Best of Rome* guide, and co-wrote *Puglia & Basilicata*. She also regularly writes on the subject of Italy for various newspapers, websites and magazines.

CONTRIBUTING AUTHOR

Duncan Garwood Even after more than a decade of living in Rome, Duncan is still fascinated by the city's incomparable beauty and hidden depths. He has worked on the past four editions of the *Rome* guide and contributed to a raft of Lonely Planet Italy titles, as well as newspapers and magazines. Each job throws up special memories; this time it was visiting a chapel in the Vatican Museums that's usually closed to the public.

Read more about Duncan at:
lonelyplanet.com/members/duncangarwood

Published by Lonely Planet Publications Pty Ltd
ABN 36 005 607 983
1st edition – June 2012
ISBN 978 1 74220 464 2
© Lonely Planet 2012   Photographs © as indicated 2012
10 9 8 7 6 5 4 3 2 1
Printed in China